I0560428

Change Leader?
Who Me?

Hard-earned wisdom for those
new to leading change

Unusual Wisdom Press

Alan Cay Culler

Change Leader? Who Me? Hard-Earned Wisdom for Those New To Leading Change is a compilation of the author's reflections on a long career in helping leaders make strategic change. The author intends this advice to be helpful to those facing the challenge of leading change in organizations. Memory is imprecise at best, so others who experienced the same events described in the book may remember them differently. Leading organizational change is difficult. People are different and every organization's history and culture are unique. These stories and methodology descriptions come from the author's experience, and are intended to inspire research into people's needs and the organization's context before beginning a change effort.

Published by Unusual Wisdom Press LLC
New Jersey, United States of America

© Alan Cay Culler 2025
All rights reserved. This book, or any portion thereof, may not be reproduced in any form whatsoever without the expressed written consent if the author, with the exception of brief quotations by reviewers or in scholarly journals. For further information submit requests through https://www.alanculler.com/contact-me
or https://wisdomfromunusualplaces.com/contact-me

ISBN
Hardcover: 979-8-9878518-5-2
Paperback: 979-8-9878518-4-5
E book: 979-8-9878518-3-8

Cover and interior design by: Lisa Monias:
South River Design Team http://www.southriverdesignteam.com

Publisher's imprint logo design Zac Culler
https://www.zacculler.com/illustration

Author's Photo by Jay Seldin Photography:
http://www.jayseldinphotos.com

Change Leader? Who Me?

Hard-earned wisdom for those
new to leading change

Alan Cay Culler

Advance praise for *Change Leader? Who me?*

Alan Culler has written an exciting new book on the evolution of change leadership. Alan was a protégé of mine, and we worked together to develop methods for identifying and training change leaders. Culler provides practical examples of change leadership from work he and I did together with Warner Burke and others. At British Airways, we identified and trained change leaders to guide the efforts to create a new organization. At Short Brothers, we identified natural change leaders who, given support, could lead the effort to save the company from bankruptcy and bring about a positive outcome: the profitable sale of the company to a world-level aircraft enterprise. At Interep, a radio advertising sales company, Alan Culler worked with presidents of member companies to bring about new ways of packaging and selling media advertising. This book: *Change Leader? Who Me?* Is a valuable tool for anyone involved in today's world of organizational change.

— **George H. Litwin, author of *Motivation and Organizational Climate*, and *Mobilizing the Organization: Bringing Strategy to Life***

In my many attempts to explain organization development, I have relied on stories to illustrate a point. Stories can be explanatory and hold one's interest. OD is highly complicated and usually involves many organizational concepts. Often, a story can explain an organizational concept better than a definition. But the story must come from the teller's experience to illustrate the point being made. Alan Culler has in abundance both the knowledge and a plethora of stories to explain OD.

— **W. Warner Burke, PhD, Professor Emeritus, Organizational Psychology and Education, Teachers College, Columbia University. Author: *Organization Change: Theory and Practice; Organization Development: A Process of Learning and Changing***

Change Leader? Who Me?" offers a refreshing and practical approach to confidently navigating the complexities of uncertainty. This remarkable guide empowers readers to master the art of change by seamlessly integrating credibility, creativity, communication, and consideration. With its insightful and comprehensive strategies, "Change Leader?" equips individuals to thrive in chaotic times, making it an invaluable resource for anyone wanting to excel in challenging times.

— **Dr. Mary Lippitt, author of** *Leadersheep: Saving the Herd* **and** *Brilliant or Blunder.*

Change Leader? Who, Me? beautifully articulates a powerful and often overlooked truth: leadership in driving change is not confined to titles or positions. Timely and topical is the empowering message within, affirming that every individual possesses the capacity to be a catalyst for positive transformation. By emphasizing the significance of recognizing opportunities, inspiring collective action, and embracing even the smallest initial steps, this book fosters a sense of agency and encourages readers to embrace their potential as change leaders in any context.

— **Dennis J. Pitocco, Founder & Chief Reimaginator, 360° Nation, Author:** *Rites Of Passage: Across The Landscape Of Our Souls,* *UN-SHELTERED-None of Us Are Home Until All of Us Are Home*

In *Change Agent, Who Me?*, Alan Culler takes us along on his journey of discovery in both life and leading change, in which he realizes that success in either means starting with changing oneself. Along the way he treats those new to the consulting world as well as those who have experienced a transformation (or two) in their careers to a clear and concise summary of the essential elements of change, levers to suit various situations and applicable tricks of the trade. Illustrated with down to earth examples from real live people Alan got to know along the way, *Change Agent, Who Me?* highlights the connections between common sense and success in managing change. It also provides a valuable summary of consulting models and resources for those new to the process and a great refresher for those who have been around this block. Alan's insights and anecdotes make for an enjoyable and compelling read!

— **Bob Yardis, HR Executive & Consultant (semi-retired)**

DEDICATION:

To my wife Billie Smith Culler, who picks me up when I fall down. I will never forget.

To my parents, Nan and Raymond Culler, my sisters Carolyn (Lynne) Culler Wilson and Constance Culler Falconer, who raised me to be loving, kind and to make a difference. I am still working on it.

To my children and grandchildren, sources of never-ending joy.

To the giants from whom I learned about organizational change, Dr. Derek S. Pugh, Dr. George H. Litwin and Dr. W. Warner Burke. I was never easy to teach.

To every consultant who survived managing me, or working alongside me. You helped me change and grow into a change leader.

To every client who trusted me with improving their organization's results and all their people who did most of the work. You kept me learning and shared the pride of achievement.

Thank you! You made this book and so much more possible.

CONTENTS

PREFACE

When I say "change," I'm talking about behavioral change, basically an individual doing something different or doing a familiar task differently. Behavioral change may require a new insight, new knowledge, and/or different skills. But what is important is that doing something different or differently happens because people choose to change. They understand the reason, the "why" of change.

Change in business starts with individual change, but it involves a group of people collectively understanding the why and acting together to change.

I spent thirty-seven years as a consultant, trainer, and facilitator of groups of leaders in business. When I started, I wouldn't have said that my chosen third career (actor, booking agent, consultant) had anything to do with leading change. I thought that I was a hired problem solver, a researcher who provided new data upon which business managers could make decisions and act.

Even as a trainer, I saw myself as a communicator of new information, not someone who helped people change. I certainly didn't see myself as a leader or think that I would change as a result of that work. I was wrong.

When I say leader, I'm not elevating the exemplary individual, the man or woman with such admirable traits that we enshrine them with a positive regard akin to hero worship. If such an individual exists, he or she might be good at leading change, or not.

Rather, I am spotlighting the individual to whom others listen, who can help others understand the why of change, and who gets people to

1

follow through on the change effort. Leading change requires a change mindset - understanding "the why," the "why now," and the penalty for not changing.

I wrote this book to synthesize what I learned over my years as a change consultant, helping leaders make strategic change, and perhaps consultants might get some value from it. However, I wrote the book for the person inside an organization who has just been asked to lead the implementation of a new strategy, or an innovation or improvement initiative, or post-merger integration. Suddenly, you hear yourself asking, "Change leader? Who, me?"

Here you will find context for change (why does it feel like we are in a period of constant change?), core traits of change leaders, and helpful change levers or tools. I have also included stories of leaders, ordinary people I've met, who embodied some aspect of leading change. There are stories of my Boy Scout Troop Leader, a classic booking agent, an Italian haircutter, my mom, and Bruce Springsteen. These are not collectively exhaustive case examples of leadership, but stories that may help you shape your values as a change leader, as they helped shape mine.

The Change Mindset

I have a passion for things Italian. I don't know where this comes from; it's strange in a Celt-WASP hybrid like me. I first noticed this penchant as a very small boy, loving trips to Boston's North End where I was pinched on the cheek by the round lady in the black dress at Mama Bertelone's. Later, in Rome for the first time, I relished the terra cotta dust on white marble and was amazed at the drivers to whom even the sidewalk was a rush-hour roadway. A warm smile grew in my heart. I used to get that feeling on Sunday mornings at La Prima Espresso in Pittsburgh's Strip District, listening to the old men roll the beautiful Italian language off their tongues. Vowels and soft tones make swearing sound like Puccini.

One of my Italian vices was my haircutter. He was good at cutting hair, but, in truth, I also went to him because I liked to hear him talk.

"'Mico' is sort of a nickname, short for Domenico. It was my father's nickname, and now it's mine. I inherited it, you could say, a family legacy. It's all right, but I would have rather had some money, say, five or six million dollars."

"Mico," I asked, "What would you do with five or six million dollars?"

"Hey, Alan, with five or six million dollars, I wouldn't have to <u>do</u> anything! I'd have enough money."

We mutually decided that, really, our lives could be immeasurably improved by the "injection of a mere $250,000 in spare cash" and laughed. The laughter was good.

Our conversation skipped lightly through politics, the arts, and food, and then swung to our ancestors: my mother's grandfather, Pleatous McCaghren, and Mico's grandfather, both immigrants.

"You could wonder how they did it," I mused aloud. "How they gave up everything to come here, eh, Mico?"

"Yeah," Mico replied. "You could wonder. People say, 'How could they do that?' I'll tell you how."

I sat back and waited, realizing that day's story was beginning.

"They could do that because they didn't know any better. My grandfather and your mother's grandfather didn't know about all the things that could go wrong. They didn't say 'what if the boat sinks?' or 'what if we get sick?' or 'what if I can't work or fit in?' They didn't know about those things. They just did it." Mico went on with a tale about his grandfather, as it had been passed down to him.

"First of all, they had <u>nothing</u> there, so what were they giving up? Then . . . then somebody they knew went, and wrote letters home: '<u>America.</u> <u>America.</u> There's opportunity under every brick in the sidewalk.' They said, 'The streets are paved with gold.' They said, 'Come and make your fortune.' They didn't know any better, so they went."

Mico's skin is the color of pecan shells; his eyes are shiny black coals, and they were twinkling almost Leprechaun-like with mischief. "Now, I'm not saying that my grandfather and your great-grandfather were stupid. No. It's not that they couldn't *imagine* all kinds of things that could go wrong. But they didn't *know* that they'd go wrong. They didn't know about trouble, didn't accept it in their hearts. They didn't let it stop them. They said things like 'we'll cross that bridge when we come to it,' or 'it'll work out,' or 'we'll find a way.'"

"You see, they had the dream: America! Opportunity! And the dream kept them from knowing any better. The dream kept them from stopping or being stopped by anything. The dream made what they had in the old country seem like nothing. The dream made it easy to give it up because it was nothing compared to what they could have. The dream kept them from knowing any better, and they just did it. They left, came to America. They did it because they didn't know any better."

Mico finished cutting my hair. He had no other customers, so we walked to our cars together. We talked about the old men at La Prima and wished each other well.

That was years ago, and today Mico's words still linger. In my work, I helped people and companies who were struggling with new strategies, and Mico had given me a blueprint for how to succeed at life-altering change:

- "They had the dream . . . ." Hold an inspiring vision of what will be after the change.
- "The dream made what they had . . . seem like nothing. . . ." Say goodbye to the past and focus on the future.
- "They didn't know any better. . . ." Don't accept obstacles in your heart. Go around them.
- "They just did it." Take action, in big steps or many small ones. ACTION, not thinking, not trying, but DOING, is what makes change happen.

I didn't know it then, but recording Mico's stories started my career as a writer.

PART I. INTRODUCTION:

"MORE CHANGE? WHAT IS GOING ON?"

Mico's analogy of the change mindset of his immigrant ancestors resonated with me. Still, as I worked in organizations, I often heard the frustration with what seemed like constant change. I was slow to realize just how much change is part of life and a key driver in business.

Take the computer revolution, for example. My mother became a computer programmer in 1956. My father was a printer by trade who spent the last twenty years of his career setting type for a newspaper on a linotype machine.

When it became obvious to him that computer typesetting would replace the linotype, he raised the issue at a Typographers Union meeting to which he brought me.

They laughed at him. "Ray, those electronic machines will never be able to line-justify like a skilled operator!"

Two years later, the entire composing room shut down, and stories were typed directly into computer typesetters.

My first independent consulting client was helping increase sales for a graphic artist who had one of the few large-format computer typesetting machines in Pittsburgh. I asked about desktop publishing.

He laughed at me. "Not enough typefaces and the output is not commercial print-ready." Eighteen months later, his entire typesetting business was gone.

It is a common story. A process is automated, or a human skill is replaced by a computer. At first, it is mocked by the skilled operators because the computer isn't as good as a human.

When I came to Pittsburgh, steel company executives told me the story of how the most skilled, but most dangerous, steelworker job in a flat-rolled mill was replaced by computer. You may have seen old pictures of a huge bucket pouring molten steel into the mill to be rolled. A human crane operator stood next to that bucket and judged when it was ready to pour. If the steel was too cold, you didn't get an even pour, and the steel wouldn't be evenly thick; if too hot, you got bubbles and compromised structural integrity.

The operator made the judgment by "feel" and color, but at a risk to life and limb because molten steel could slosh. It took two years for the computer to get as good as a human, during which time many who'd held the job denigrated the technology. But computer programming continued to improve and ultimately saved lives.

Now you can see this same phenomenon with machine learning or generative artificial intelligence. People will mock the quality of writing or video produced until they don't. This has been true of every technological change.

"A good horse will always be faster than this automobile toy."

"Why would I want to carry a phone everywhere I go?"

"Self-driving cars? Pu-lease!"

Technology changes people's lives, sometimes for the better, sometimes not-so-much.

But as you'll see in the next chapter, technology isn't the only change trend that aspiring change leaders must help people adapt to.

CHAPTER 1

LEADERSHIP CONTEXT: THE WINDS OF CHANGE

In the 1990s, during my first incarnation as an independent consultant, I observed a decade of earth-shaking, mind-numbing, blurred, rapid-fire change.

I wrote a white paper entitled "The Winds of Change" for a client leadership team planning a new strategy. I suggested that thinking about trends might help them anticipate the future. The trends I saw then were:

- **Emerging and converging technologies** – the blending of hardware and software in computers, television, film/video, music, etc.
- **We are one; we are many** – globalization and its counter-trend of tribalism.
- **"Comm-Ent"** – combining information (news, data) with entertainment meant moving from the organizing principle "Is it true?" to "Does it hold my attention?"
- **Gradual global greening** – environmentalism and the reaction

to it weren't new in the 1990s, but I thought environmentalism was winning.

- **Changing demographics** – the United States was getting older and less white; the rest of the world was getting older.
- **Changing psychographics** – changing attitudes toward work-life balance, working from home, and childcare.
- **Changes in ownership** – mergers, acquisitions, leveraged buy-outs, spin-offs, and the impacts on the work contract and corporate culture.
- **Speed learning crisis** – all these changes required learning at lightning speed, most especially learning how to learn.

The Winds of Change are now a tornado.

Technological change is accelerating. Since the 1990s, we've seen the rise of the Internet, smartphones, social media, generative artificial intelligence (AI), DNA crisper technology, EVs, etc. The changes in transportation, communications, and the transfer of information have shrunk the world.

The globalism-tribalism pendulum is still swinging. The export of communications and entertainment products from the developed nations created a homogenization that some found offensive. There was a resurgence of identification with local identity, nationalism, and in some cases, a kind of tribalism.

"Comm-Ent" materialized and solidified. In some cases, the news looks like Reality TV. Production has moved to the audience with sites like YouTube, Instagram, and TikTok. This technology, combined with AI and social media, is giving us deep fakes and nanosecond attention spans. As a result, conspiracy theories, misinformation, and "fake news" abound.

Environmentalism has morphed into hair-on-fire climate change panic in some and defiant denial in others. Mass migrations are underway, exacerbated by economic inequities from globalization. These shifts in populations have triggered resistance to immigration and the aforementioned tribalism.

Add to this a global pandemic that accelerated the work-life balance concerns of younger generations who, with lesser numbers, are supporting aging Baby Boomers, many of whom are unprepared for retirement.

Mergers and acquisitions have created global mega-monopolies that focus exclusively on shareholder return, adding dramatically to economic inequity.

The sheer pace of change requires individuals and organizations to acquire information and adapt rapidly. Innovative thinking and continuous improvement are tickets to admission. Unfortunately, in many countries in both the developed and undeveloped worlds, the basic education system has ossified. In the worst cases, we are crippling whole segments of our population by depriving them of the tools for success in the fast-changing world.

We all better start speed-learning or we'll be replaced by AI that learns faster than we do.

This list is not mutually exclusive nor collectively exhaustive. The trends overlap and influence each other. Many other variables contribute to these trends - specific local, political, and regulatory issues, as well as issues unique to particular industries or stages of development.

In my career, I saw some companies fail to see what was coming, like the Typographers' Union and later my graphic artist client who missed the same trend. However, I've also seen some companies that responded quickly to change.

For example, an office interior design and construction firm looked at changing psychographics in their industry and saw a trend toward telecommuting, which would decrease the need for office space but increase technological connection facilities, data centers, and video walls. Focusing on this trend early created business opportunities during the COVID-19 pandemic.

A pharmaceutical firm looked at emerging technologies and concluded that biotechnology firms had an inside track on genomic medicine. The alliances they forged have led to new drugs and vaccines developed in record time.

I'm going out on a limb to say that we are in the middle of a huge transitional age for humanity. Such ages have happened before, of course; farming and trading towns and cities eclipsed hunter-gatherer clans, the Gutenberg Press ended the church-nobility monopoly on information and accelerated the Renaissance, and the industrial revolution transformed the creation and transport of goods.

This transitional time will shake nations and international relations. It will reverberate in the business world, offering both danger and opportunity. It will also change how individuals define themselves and their relationships with others and how they act at work and at home.

This kind of change will require leaders who never thought they'd lead change. It will require leaders who speed learn and competently lead change.

I recommend that leaders and leadership teams make time to consider context. Discussing and planning for the winds of change <u>before</u> they blow your house down is time well spent.

CHAPTER 2

"WHAT'S A CHANGE LEADER?"

This is a common reaction of people upon whose shoulders the task of leading a change has suddenly landed. Change is daunting; it is unknown territory. The idea of leading it is even more formidable.

Changing yourself is hard. Think about how hard it is to lose weight, quit smoking, or start exercising. First, you must:

- Internalize the reason to change (now),
- Say goodbye to the old way,
- Envision the new way,
- Act,
- Ignore or overcome obstacles,
- Measure results and
- Act again.

Even change in a company comes down to individuals **doing more of something, less of something, or doing something differently**. That ain't easy. (If it were, I'd be skinnier.)

For a group of people to break an old habit or learn a new way of being in the world is exponentially harder. It helps if someone goes first to try out the new way and encourages others to follow. Change requires leaders.

What is a leader? Is it different than a manager? During my career, I read about leadership, thought and talked about it, and observed leaders in companies going through change.

I came to the view that leadership and management are different capabilities. Some people have both skillsets, but not everyone in a management role is good at leading change.

My perhaps over-simplified differentiation of managers and leaders is:

Managers:

- thrive in a relatively **steady state**
- are accountable for **getting work done**, and
- **Develop people** to ensure they are capable of getting work done

Leaders:

- thrive in **abnormal circumstances** such as change, emergencies, war
- are accountable for **giving direction**, "This way!"
- **attract followers,** "Follow me!"

Perhaps the best Illustration of the difference between management and leadership comes from an interview conducted by my friend and mentor Dr. George H. Litwin. During a project with the US Navy, as George tells the story, he was interviewing an admiral:

> He asked me if I knew anything about the five-inch 127-millimeter gun on the forward gun turret of a Burke class destroyer. I replied that I didn't. He went on to say that "aiming and firing this weapon is a complex operation with many steps, missing any one of which could result in a safety incident, misfire, or missed target. Getting a gun crew to safely and accurately fire this gun requires good <u>management</u>. Getting the crew to fire

that gun when they are themselves under fire, that requires <u>leadership!</u>"

The military talks a lot about leadership because what could be a more abnormal circumstance than war. Rarely in change do lives depend on it, but leadership is still required.

A change leader might be a great speaker who inspires others. Or might express empathy for the struggles others face as a result of the change, and then instill confidence that they can change. Or he or she might be a teacher who develops new competencies in others.

Leaders might also be good managers who organize and control the work of change so that the steps are easy to follow. These manager-leaders might use their positions to hold people accountable for the change. But not necessarily. Often, change leaders emerge who are not invested in the old power structure or the old way of doing things.

Whoever the leader is and however she or he leads, the first defining characteristic of a leader is that others <u>follow.</u>

We lead toward something or away from something, so the direction or destination is important. This is why so much of what has been written about leadership involves vision, the clear and inspiring picture of the desired future state. Sometimes the vision is the reason people follow.

But leaders must be <u>followed</u>. When I ran a change leadership workshop, I used to joke, "If you think you are a leader, look over your shoulder. If no one is there, you might just be delusional."

So the first question for any would-be leader is, "Why would anyone follow you?"

The context for leadership is an abnormal environment. This is why the military touts leadership; what could be a more abnormal environment than war? In business, an abnormal environment is a time of change - change in customers or competitors, change in ownership (mergers and acquisitions), change in technology, etc.

However, regardless of the context, you want the leader to say, "This way! Follow me!" Those are the two primary accountabilities of leadership: direction and followership.

In leadership literature, direction gets a lot of ink. There are many articles on vision, mission, values, and purpose. Start-ups also require leaders. Entrepreneurial literature also discusses vision and buzzwords such as "pivot," the change in direction when the first one isn't working.
The important things that leaders communicate are:

- The **why** of the change – "We can't go on this way and we can't go back because. . . competitors have lower costs or different technology. . . the community will not put up with our pollution anymore. . . customers' needs have changed. . . or. . ." This is sometimes called the "burning platform"; i.e.," "jump, we can't stay here." (I learned to substitute "change case" for "burning platform" "when working in oil production, a term with less painful connotations.)

- The **destination** – one of my favorite vision statements is "the land of milk and honey" from Exodus. Can you imagine anything more compelling for Moses and his desert nomads than green pastures for goats to graze, breed, and give milk, and an orchard for an apiary? Vision statements are often sensory-rich and emotionally laden to engage people to follow. Vision-led leadership is always more engaging than threat-driven leadership because some people freeze when they are afraid.

- Sometimes the **what or how** of the change, but often this is the work of followers.

Speaking of followers, why do people follow a leader?
- The case for change is compelling.
- The vision is engaging and exciting.
- They believe in the leader, often because of a track record.
   o She's proven that she is competent; she'll get us there.
   o He understands my needs – he's always been empathetic and supportive.

o   I trust him or her. Trust can come from many things: affinity ("she is like me"); reliability ("he is a straight shooter who does what he says he's going to do"); timely, accurate information; transparent decision-making; and a history of kept promises.

These things are important for the manager as well, but a manager may have systems and processes to fall back on, whereas leaders are in a new environment and must improvise.

Reluctance to lead

Leaders must also be prepared to change themselves.

Early in my career, I conducted a series of leadership workshops for a company going through a large change. These workshops were called training, and there were some competency-building exercises, but the real purpose was for participants to internalize the need for change and commit to it. We used the term "change leader," and I remember one participant saying, "Change Leader? Who, me?" He was a middle manager, not an executive, and my co-facilitator and I pointed out how many people he influenced. He was clear that he thought change leadership was the job of "those guys up there," which he said, pointing at the ceiling.

At the end of the week, he said, "You know, I finally get it. Change in this huge corporation does come down to guys like me doing something differently." My co-facilitator and I congratulated ourselves, a bit smugly, if I'm honest.

A couple of weeks later, at another session of the same workshop, I was quite critical of a team that I thought wasn't taking the change seriously. I used the term change leader and one of the members said, "You're the change leader and not a very good one, either."

I heard myself say, "Change leader? Who, me?" Even now, I feel the cringe as it came out of my mouth, followed by something really snarky. My co-facilitator just looked away, apparently finding something fascinating on the wall.

On a break later in the week, after I had given my lecture about leaders being open to change, two members of the recalcitrant group pulled me aside.

"Alan, you may not think you are a change leader, but you are leading us in leading change. That requires that you change along with us." They gave me pointed feedback on my lack of empathy and how my sarcasm made me less than authentic and a bit mean-spirited.

I have worked on that feedback ever since.

CHAPTER 3

CHANGE CRAFT: THE BASICS OF LEADING CHANGE

What is a craft?

The English word "craft" has its origins in the Anglo-Saxon *cræft*, which comes from the German *kraft*, meaning "skill or strength at planning and making." When we think of craft, we think handmade, or small batch production, like handmade tables, hand-woven blankets, or craft beer.

Craft is based upon unique knowledge and skills, or competencies, that the craftsman uses to plan and make with quality. That craftsman increases competence with focused practice.

The phrase "focused practice" is critical. It is practice focused on improvement, breaking down the craft, practicing each part in isolation, getting rigorous feedback and practicing again, then putting all the craft segments back together.

In that same vein, Malcolm Gladwell in his book *Outliers* describes K. Anders Erikson's research at the Berlin Academy of Music to posit that it takes 10,000 hours of focused practice to become world-class at anything.

Is leading change a craft?

Does leading change have unique competencies? Absolutely. In the past, however, there was no time for or interest in focused practice, and most managers had few opportunities to learn to lead change in their careers. Plus, change leadership was a rarely used capability that could be left to consultants, staff, and other specialists. As a result, some managers think a new technology implements itself, or that entering a new market on the other side of the world is about language translation, or that people should "just suck it up and work all the time, like I did."

But times have changed, and now, with constant change, change craft has become a useful skillset. And the first step in learning a craft is the desire to learn it.

The basics of change craft

Begin with the most important question: Why?

In his best-selling leadership book *Start with Why*, Simon Sinek makes the point that stating the compelling case for change and expressing gratitude are ways to attract and enroll followers to make the change happen. This is akin to a story I heard so many times during the British Airways privatization project in the 1980s that I thought I had witnessed the meeting. Prime Minister Margaret Thatcher, who privatized the airline, gave the gathered executives a choice: be broken up and sold for scrap or be transformed into a profitable airline and sold in a public offering "like a proper company." This was the first and maybe the best compelling case for change in my career.

Late in my career, I worked at another of Mrs. Thatcher's privatizations, British Petroleum (BP). I helped with Continuous Improvement work to improve process safety. The compelling case for change in that project was twofold: accidents at the Texas City refinery and at the Deepwater Horizon drilling platform in the Gulf of Mexico. No one had to tell that story repeatedly; one only had to mention the name of the sites to focus everyone on change.

For some changes, the answer to why is obvious: because the customers changed - different needs, wants, or expectations. Or competitors changed - different providers (e.g., international), or they are better, faster, cheaper.

Or there is a new technology, an opportunity for us to be better, faster, cheaper. Or the rules of the game have changed - new regulations, community standards, a new owner with new targets.

For other changes, the leader may have to dig deeper, look at the trends described in the "Winds of Change" chapter, and/or other relevant changes in your industry.

The change mindset

After asking why change, the next question is: do we have to change? Is *not* changing an option? What is the impact of not changing? Some see these questions as resistance to change, but they are fundamental to the change mindset. They help people choose to change.

Exploring why and the impact of NOT changing together make the compelling case for change, and are the underpinnings of the change mindset.

My Pittsburgh haircutter Mico introduced me to the change mindset when he explained how his family emigrated from Calabria.

"They had the dream, and the dream made what they had seem like nothing."

Immigrants are a good example of <u>choosing</u> life-altering change. They reject where they live and move to an uncertain promise of opportunity. These are the three elements of a change mindset:

- **Rejection** of the status quo (case for change)
- **Promise** of the future (vision)
- **Choice** (people may reject <u>your</u> change if they feel it's imposed upon them, but if they choose, then it's **their** change)

Of course, you have to act. You have to sell what you own, get visas, buy tickets, get on the boat. No change happens until you <u>do</u> something, but action without the right mindset is unlikely to succeed.

Sometime later, I learned about a formula that crystallized the change mindset.

The formula for a change mindset

This formula for change is usually credited to Richard Beckhard, who published it in 1977 in *Organizational Transitions*. The formula was developed by David Gleicher while at the consulting firm Arthur D. Little.

$$C = D \times V \times F > R$$

Change happens when the products of...

Dissatisfaction with the current state, and a

clear **V**ision of a more compelling possible future, and

practical **F**irst steps towards a different future

are greater than the **R**esistance, the pain or cost of change

Dissatisfaction (rejection of the status quo) is the push of change, often called the compelling case for change – the why and why now we can't stay the same. It is multiplied by the pull of change, the future promise (vision),which leads to first steps. These three elements together must exceed resistance to change. In the original formula, resistance was the cost of change; in 1980, Catherine Dannemiller changed cost to resistance, and in 2014, Steve Cady added an S for sustaining the change.

What I like about the formula is that it lays out the mindset (push and pull) and actions necessary to overcome the inertia of the status quo. Also, the formula is not additive, but multiplicative, demonstrating the exponential difficulty of change.

There is both the dissatisfaction (rejection of the status quo) <u>and</u> the vision (future promise). The dissatisfaction is often called the compelling case for change – the why and why now that we can't stay the same.

I have seen leaders in business and politics pitch the threat that not changing is the road to ruin, the end of life as we know it. Danger can scare us into action, but over time constant threat gets normalized, doom and gloom depress people, fear freezes people, and action is forgotten.

Vision-led change is always better and more lasting than threat-driven change. The grit of marble dust might wear your teeth and spirit down, but without the "golden sidewalk," you don't get on the ship.

Vision statements are often emotion-laden and sensory-rich:

"We hold these truths to be self-evident . . . all men are created equal . . . life, liberty, and the pursuit of happiness" . . . "We the People."

"I have a dream."

Dissatisfaction pushes; vision pulls you. Dissatisfaction, rejecting the current state, is a reality-based problem definition. Vision is opportunity and solution finding.

A vision isn't a daydream. "Pie in the sky by and by" doesn't cut it for long. There must be a plan and milestones, as well as mid-journey measures to show your change is proceeding as planned.

What happens when you know you can't go on the way things are and that you must change, but what's ahead is unclear? How can you leap empty-handed into the void? Big change is often like this. We think we know the opportunity, but if we are clear-eyed, we also see the risk. The phrase "jumping from the frying pan into the fire" is a cliché because it's a visual reminder of what frequently happens.

Entering the unknown, where we don't know what we don't know, relies on values:

- **Do what is right** – Clean air and water, remove shortcomings . . . make amends, taking care of customers, people matter, and results count.
- **Resilience** – "we'll get through this," "we'll cross that bridge when we come to it," one day at a time."
- **Support** – "What if the sky should fall? As long as we're together,

it really doesn't matter at all."

The push from dissatisfaction, the pull of vision, and the opportunity that opens to values must overcome what Beckhard and Gleicher call resistance to change.

People may resist change that they haven't chosen. Resistance may be fear of loss or just plain old inertia. Remember Newton's First Law of motion: "A body in motion tends to stay in motion and a body at rest tends to stay at rest unless acted upon by an outside force."

That's the thing about change; it produces reactions. Newton's Third Law, "Every action produces an equal and opposite reaction," applies to social systems as well as physical bodies.

Some people say this is because people fear change. But if that were absolutely true, no one would ever leave home, get married, have children, move to parts unknown, or do anything difficult that might mean they might be a different person.

People don't fear change; rather, they fear loss – loss of job, power, or status. Some people also see the potential for loss in the unknown more than others.

Mostly, though, people don't like to be compelled to change. They fear a loss of autonomy. They don't fear change; they fear your change. They fear potential loss when they don't have a choice to make it their change.

That's why the formula included first steps that reduce friction, ignore gravity, **and prompt you to kick yourself in the butt to do something. The focus is on Action.**

If you are the change leader, this is the path for you and to help others: Change mindset first, draw on values, and then take action. And if you find you've jumped from the frying pan into the fire?

Get out of the fire. Get everyone to a safe position. Refocus.

Who will help make this change happen?

John Kotter, Harvard professor and author of several books on change leadership, has a change requirements model that includes the usual concepts - vision, urgency, communications, short-term wins, etc. Kotter, though, recommends "Building a Guiding Coalition" for the change. He describes this as a diagonal slice of the organization that includes executives, middle managers, and opinion leaders. In my experience, these are often people who are outside the current power structure and may be people who have been vocally critical of the status quo.

Jim Collins, author of *Good to Great: Why some companies make the leap. . . and others don't*, recommends the first step of change is to "decide who's on the bus." Even individuals making personal change can benefit from this analysis. Who supports you in the change you want to make? Who can help in ways beyond moral support?

So, who is on the bus? My list of criteria includes people who:

- Have internalized the "Why" of the change.
- Are true problem solvers who invest the time to define and analyze a problem, not just suggest solutions before having the facts.
- Have extraordinary communication skills – looking for clarity over eloquence, and simplicity over sounding smart.
- Others listen to. (This often has nothing to do with positional power, but everything to do with "craft capability.")
- Immediately jump to the "worst case scenario." This is your risk assessor, your seer of unintended consequences. You don't want a whole team of doom and gloomers, but one or two people with this view – and a sense of humor - can help avoid disaster.

What and how?

Ultimately, a leader must explain the change. The leader may describe a type of change, i.e., more innovation, improvement, or integration. The leader may describe levers of change like a new strategy, technology, operational processes, people-stuff like training, or organization. The lead may describe the change in simple from-to statements, e.g., "we are changing from logistics rules focused to customer service focused."

The leader may describe personal values, e.g., "we will take care of displaced people." The leader should go out of his or her way to understand the impact of the change on people and to express gratitude.

The late Max De Pree, former CEO of Herman Miller, the high-design office furniture maker, in his book *Leadership is an Art,* said it well:

"The first responsibility of a leader is to define reality; the last is to say thank you."

Recognize that everyone, even the leader, will change

In the 1980s, I watched Colin Marshall, Chief Executive of British Airways, transform. When we first met, he was impeccably dressed in a custom suit and French cuffs and barked his demands for tea to underlings. Three years later, I saw an almost humble leader with rolled-up sleeves listening to his mid-level leaders who were driving the change effort. He often acted on their advice. New thoughts change you and make it impossible to be aloof or to delegate change.

Finally, don't give up!

Expect backsliding, missed targets, and failure. When that happens, reframe, regroup, and restart. With some focused practice you can be a change craftsman.

Who me? Yes, you.

PART II

WHAT DO YOU MEAN BY CHANGE?

"We just want a new strategy. . . or a new system. . . or to train some people. . . ."

Consulting is always about change, but there was a time when you couldn't use the C-word.

People might have recognized that they were amidst the kind of massive trends we discussed earlier. Maybe their home market was under attack by new global competitors. Maybe multiple manufacturing lines meant rising costs and missed deliveries. Maybe demographic and psychographic shifts made it harder to get consistent communication across business units.

But they still weren't buying the notion of "change." Instead, they were innovating new products, or improving quality, or training people on how to get things done without direct lines of authority (influence management).

Consultants, too, assiduously avoided the word. "Change scares people," a senior consultant told me. Now, more people accept the fundamental truth that change is about altering behavior – people must do things differently or do different things. And that includes the leaders.

I get it. As described earlier, I was slow to define myself as a change leader. I started as a trainer. Sure, I was helping people change their behavior, but that was about them, not me. Or so I thought.

I started facilitating leadership groups using my training skills. At first, it was conflict resolution. Later, I was asked to get everyone to agree on a new strategy. I led quality circles to gather workforce views about how to improve operations. Someone saw me facilitate brainstorming and asked me to facilitate sessions on new product innovation.

I began to think of change as a process around the time that Mico told me the story I shared in the Preface of how immigrants managed to change so radically, "dream, let go of the old, don't accept obstacles in your heart, and act."

Over time, I read articles and books on change that touted many different change models. Later, I began to categorize these models into four distinct types: Phase models, Requirements models, Diagnostic models, and Planning models.

Phase models

The change process has three distinct phases:
- An awareness of the need for change and a growing urgency to act
- Concrete actions that are often experimental and evolving in nature
- Reinforcement through mindset, behavior, measurement, and discourse

Phase models outline the steps of change, beginning with Kurt Lewin's three phases of change in 1947:

Unfreeze – Change – Freeze

The idea that a leader must prepare the organization for change, change it, and then integrate change into day-to-day operations has guided change practitioners ever since.

Many researchers have renamed the phases.

William Bridges: Endings – Transition/ Neutral Zone – New Beginnings

Noel Tichy and Mary Anne Devanna: The Gathering Storm, Vision and Commitment, Institutionalization

Jeff Hiatt of Prosci: Preparing for change, Managing change, Reinforcing change

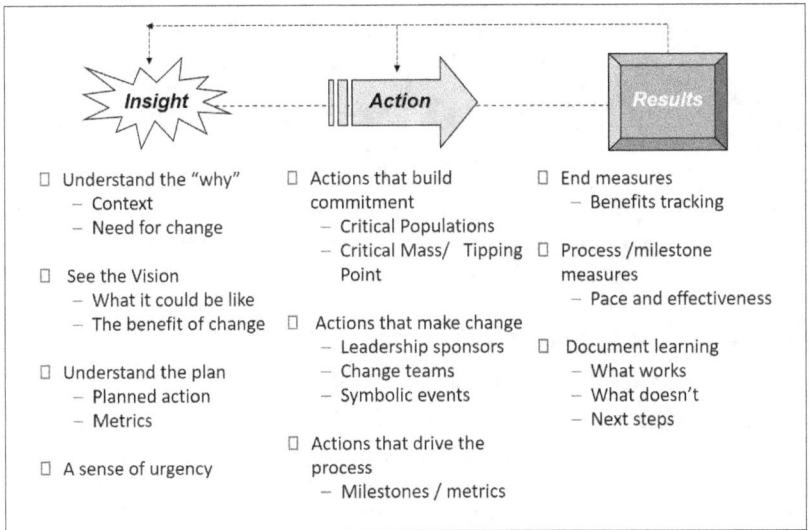

A model that I have used is **Insight-Action-Results.**

The underlying assumption of all of these models is that change is a process with inputs, activities, and outputs. Each step of the process can be measured and monitored, with a feedback loop back to inputs.

Lewin maintained that the change process was one of "action research." Try – collect data, fix, and try again.

The change process is filled with uncertainty. Often a change leader changes one thing and something unintended happens with a supplier, or a different customer. So the action research approach is very useful. The unintended consequences I encountered in my change career certainly confirm that hypothesis.

Phase models provide a "you are here" map for leaders.

Step	Action	Observed Behavior
1	Increase Urgency	People start telling each other "Let's go! We need to change things!"
2	Build the Guiding Coalition	A group powerful enough to guide the change starts working together well
3	Get the Vision Right	People are talking about the vision
4	Communicate for Buy-in	Fewer 'What' and 'Why' questions; More 'How' Questions
5	Empower Action	People act to improve without asking for permission
6	Create Short Term Wins	People feel a sense of success and talk about the quick wins
7	Don't Let Up	Improvements come in waves
8	Make Change Stick	New behaviors stay when leaders change

Requirements models

Requirements models delineate what a leader needs in order to make change. Earlier, I mentioned the model put forth by John Kotter in his book *The Heart of Change*. Essentially, he says that successful change needs "felt urgency, a guiding coalition of leaders, a vision, buy-in, empowered action, short-term wins, and long-term commitment to make change stick."

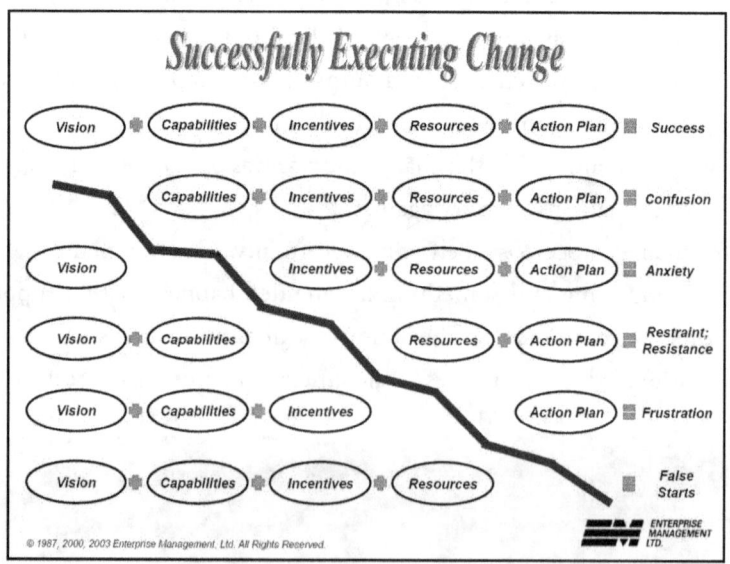

Another of my favorite models was created by Dr. Mary Lippitt of Enterprise Management. It explains requirements in terms of what it feels like when a required element is missing. Frustration, anxiety, and confusion are not the desired results and actually inhibit the intended change; they also suggest where the problems lie.

Requirements models make good checklists for leaders or change practitioners. Phase models can be "we are here now" communication tools for practitioners and perhaps the general population, with one caveat: when communicating with the general population, use only one model and explain it step-by-step in words with examples.

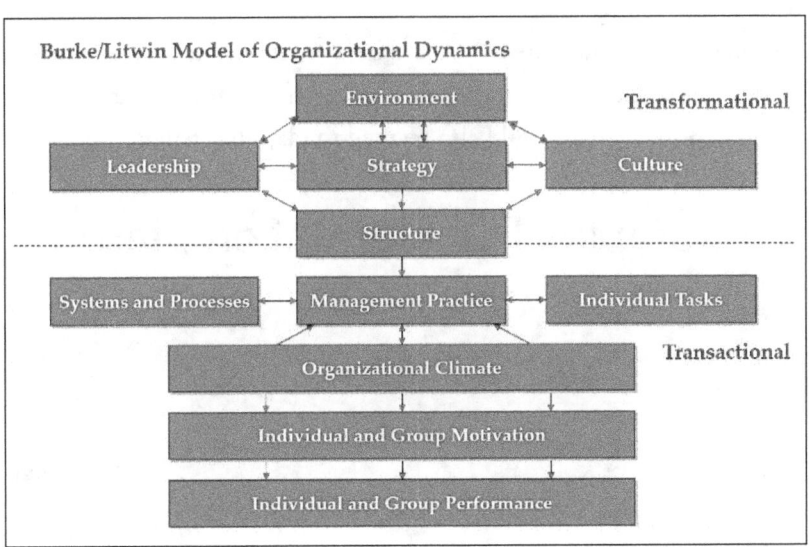

Diagnostic models

These models are especially useful because they help change practitioners think through the why and what of the change. Early in my career at the privatization of British Airways, 1984-1987, I witnessed change experts at work, Drs. George Litwin and Warner Burke, among others. George and Warner discussed this project, and sometimes I overheard and later joined discussions, as I worked behind George for ten years. These discussions evolved into the Burke-Litwin Model of Organization Dynamics pictured here, and published as "A Causal Model of Organizational Performance and Change" in the *Journal of Management* in 1992.

The model explains the many elements of how an organization works (the boxes) and the interactions and feedback mechanisms between them (the arrows). The day-to-day business (transactional elements) is dynamic enough, but when you wish to change an organization, you must start with the why of the change, which is often found in the interaction between the external environment and the organization (transformational elements).

The Burke-Litwin Model guided a lot of my work over my thirty-seven years in consulting.

While Phase models are a "you are here" snapshot and Requirements models are a checklist, Diagnostic models help gather data to make change. Burke-Litwin could also be used to plan the change.

Example: Transformation Map

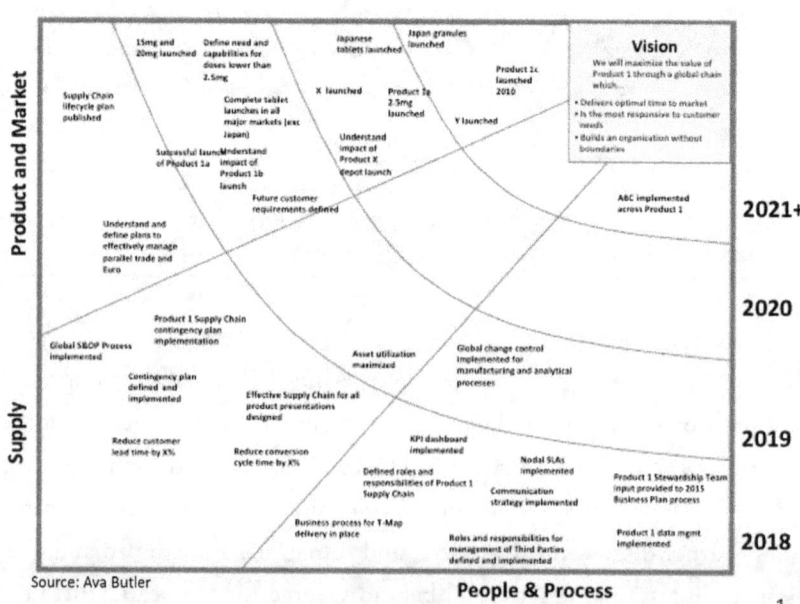

Source: Ava Butler

1

Planning models

These models are meant to engage the client in planning.

At Gemini Consulting, we used a transformation map as described by Francis Gouillart and John Kelly in their book *Transforming the Organization*. This tool allowed teams to plan actions on a variety of variables or disciplines.

Both Phase and Requirements models can take a somewhat static view of change. Transformation mapping and other planning models can be more action-oriented, but they often assume a linear path that will not change.

A transformation map begins with describing the outcome, the vision, and then agreeing on the elements that must change to achieve the vision. (It's also important to identify what won't change.) Then, for each element, the leadership team identifies where they currently are and walks through phases, milestones, and interim metrics (the lines radiating toward the vision). This forms a picture of the overall change plan.

Caveat:

Change models are extraordinarily useful to people who think in a certain way. People who are highly visual, who are comfortable taking in information in whatever order they find it and then structuring their decisions in an ordered way, tend to love change models and other frameworks. In the Myers-Briggs typology, these are intuitive thinkers or NTs, like me.

The problem is that people like me are in a group that represents 26% of the general population. This means that three-quarters of people don't think in frameworks and models easily. So if this discussion totally lost you, don't worry; you're in the majority. If, on the other hand, you're saying, "all this finally makes sense," I offer this caution: be careful about talking from frameworks and models, as you are likely to be facing glazed eyes.

Over time, my thinking about change evolved. I saw change in organizations as a capability required for growth. Context was important.

Had something in the marketplace changed so fundamentally that a step change was required to become effective again? Had the organization gotten a little scattered doing the same thing in different ways, or by not following known procedures? Were there many different views, interdivisional conflict, and lots of finger-pointing and disarray?

I began to see change as being of different types and requiring different growth capabilities:

- **Integration** – alignment, getting everyone on the same page
- **Innovation** - creating new products, markets, and ways of operating
- **Improvement** - getting measurably a little better each day, week, month, and year

Both innovation and improvement are disciplined processes that use creative idea generation, analytical evaluation, and rigorous implementation, planning, and control.

Innovation allows for step change, an entirely new strategy or process that produces dramatically new results and alters the trajectory of the firm. Improvement, on the other hand, is gradual, incremental, and iterative, a slower type of change. Some firms are better at innovation; others are better at improvement. The best firms are good at both and their leaders encourage rapid integration of innovations and improvements into the operations of their firms.

Of course, there is one more "I" to change: Implementation. Change isn't about decisions and plans. It's about action, actually <u>doing</u> it.

All three types of change are processes and require skills, some of which overlap.

These capabilities turn out to be the sole responsibility of leadership. Leaders decide:

- How to build each capability
- What to apply when
- How to organize for it
- How to use each capability to improve your own leadership

Many leaders think that they can delegate change. Unfortunately, because people follow your footprints, that turns out to be a failure mode. If there are no footprints, followers do their own thing, and results are scattered at best and chaotic at worst.

In my consulting work, I was often called in to fix a failed change effort. In most cases, the cause of the failure was that the leaders had underestimated the people side of the change and had devoted little energy to changing themselves. Perhaps the leaders or their people had developed change fatigue and went looked for yet another methodology. Perhaps they hadn't established interim metrics to show when they went off track. My approach was always the same: get back to the objectives of the change and look for ways to achieve interim results.

Let's dig deeper into those types of change.

CHAPTER 4

INNOVATE, INTEGRATE, IMPROVE (REPEAT)

A s I helped leaders change their organizations, I used this model to show how people change:

People (either individually or collectively) come to an **insight** about the *why* and the *how* of change. They take **action** and they get **results**. Things most often break down between insight and action. People know what to do, but get stuck. And what I learned as a consultant was that sometimes organizations need help with this as well.

Clients often hired me and my colleagues when they perceived a need for help with insight (strategy development projects) or action (organization design, training, process development) or when they weren't getting consistent results (alignment and refinement projects). However, what we often ended up doing was helping the client develop or fix one of three core growth capabilities:

- The way to **Innovate** – come up with new ideas for products, or how to reach customers
- The way to **Integrate** – build focus and unity in their organizations
- The way to **Improve** – get better, faster, cheaper at what they do every day

These three growth capabilities are central to the health of an organization, and when any one of them is functioning sub-optimally, a company can run into trouble.

These growth capabilities also follow the business lifecycle order. First, a startup generates a new insight, often a technology that makes something newly possible (Innovate). They form a team to deliver this innovation (Integrate). Then, as they get feedback from customers and suppliers, they work to make their offering better and/or cheaper, or to produce it more quickly (Improve). Then, as competition increases, they start the process over again (Innovate-Integrate-Improve-Repeat).

I call these growth capabilities because each leads to growth in revenue or profit, and sometimes both. They are organizational capabilities, a unique combination of the competencies of **People** and organizational **Processes** to ensure consistency. The DNA of these capabilities is an engaging people-centric process, but each methodology is different. Often, the kinds of people who do them well come from different disciplines.

Innovation

It is hard to pick up a business magazine without finding an article on innovation. Most discuss disruptive innovation – the changes to an entire industry by some new technology-enabled business model. Apple, Google, Amazon, and Tesla make everyone's "most innovative companies" list, but innovation does happen outside of Silicon Valley. Google still has a policy allowing employees to spend 20 percent of their time working on new ideas that interest them, but 3M started that practice in the 1970s.

Innovation process combines vision and creativity with discipline, detailed development, and planning. This process is the interaction among:

- Ideation – finding opportunity or coming up with new ideas, either from analyzing technology or customer trends, or from using techniques like brainstorming or lateral thinking.
- Development – screening, experimenting, prototyping, and testing form the bridge between the raw idea and new product or business model.
- Implementation – bringing the new product to market, gaining customers, and transitioning from the new to "business as usual" are often overlooked. Integrating innovations into normal operations and improving them frees the organization for the next innovation.

Rigorous evaluation is critical at every stage. The Real-Win-Worth analysis, developed at Rockwell International and adopted by 3M, was one of my favorite tools. At each stage of development, the innovation is evaluated to determine whether there is a real product or service and real customers who might buy it. Then the competitiveness of the company offering and the available return are rigorously analyzed. Can our product win? Can our company win? Finally - is it worth it? What are the potential rewards? Sales? Profit? Prestige?

With increasing data requirements at each stage of development, the innovation faces a go/no-go decision based upon questions generated by the Real-Win-Worth analysis.

My colleague Roopa Unnikrishnan had a sweet offering that introduced innovation process in a one- to two-day workshop. What I really liked about her approach was that she:

- Linked clearly to business priorities.
- Tested assumptions and the dominant industry logic.
- Included both ideation and detailed development planning. Participants left with real action items and next steps.

The danger of this approach was that an organization might see the workshop as an end in itself and miss the opportunity to build it into a repeatable process. An innovation system includes a mechanism to collect ideas, evaluate them, and fund them, like the Thomson Reuters' Catalyst Fund or the Royal Dutch Shell Game Changer process. Each of these initiatives operates like an internal venture capital fund. They provide seed capital for ideas to be developed, mezzanine financing to bring ideas to testing, and launch capital to bring ideas to market.

People and organization

Innovative people are a study of both/and, i.e., they are both creative and disciplined, both intuitive and analytical, both curious and doggedly persistent. This is a difficult individual talent specification, which is why so many organizations rely on innovation teams. For example, at Apple, Steve Jobs, Johnny Ive, and Tim Cook worked collaboratively on new products. Ive was the designer, but Jobs and Cook often contributed as much to design. Cook was the operations guy, but Jobs and Ive contributed equally to practical questions like scale-up and so on.

Organizing for innovation is tricky. Because innovation is a fragile process, many companies separate it from day-to-day operations. Steve Jobs famously gathered a crew of engineers in a Quonset Hut to design the Macintosh. The advantage of these innovation centers is that innovation can flourish; the disadvantage is that integration into mainstream operations becomes difficult. The Macintosh designers had a tight culture. They called themselves "pirates" and openly mocked the engineers of the previous flagship product, the Apple II. Macintosh was always intended to replace the Apple II, but the slash-and-burn process of Steve Jobs and the Macintosh pirates caused many developers from the Apple II team to leave. It also completely ignored the innovations of the Lisa, the computer designed by the Apple II team.

Integrating innovation into the organization, e.g., Google's 20 percent time, has the advantage of developing everyone's skills, but misses the focus of having a team whose only job is innovation. Some organizations have adopted both separate and integrated innovation strategies; Google has Google X (the separate innovation lab working on "moon shots") and its 20 percent time initiative.

Integration

The growth capability of integration involves bringing disparate points of view together in order to unify the organization. If everyone is on the same page, then people can focus on innovating or improving the product <u>and</u> acquiring customers at the same time. The increased focus of a truly aligned organization can lead to the Holy Grail of every business: profitable growth.

Process

Integration is a process of sharing information and decisions. There is much in management literature about alignment, but in my experience, this only happened by intentionally creating meetings and processes to share information and make joint decisions.

I stole my colleague Walter Simpson's term "silo busting." Walter does a lot of turnaround business with companies in Chapter 11 bankruptcy (needing to restructure debt). In the high-pressure arena of saving a failed business, Walter gains agreement on core products and core customers and eliminates overlaps that cause a company to decline. It's integration on steroids.

Integration is also critical in the post-merger world. Leaders who have never worked together must decide what operations should be left alone and which have such strategic interdependence that they must be integrated quickly and carefully. During my career, I was around fourteen of these, including two where I was an acquired employee. I can tell you that the emotional and political dimensions of post-merger integration often overwhelmed the rational and technical ones.

People and Organization

Integrative people are the diplomats of the organization. They naturally look for points of agreement before talking about differences. This simple discipline can be taught and enforced by meeting ground rules, such as *pluses before deltas*:

"Let's talk first about what we like about this idea, before we talk about how we might change it."

Integration should be baked into every organization design as the horizontal organization of information systems, networks, forums, and cross-divisional teams, which bring ideas from different functions together for discussion.

Improvement

The fundamental principle of improvement is measurement. Measure today's performance, cycle time, quality defects, and volume. Determine why problems exist: Is the process unclear? Is there rework? Are redundant approvals slowing the process? Take action and measure the results. Then repeat the process. The <u>continuous</u> part of continuous improvement, or CI, is where the money is.

Process

There are many improvement methodologies: Plan-Do-Check-Act, Six Sigma's Define-Measure-Analyze-Improve-Control, and Lean's Sort-Straighten-Shine-Standardize-Sustain. I don't advocate one over another. What's important is that an organization <u>has</u> a structured improvement process that all people understand, that is used in a disciplined way, and that sustains improvements over time.

My late colleague, Dr. Richard W. Taylor, was a Six Sigma Master Black Belt. Ric was an engineer, a statistician, and a Minitab whiz who had forgotten more about metrics and measurement than I ever learned. My focus was on people and soft skills. When we worked together, we joked that between us, we were a whole person. One of the most meaningful things I learned from Ric is that true improvement happens when you control the inputs. The whole idea is to move upstream to the leading indicators. You should monitor the outputs, of course (measure and track results), but first control the materials, people's knowledge and skills, and activities that produce what the customer values.

People and organization

Anyone can learn CI methodology if they are disciplined and process-focused. They must see the work in terms of inputs, activities, and outputs, and be prepared to find the cause before jumping to a solution.

As with innovation, there is a tendency in organizations to create "improvement experts," i.e., permanent Six Sigma Black Belts, Continuous Improvement coaches, or Process Excellence Engineers. However, improvement departments can quickly become a career backwater and often spell the end of consistent business-focused improvement.

Instead, I believe that continuous improvement is everybody's job. Organizations that are famous for improvement (Toyota, General Electric) teach everyone these skills and often require senior leaders to conduct a major improvement project to attain a senior role.

Learning from failure and success

For organizations to get better at the three "I"s of change, people must stop and evaluate what was done well and what should be done differently next time. One of the simplest yet most effective processes I learned came from the US Army, the "After Action Review" or AAR. The AAR was designed for field operations to quickly review success and failure of an operation, either a battlefield engagement or logistical movement, or other operation. It consisted of several questions and subsequent documentation and communication. Accountabilities for documentation and communication are decided in advance of the discussion.

- What did we intend?
- What actually happened?

○ What went well, or worked?

○ What went less well, or didn't work?

- What actions need to occur to reinforce gains or correct problems?
- What would we do differently next time?
- Who else needs to hear about this?

Because it was designed to be used in the field, it is a simple process. I have used it for lower level tasks or entire change efforts.

Innovate, integrate, improve (repeat)

In my view, what helps a business grow is that there are three well-developed growth capabilities, each used at the appropriate time in an iterative fashion. Each has a different objective. **Innovate** focuses on creating New; **Improve** is concerned with making something Better; and **Integrate** is tasked with bringing it all Together. Ideally, a business will create something new, integrate it into normal operations (getting everyone to work together to deliver consistently), then continuously and systematically improve it (integrating each improvement) as they go.

What makes these growth capabilities similar is that they unite competencies (skills and knowledge) with a structured process. They are all measurable. They all engage people. They require individual and collective discipline and, in the aggregate, create insight, inspire action, and ensure results.

PART III

TYPES OF CHANGE: INNOVATION

W hat is your favorite innovation story? What is a product invention or a new process that radically changed your life or others' lives? Everyone could have their own list.

When I asked my parents that question, they named the home refrigerator because it meant they could shop once a week rather than every day. Today's generation might name the iPhone, TikTok, Twitter (now X), YouTube, Facebook, or AI.

If you are medically minded, maybe you'd name vaccines, X-ray, penicillin, birth control pill, or DNA genome mapping.

Types of innovation

The earliest innovations were about harnessing nature, fire, and farming: the water wheel (240 BCE), the windmill (500 CE), the compass (China 200 BCE, for marine navigation 1000 CE), marine chronometer (1767, enabled longitudinal measurement), Ben Franklin's lightning rod (1752), the solar panel (1883), and nuclear energy (1942). This experimentation continues.

We most often think about technology-driven product innovation:

- Transportation: wheel, steam train, automobile, airplane, space shuttle

- Building: wood and stone, concrete, plastic
- Language: spoken language, alphabet, movable type printing press, computer word processing, emojis
- Time measurement: sundials, candle clocks, mechanical clocks, quartz watches, atomic clocks
- Lighting: torches, candles, incandescent lightbulbs, light-emitting diodes (LEDs)
- Recorded music: wax cylinders, records, tapes, CDs, MP3s, Internet Streaming
- Portable music: transistor radio, Walkman, MP3 player, phone, Spotify

But there are also innovations in process:

- Renaissance painting workshops and the guilds' division of labor
- Steam engine-powered, belt-driven factory
- Assembly line
- Neighborhood store, Big Box store, warehouse store, eCommerce
- Hansom hacker, taxi, ride-sharing

Innovations can change lives. They also radically change businesses and industries. The Gutenberg press eliminated the scribe trade. Computer typesetting and desktop publishing made the linotype hot metal typesetting machine obsolete. Perhaps generative artificial intelligence will replace writers.

What is innovation?

The word innovation comes from the Latin *novus,* or new, so it means to "make new." Newness for its own sake is counterproductive, so the innovation has to be useful. It has to do a job, or meet a customer need, in a new way that gets better results.

A Sony Walkman allowed me to carry one album or a mix of albums on a cassette tape; Spotify allows me to carry much of the music of the world on my phone, which I'm carrying anyway.

Newness is central to innovation, and so is functionality. Newness is often more important to early adopters who enjoy proving or disproving the functionality of the latest gadget. Functionality is the prime criterion of late adopters like me.

Newness is often a matter of scale. A jet engine, enlarged and turned vertically, becomes a rocket that will take us into space. Or a Walkman shrinks and becomes an iPod Nano. Or vacuum tubes shrink to transistors and then to integrated circuits carved into a silicon chip.

Sometimes an innovation is a matter of scope. The Swiss army knife or the Leatherman multi-tool does more jobs than a pocket knife. I have an oscillating multi-tool, which, with a quick change of blade, replaces a paint scraper, router, saw, and shaping rasp. Bar codes and scanners have many uses, but they revolutionized inventory management and warehousing.

Newness can also be an entirely new concept: the *idea* of portable music, the *idea* of light produced by electricity flowing through a filament rather than a flame of some kind. Or it can be something produced in such a new way that it makes it difficult for traditional competitors to duplicate, a prime example being digital transformation. But we'll talk more about that when we discuss business model innovation.

So, how do you make a company more innovative? What processes are needed?

What is a successful innovation process?

A process is inputs, activities, and decisions that produce predictable outputs. We often start with outputs, the "job to be done," e.g., more portable music for an individual, or faster, cheaper, better distribution. Once the output is defined, innovation is a process of thinking of ideas (ideation) and then evaluating and testing those ideas. This is an iterative and disciplined process.

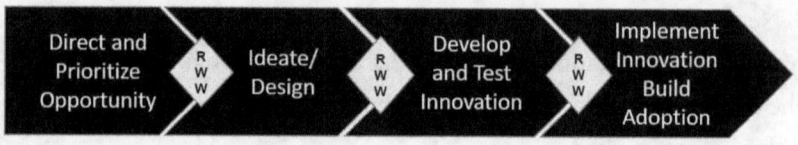

Here is one model I used:

This model has several elements I like:
- It begins with defining the problem you are trying to solve or the opportunity you wish to capitalize upon.
- It ends with adoption, which to me is the measure of success.
- The model differentiates between idea generation and testing of ideas or designs. In practice, there is often no bright line between these steps, but I find that showing them separately ensures that ample attention is given to each activity.
- The model shows evaluation decisions between steps (gray diamonds). Evaluation must happen at multiple stages in the process. Innovation is as much a matter of "killing" unpromising ideas as it is investing in perceived winners. The R-W-W evaluation step is composed of three questions:
  - **R - Is it real?** (Is there an opportunity for this idea with these customers? For anyone?)
  - **W - Can we win?** (Competitiveness of the product and company)
  - **W - Is it worth it?** (Reward—profit vs. risk)

  R-W-W is a simple evaluation that gets more detailed as investment grows.

The Define and Prioritize step identifies the problem we are trying to solve. The inputs to this process can be regular competitive analysis, environment scans for new technology, and changing customer needs. Sometimes, Define and Prioritize bleeds into Ideation. Sometimes we find a technology that could completely eliminate some of our core processes, and so we begin to examine how we'd utilize it. Sometimes we examine the underlying functionality or job to be done and challenge the existing paradigm. For example, someone at Sony looked at the job to be done of listening to music and asked, "How could we make it portable?" That question gave birth to the Walkman. Steve Jobs asked, "How could I carry more of my music?" He introduced the iPod, with the tagline "1000 songs in your pocket."

Similarly, Ideation sometimes bleeds into Testing. Rapid prototyping, to learn from failure quickly, greatly hastens the process, assuming risks are low and there is a clear process for learning. Without systematic learning, innovation groups become chaotic and tend to reinvent the wheel. One good learning process is the US Army's After Action Review, described earlier.

The Implementation step can include testing. Many of us have had the experience of using a new software release that we say is just a buggy beta version, where we're expected to find the bugs. It is faster, but may not produce a beautiful customer experience.

Adoption is not just a matter of customer adoption. Integrating a new product, service, or methodology into the operations of the innovating organization can be extraordinarily tough. The degree of difficulty is related to the size of the change, but sometimes the smallest change can produce phenomenal resistance. "Where are we storing copier paper now?. . . Why?"

When resistance occurs, it is a sign that you have undermanaged stakeholders' expectations or involvement in the process. Once resistance occurs, listen and summarize what is said before responding. Then, clear up misunderstandings, acknowledge shortcomings, and be supportive in emotional and political issues.

How does a company implement innovation?

Implementing innovation is simply planned change, and like other types of planned change, it follows a process:

- **Establish the why of change**. What evolving customer needs are we trying to meet, or what competitive threat or disruptive technology are we responding to?

- **Establish the how of change.** What are the expected results, and by when? Gain commitment to your version of the process described above, plus organization, roles and responsibilities, funding, decision structures, metrics, and rewards.
- Monitor results and improve the process.

Now that sounds really easy, doesn't it? It's not. Here are a few issues to think about:

Organization: There is always a debate whether to insulate innovation in its own organization - the Lockheed Skunk Works, Macintosh Pirates, Xerox Palo Alto Research Center (PARC), or Google X - or to hold everyone accountable, like 3M or Google's 20 percent time for new ideas. The separate organizational unit creates focus, but creates an integration problem later.

The Xerox Palo Alto Research Center was and is an amazing innovation facility, inventing new technologies such as the graphical user interface (GUI) at the heart of Apple and Microsoft Windows, object-oriented programming, WYSIWYG text editing, and many more. Xerox PARC produced more innovations than Xerox could use, e.g., Apple bought its graphical user interface, and many companies built on the Dynabook or laptop. Unfortunately, few PARC inventions were ever integrated into Xerox products. So while the advantage of focus at PARC is undeniable, the disadvantageous lack of integration is also apparent.

On the other hand, the "everyone innovates" model is inclusive and can produce some surprising results, but it requires massive infrastructure to manage.

Funding: Whose project gets money and whose doesn't can be a huge issue. I've seen several organizations that set up an internal venture capital structure to manage this quite successfully. The most important success factor seems to be transparency – communicating why one project got funded and another didn't.

Metrics and rewards: Measuring the percentage of new products as part of the mix is a good approach. 3M's strategy was 25 percent of sales from products that didn't exist five years ago. Coupling that with stage gate is better (A stage gate is the go/no go decision point between stages, represented on the diagram as the RWW diamond), e.g., how many ideas, how many working prototypes, how many successful market tests.

My favorite metric and reward is the W. L. Gore annual award for the idea that looked the best on paper, but was the most spectacular failure. My friends at Cowden and Associates, a Pittsburgh-based health and welfare consulting firm, had some fun with this approach and ultimately added ideas as well as more discipline to their planning.

Business model innovation: Friends with more recent MBAs than mine can't believe that "business model" is a relatively new term. It came into use in the late 1990s and early 2000s with the Internet boom, and is used by entrepreneurs and venture capitalists alike.

The term is a succinct definition of how you make money. One can further break it down into component parts: Business Concept, Revenue Model, Cost Model, and Profit Model.

Business models today are usually discussed in the context of disruption because of a new technology. Kodak had its business model disrupted by digital cameras that enabled sending pictures by email. Blockbuster's business model was disrupted by Netflix, which first mailed DVDs and later sold streaming so customers didn't have to leave home to watch a movie. Borders was the first big bookstore to fall to Amazon's online bookstore business model.

Business model innovation is a special case process. It relies on scanning technology, understanding future customer desires, challenging assumptions in the existing paradigm, and experimenting a great deal. You can also use Blue Ocean Strategic thinking, where you look at each element offered in the industry and carve out space where there is no competition. Cirque du Soleil created a circus that eliminated animals, but had elaborate costumes, sets, and lights built around acrobatics and a theatrical story.

Changing to an innovative culture: Culture change is hard, but not impossible. Companies that succeed in changing culture over time do it by changing behaviors and the organizational support (like rewards and recognition) for different behaviors.

Sometimes, culture is embodied in slogans such as IBM's THINK signs that founder Tom Watson placed around the office. However, cultural values must go beyond slogan ink.

The norms of the organization must also recognize and nurture the different kinds of thinking involved in the innovative process. When the team is creating, no idea is bad. Judgment is suspended. When the team is evaluating, deciding, or implementing, the culture must support a tough-minded "let's get it right, let's get it done" approach.

Organization success stories perpetuate innovation. Singer Sewing Machine employees used to tell the story of the birth of the company's early marketing innovation: the demonstration. This approach was born when an employee took her sewing machine to a quilting bee. Likewise, any Sony employee can tell the story of Akio Morita finding a one-column-inch story about the invention of the transistor. Morita flew to the U.S. and licensed the technology from Bell Labs for $25,000. The rest is history.

Innovation cultures continually scan for new technologies, processes, and products that might be used. There are pitfalls to this approach, so controlling the process is important.

Two such pitfalls to the innovation process are:

The cult of creativity: Loving ideas so much that you are not paying enough attention to delivering results. I worked for a CEO who was a font of new ideas. When turning his ideas into a plan, he'd say, "That's just a detail." He adopted every divergent thinking technique that had been invented and was always buying new books on creativity. He made brainstorming a religion.

Unfortunately, many projects got started, but few delivered results. There was little cultural support for winnowing down ideas, evaluation, testing, and building adoption. Most people agreed that it was a fun and exciting place to work, but the firm eventually went bankrupt.

The corporate crunch: Setting unrealistic hurdle rates and holding nascent projects to the same standards as established businesses. This often happens in multidivisional companies that have been in business for a long time. Divisions are held to rigorous performance standards on their day-to-day businesses, and the Capital Budgeting Process is run by the controller. "Why should we invest money in a business that does not promise rewards that compare to our best businesses today?"

As any entrepreneur will tell you, new businesses frequently lose money until people manage their way down the experience curve, reducing costs as they learn. Holding new businesses to the returns of long-established businesses is unrealistic and means that the company won't innovate, or that innovators will learn to be extraordinarily optimistic in revenue projection in order to garner investment. Innovators are an overly optimistic lot to begin with, and encouraging them to stretch their optimism is a recipe for loss.

PART IV

TYPES OF CHANGE: INTEGRATION

I s integration a type of change or a step in the change process? It's both.

When I conducted leadership team facilitation, I was often hired to get people on the same page. When I ran innovation initiatives, integration was called adoption; in improvement initiatives, it was called control. In both cases, it was the final stage in the change process that ensured that changed processes and procedures were followed and that changed results were sustained.

Integration is clearly visible in its absence

"We're a gaggle when we should be a flock."

"Huh?"

My client continued. "You know those Canada geese that we're always chasing off the campus in the fall and spring? When they're a gaggle on the ground, they run every which way, honking incessantly."

"When geese migrate, they become a flock, flying in a perfect 'V.' This formation cuts down on wind resistance. If you watch a flock of geese in the air, you'll notice that they are quiet for a while. When they honk, the goose at the head of the 'V' peels off and goes to the back, and a new goose moves to the front to take the heavy winds. The flock collaborates, and it moves as one. We're a gaggle when we should be a flock."

I am not an avian biologist, but the analogy stuck with me. A group moving as one is a powerful image.

There are many reasons for integration failure. It could be due to poorly designed information flow or a lack of transparency in decision-making. It could result from an internal competitive atmosphere or conflicting measures, i.e., "We say we are devoted to customer service, but I am evaluated on unit profit."

Different organizational functions or divisions may have conflicting goals and reward structures. Or there may be no system to gather input, circulate information, or share decisions that have an impact outside of the unit in which they are made.

Integration as a step in other change processes

In innovation and improvement initiatives, the integration process includes procedures to be followed and outputs to be measured to ensure that desired results are achieved. Interim process steps are measured so that inputs can be adjusted if the process is off track, e.g., checking on new supplier quality in improvement, or technology stability in innovation.

Mergers and acquisitions are one area where integration is the primary form of change. After all, you start with two or more companies and hopefully end as one.

There are many different tools (change levers) that promote integration. These tools may include:

- **Shared goals and rewards.** In my first large-scale change project, the 1984-87 British Airways turnaround and privatization, all executives, regardless of location or function, were evaluated on customer service as measured by J.D. Power and total profit of the airline. They had 50 percent of at-risk compensation on these shared goals. It promoted a significant spirit of collaboration. "We're all in this together."

- **Organization structure.** The matrix structure – e.g., divisional vertical boxes and wires and horizontal dotted line relationships by function - has been adopted by many global corporations so that all marketing, human resources, or operations people share information. This creates a two-boss management structure that requires high-level communication and negotiation skills, e.g., in what situations (safety or regulation, for example) does the dotted line predominate?
- **Informal structures and processes.** These are powerful ways to promote collaboration and integration. Use forums and networks to share information, and transparent procedures and systems to solicit input and communicate decisions. Carefully define hand-offs in cross-unit processes, e.g., specify the output from the sales process (the order) to meet the input needs of operations scheduling (specifications and customer delivery requirements).

Some watchwords for integration

- **Early and often.** Don't wait until the end of the change process to think about integration.
- **Balance competition with collaboration.** Many leaders see value in a little healthy internal competition. Some organizations overdo this and destroy organizational integration. Strike a balance intentionally.
- **Measure integration.** As the saying goes, you get what you measure. You can do this with shared goals as British Airways did. You can implement integration process control measures, e.g., the number of internal vs. external leadership hires for the leadership development forum, or interdivisional shared process improvements.

CHAPTER 5.

SILO-BUSTING: INTEGRATION IN ACTION

"You know the problem with this place? We're all stuck in our silos, our stovepipes. People compete with <u>each</u> <u>other</u> more than [XYZ competitor]."

When a new leader (or a consultant) first shows up, people sometimes take the opportunity to whine. The Brits and Aussies call this "whinging," but whine is much more onomatopoetic. Take the example of a corporate division executive:

"We run our own business; we've always been told we're entrepreneurial. Why should we have to fight for capital along with every other division?"

The word sounds like what it is - a W-H-I-N-E.

A leader might just chalk whining up to human nature, and, to be fair, nothing is more human than a good whine every now and then. However, silo-whining, though not unusual, is a symptom of a deeper problem to be solved - a lack of integration and a lack of unified focus that's likely to undermine performance. On one project, I was helping implement a company-wide change, and my approach was to work with one division at a time. In the initial interviews, people kept telling me,

> "We have a real Not-Invented-Here culture. There's no way our people would accept doing what [division X] does."

> "It became clear that silos would impede the implementation, so we changed the plan to work in cross-divisional groups to break down the silos."

"Silos" or "stovepipes" is shorthand for a lack of organizational integration across functions, divisions, products, regions, customer groupings, or other organizational units, and is a great thing to whine about. Virtually all organizations have silos, different units with differing priorities behaving in their own self-interest, the perfect ground to wallow in the swamp of We-They-ism.

> "They don't get it. Marketing's 'customer focus' means manufacturing's shorter production runs and higher costs. They want to be customer-driven and low-cost producer at the same time. It just doesn't work."

A silo isn't necessarily a bad thing. Each organizational unit has its own goals, operations, and culture that support those goals. However, I think silos become problematic when the lack of integration starts to hurt people's careers or when internal win-lose behavior prevents all units from performing at their best. For example:

> "Yeah, I'm sure it's a great opportunity for her, but she is one of our best people. There's no way I can release her from this division, no matter how much they want her. Something will turn up for her here eventually."

If you determine that silos are getting in the way, here are some processes to mitigate damage and increase integration.

Leadership alignment

My work in leadership alignment often supported a large change. Sensing a lack of agreement, the CEO or COO hired me for leadership alignment of the C-suite team. Vastly simplified, my process was to interview everyone, gather additional data as needed, and surface points of agreement and points of discussion (purposefully <u>not</u> called disagreements). I fed back the results of the interviews, and we discussed critical issues and came to agreement.

The idea was to:

- Make shared goals and other agreements visible
- Bring differences out in the open, without value judgments
  - ○ Understand the whys behind the differences
  - ○ Evaluate whether the differences matter in terms of agreed-upon outcomes
- Discuss to foster understanding
- Come to agreement (not necessarily consensus)
- Agree to support the decisions made

I used variations of this process in strategic planning, organization design, leadership development, post-merger integration, and change management. But here is a secret: it needn't be run by a consultant. In fact, I believe this process is a critical leadership capability that results in successful integration in an organization. The leader can run this alignment exercise or ask an internal third party (from Human Resources, for example) to conduct the process. The only requirement is objectivity in the data collection, feedback, and discussion.

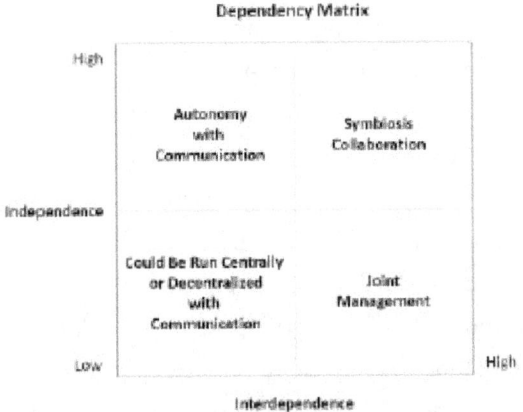

Dependency Matrix

Symbiosis analysis

There are many tools available to guide leadership or interdepartmental alignment. One that I often used is a version of a 2x2 matrix based loosely on a matrix from David Jemison and Philippe Haspeslagh's book *Managing Acquisitions: Creating Value Through Corporate Renewal.*

The matrix answers the question, "Which parts of the business can be managed independently and which decisions or actions need to involve others?" I used this tool to discuss the benefits of collaboration, especially where there is mutual benefit. It can be used at leadership levels or as a communication/discussion tool at lower levels.

The goal of discussion is to show the advantage of sharing information and coming to joint decisions across organizational silos.

Structured resolution

Sometimes silo walls are thick, or the internal competition has gotten to a point where formal conflict resolution is required. Interdepartmental pranks can be fun. Who doesn't like stealing the toilet paper from Engineering's bathroom or gluing all of Marketing's Post-it notes together? But if this kind of internecine warfare is a regular occurrence and is impeding real work, then something probably should be done to manage the conflict.

One structured process I used is called the Two-Way Mirror. It is based upon a Confrontation Meeting run by Dr. Richard Beckhard, one of the leading lights of organization development.

Each organization (department, function, product group, or unit) is asked four questions:

- Us: How would we describe ourselves: organizational purpose, strengths and weaknesses as a group, kinds of people we are, etc.?
- Us: How do we believe that the other group would describe us: organizational purpose, strengths and weaknesses as a group, kinds of people we are, etc.?
- Them: How do we believe the other group would describe them-

selves: organizational purpose, strengths and weaknesses as a group, kinds of people we are, etc.?

- Them: How would we describe the other group: organizational purpose, strengths and weaknesses as a group, kinds of people we are, etc.?

The answers to these questions are placed on flipcharts, and the groups brought together. The leader asks for the self-descriptions first, then the imagined descriptions by the other group. Most groups are reasonably self-aware, but may miss entirely when assessing how the other group sees them. There is often an overlap in how one group thinks they will be seen and how they see the other group. The discussion evolves to the need for collaboration and the horizontal organization systems and structures that ensure that the two groups keep talking.

Horizontal organization

Each of the processes above are event-based silo busting: a leader perceives a lack of integration and plans an event to overcome the problem. This may be a necessary, but certainly not sufficient, solution.

Most organizations are designed for vertical alignment. The hierarchy contains goals and key performance indicators (KPIs) that cascade from executive to manager to supervisor to worker. Cross-unit integration is frequently ignored. Structural cross-unit integration is often accomplished through the "matrix" organization. This most often applies to functions. For example, divisional finance has a solid-line reporting relationship to the business and a dotted-line reporting relationship to corporate finance.

Sometimes these dotted-line responsibilities are carefully spelled out with performance appraisal implications (e.g., 65 percent of bonus based upon business evaluation, 35 percent based upon corporate evaluation); sometimes not so much. When left undefined, dotted line relationships contribute to confusion, conflict, and a lack of trust.

The best organizations go beyond well-defined matrix structures. They use regular forums to decide shared goals, strategy, leadership development, capital budgeting, innovation, and continuous improvement solution exchange.

These organizations create shared information systems and databases to facilitate free flow of information. They often institute internal social media, using platforms or networks and forums around key demographic groups and key issues. They create cross-unit problem-solving teams and frequently rotate people among units to break down the deleterious effects of silos and to ensure working together on an ongoing basis.

Sometimes during change the silos form not around organizational groups, but around points of view or opinions about the change. Getting all groups "on the same page" about the change may call for some unusual strategies for silo busting.

The aircraft manufacturer Short Brothers of Northern Ireland built the first aircraft for the Wright Brothers. Shorts was nationalized during World War II and was among the firms privatized under Margaret Thatcher. It turned around financially and was to be sold. There were those in the company who were adamant that Shorts should still build whole aircraft. One of the strongest advocates for this position was a division CEO, a manager with a volatile personality who could verbally eviscerate someone when angry.

Finally, the Canadian company Bombardier put a deal on the table, and Shorts' role was to build only the fuselage for the Canadair regional jet. The division CEO had privately accepted this outcome, but his extended management team, unaware of his change of heart, pushed back. Further, they were concerned about the coming explosion from their CEO, whom many in pre-session interviews described as Genghis Khan.

To his credit, the CEO took this feedback well. "I'm not proud of how I react sometimes, and I see that this behavior will not work to bring us together behind this sale. Let's have some fun with this. I'll bet the Mongols thought better of Genghis Khan than the conquered did."

I did some research and produced a white paper on Genghis Khan, and from that, we crafted an exercise that allowed all groups to agree on the culture and leadership behaviors they wanted in the new organization. In the process the silos broke down and people supported the Bombardier deal.

People will still whine, of course. But perhaps they'll whine about the coffee in the shared break room rather than those "arrogant idiots" on the other side of the silo wall. And that's better. You can try another brand of coffee and another. And then go back to the first.

Then you'll have an integrated coffee whine system but permeable silos.

CHAPTER 6.

INTEGRATION CHALLENGE: MERGERS AND ACQUISITIONS

I ntegration may be the most difficult type of change. It involves people actually doing new innovative behaviors or sticking with the improved process while collaborating and sharing information and decision-making. Innovation and improvement are about people, processes, and technology; in integration, the people are always center stage.

Now, imagine the challenge of combining two organizations, with the people of each having to change. The degree of difficulty for change leadership goes up exponentially.

Why acquire?

There are two ways to grow a business: build or buy, organic growth or acquisitive growth. Organic growth is hard. You must find the customer's need, innovate to make the product or service profitably, and then integrate, improve, and integrate again.

Acquisitive growth looks easier. The opportunity to acquire often occurs serendipitously. Two CEOs meet on the golf course. An investment banker calls out of the blue. You buy a going concern with products in established markets, and the money rolls in. It seems like a no-brainer.

"Double in size overnight – easy-peasy," said the investment banker to my client. He was relaying this conversation to me six months after the close, when people from both firms were leaving, and he couldn't get any data about performance because the systems migration blew up.

Every few years, a large consulting firm publishes research showing that a large percentage of mergers fail (75 to 85 percent usually). The research typically defines failure as when the value of the combined business is less than that of the pre-acquisition businesses individually.

By now, it would appear to be an accepted fact that, by that definition, **most acquisitions fail.** But companies keep acquiring, and executives keep getting huge bonuses for what is essentially value destruction. Shareholders and boards keep approving big mergers, and the business press loves them.

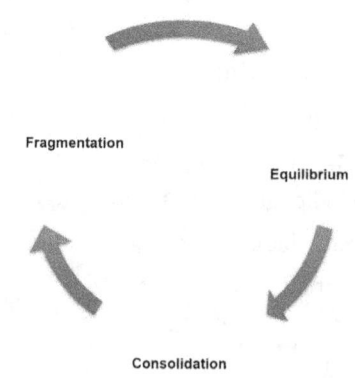

Fragmentation

Equilibrium

Consolidation

Acquisitions are a natural part of the business cycle. A startup company finds a need, creates a product, and is followed by many others selling similar products, with no one firm dominating the industry. Some industries reach a kind of equilibrium with many firms competing.

Then technology changes, or the business slows down, or a firm locks up a supplier. Organic growth becomes difficult. Firms start to lose business, a consolidation cycle begins, and acquisitions happen.

There are some companies - Cisco Systems comes to mind - who are serial acquirers. These firms have a process to buy much smaller firms, fold them into the acquiring culture, and move on. Leaders in these companies develop a core skill at integration.

For most managers, change leadership opportunities show up infrequently in the best of circumstances. Post-acquisition integration opportunities are even more rare. Most managers get one such opportunity in an entire career, which is probably why most acquisitions fail.

Mergers or acquisitions?

In my career, I was around fourteen acquisitions. Three times, I was a consultant doing work at a client when they acquired another company, which affected my work; and twice, I worked for a client who was acquired, which effectively ended my work. Seven times, I was hired to help with integration. Once I worked at a consulting firm that acquired another, and another time I worked at a consulting firm that was acquired. I saw a lot of mistakes and made my share of them.

You may note that I have consistently used the word acquisition and not merger. **There are no mergers.** Acquired companies and leaders trying to placate the managers of an acquired company use the word merger. There is almost always a buyer and a seller, an acquirer and an acquiree. Sometimes, the attitude that goes with this reality gets really nasty.

"If you're so great, how come we **BOUGHT YOU?**"

As I think is obvious, this is a value-destroying attitude. An acquiring company acquires to add value to its firm, and **all value is created or destroyed in integration.**

To be fair, there may be some true mergers. Despite this fact, however, leaders in an acquisition integration should behave *as if* it were a merger, *as if* two firms were coming together equally to build a third, better firm. In this idealized world, the following would be true:

- Both parties are **clear** and honest about the **purpose** this partnership serves for them.
    - Acquirers often want access to proprietary technology, products, or markets and overpay to get them.
    - Acquirees often want access to investment capital and are disappointed that less is available because of the purchase price.
- The **process** of integration is **transparent.**
    - Acquirers may be thinking of spinning off certain underperforming businesses, or locations.
    - Acquirees might believe those businesses are core and autonomous.
- **Decision rights** are clearly delineated.
    - Which decisions will acquirees have input to?
    - How will deal-breaker decisions be surfaced early in the integration process?

Change leader roles

Of course, responsibilities for integration will vary depending on where you sit in the organization.

Executives will have more decision rights concerning the purpose of the acquisition. Integration managers will be held accountable for the integration plan and its results. There likely will be teams looking at various functions or businesses.

How these roles work together is a critical success factor for the integration overall.

The integration process

Regardless of the part of the process for which you are responsible, follow a planned process. Clarify purpose, how you will work and deliver value, and then plan and monitor results.

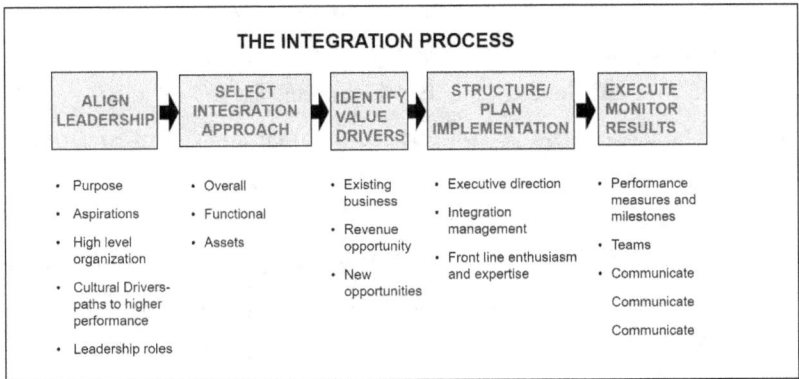

The Jemison-Haspeslagh matrix introduced in generic form in the last chapter is a good start for discussing value. It helps to decide which functions or businesses can be left alone and which should be integrated.

While it's important to communicate decisions you make, I don't recommend using this tool for that purpose because many people don't find such drawings useful.

	Low ← Need for Strategic Interdependence → High	
High — Need for Organizational Autonomy	**Preservation:** Interdependence is not necessary just now, but culture maintenance is required	**Symbiosis:** High degree of interdependence is required and culture maintenance is critical to sustaining and creating value
Low	**Holding:** Units with low need for autonomy and interdependence are held now, but may be spun off or closed down later	**Absorption:** High degree of interdependence is required to create value, but maintenance of culture is not critical

Source: Managing Acquisitions, P. Haspeslagh and D. Jemison

Things Leaders in Mergers & Acquisitions Should Never Say

- **"Don't worry."** Of course, people will worry. Maybe they'll worry less if they have information, but they'll worry anyway.

- **"Nothing will change."** Of course, things will change. Otherwise, why did you do this deal? Trying to lessen worry with an untruth isn't helpful.

- **"No one will lose their job."** Come on. Even with the best redeployment plans, there will be redundancies. If you must promise something, promise that those let go will be notified as quickly as possible and treated fairly.

- **"This is a merger of equals."** Even with the best of intentions, even with the best integration processes, this will turn out to be a lie.

- **"We will share information on a need-to-know basis."** Yeah, that might work in the CIA, but in business, people resent being told that they aren't important enough to be informed. Sure, some strategic information will need to be kept close to the vest, but a much better posture is, "If we have information that affects you, we will tell you what we know as soon as we know it."

- **"Don't believe the rumors."** When my wife worked for a small hospital acquired by a large university healthcare system, she had an epiphany. "The rumors are <u>always</u> <u>true</u>." No matter how much you try to hide information, people talk, and the secret is blown. It's also true that, in the absence of information, people make stuff up that is worse than the truth. Get a handle on rumors. Create an anonymous rumor hotline where people can record a rumor, and you can respond within a day.

- **"We are looking for synergies."** The word synergy means a combination greater than the sum of the parts. Unfortunately, my consulting brethren have changed synergy to mean cost reduction aka people taken off the payroll.

- **If it ain't broke, don't fix it."** By definition, an acquisition broke all processes from both legacy companies. Use the opportunity to redesign and improve, and ensure ownership by all parties.
- **"The integration is complete."** I have seen companies where, years after an acquisition, legacy company uniforms, letterhead, logos, and processes were alive and well. Some of that is fine. People need to remember where they came from. But if it gets in the way of everyone working toward shared goals and feeling a part of a united company, memorabilia needs to go.

Leadership integration priorities

As hammered earlier, most acquisitions fail. Remember "Double in size, easy-peasy"? That's a statement of top-line growth that ignores difficulty and value destruction.

Failure is often blamed on a culture clash. Integration processes should be inclusive and rational as a remedy to the clash. Doing real work together would go far in joining disparate cultures.

People are important, but real work is more so. Leadership priorities are in this order:

- **IT systems first** -you need real data that people believe in, P&L, management accounting, sales, production, and HR. Run both sets of systems until you are sure the integration has lasted for three months.
- **Customers** - here I mean real customer relationships, not just the reams of data collected on customers, and sales should not be the only point of contact.
- **Suppliers** – I have seen too many supplier agreements thrown out for synergy, which crippled the company's delivery to its customers.
- **Operations** -operating processes can always be improved, but they need to be maintained and integrated slowly. Often, both manufacturing and service quality decline during integration.
- **People, Organization, Culture** – Why does a change guy like

me put culture at the bottom of the list? Especially when companies may have twice the people they need in some functions? In surveys about acquisition success or failure, respondents often say that culture and organization, i.e., people issues, are the most important. But if you address these issues by themselves, they quickly turn into be-nice-to-each-other workshops.

Most people issues can be addressed as you do other work. Shouldn't you get to know the people you acquired before you sacrifice them to synergy? Success in people issues comes from how you work together, <u>actions</u>, and not from patronizing high-sounding words.

Leaders, if you take only one thing from this discussion, make it this: **Please stop thinking that acquisitions are easy.**

In an acquisition, two groups of people who don't know each other must act differently and start from different places. Change, innovation, or improvement must be integrated into day-to-day operations, and mergers and acquisitions are always about integration.

Easy-peasy it is not.

CONTINUOUS IMPROVEMENT (CI)

I'm a "fix and repair" guy rather than a "discard and replace" guy. I keep things forever, tweaking and improving. I still play the Regal guitar that was my thirteenth birthday present. I have adjusted the action, replaced the bridge, and found the perfect strings. It wasn't an expensive guitar, but people are amazed at how good it sounds.

So my affinity for improvement change methodology comes naturally.

Many companies attempt disruptive large-scale change because they are looking for the next bright, shiny thing. What they really need is a "make it better" ethos.

I worked in Continuous Improvement for so long and saw so many different approaches that I became methodology agnostic. All methodologies use a rigorous problem-solving process, teams, and actions to ensure sustainability. I tell people: pick <u>one</u> methodology and stick with it. What doesn't work is constantly switching methodologies.

The basic process for Continuous Improvement (CI) is:

- **state the problem: what is wrong (defect) with what (object, or process to be improved) and so what (the impact of the problem)**
- **measure where you are,**

- **plan to improve,**
- **measure where you got to, and**
- **repeat.**

It isn't rocket science, but it does take disciplined execution.

I can predict how successful an organization will be at CI by some simple observations:

- Do executives habitually think in two or more comparative numbers (this week's performance vs. last week, or vs. a benchmark)? Comparing is how you know you are improving.
- Are performance numbers posted for all to see? Are those charts actively updated? Improvement is everyone's responsibility, and visibility is critical.
- Do the improvements actually fall to the bottom line in a meaningful way? Revenue up consistently, costs down consistently? This shows that the organization is picking the right projects and following through in a disciplined way.

CI also requires process focus and disciplined leadership, which are discussed in the following chapters.

CHAPTER 7

LEADING CI: PROCESS FOCUS

O nce, I found myself struggling to help a client and her organization become process-focused. This organization was almost religious about the old Tom Peters and Bob Waterman's "Bias for Action" (task-focused methodology). They got a lot of stuff done quickly.

But when they applied this "To-Do-List on Steroids" approach to process improvement, it failed. Multiple teams worked on overlapping improvements, there was a lot of rework, and customers were complaining about product defects and missed shipping deadlines. The client teams kept jumping to solutions before they understood the problem. I explained the difference between task and process focus to this leadership team using the slide below:

Task Focus	Process Focus
Task	**Input >> Activity >> Output**
· Most appropriate for ad hoc or discrete work or one-of-a-kind projects	· Most appropriate for routine work, interconnected or continuous projects
· Objective: Completion	· Objective: Efficient Flow
· More often individual work, easy to manage	· More often the work of several individualsdifficult to manage
· Requires planning and scheduling (what to do, how to do it, and who does what by when)	· Requires thinking about why we do something and for whom, and how to do it better, faster, cheaper, as well as planning and scheduling
· Gets stuff done - "it's all about the check mark"	· Appears to take longer - might seem like bureaucracy
· May cause "unintended consequences"; eliminating one defect may create a defect elsewhere, and financial or compliance risk	· Is foundational to continuously improving efficiency and effectiveness, and delighting customers (members).

My challenge was to help my client and her people move beyond seeing their operations as just a set of discrete activities and instead look at the inputs and outputs of those activities. I wanted them to understand the flow between those who provide inputs (suppliers) and those who receive outputs (customers).

There is nothing wrong with task focus. Most of us get through our weekend with a long to-do list. It works for discrete work and one-of-a-kind projects, where the primary objective is completion. There is tremendous satisfaction when the job is complete and we can cross it off our list. (Some of us are so motivated by the checkmark that if we do something that isn't on the list, we put it on the list in order to cross it off - silly, but it still feels good.)

Process focus requires thinking about <u>why</u> we do something, and <u>for whom</u>, and what output each customer of the process expects. It also requires considering the connections between activities and the overall flow of the process. And, probably most importantly, these things are

measured for quantity, quality, and timeliness.

Seeing the world in process terms is both a blessing and a curse. The blessing is that it is easier to make lasting improvements; the curse is that process awareness is very difficult to turn off, which makes renting a car or checking into a hotel potentially frustrating when the process isn't clear or the flow is confusing.

These leaders still had a hard time getting this distinction. So I shared how process focus finally came home to me in the lunch line at DuPont.

I led training for engineers at DuPont, which was founded in 1802 to make gunpowder. As a result, DuPonters are known for safety and are very process-focused. "If we got the process wrong, we blew people across the river."

My training class returned the first day from their forty-five-minute lunch break, complaining bitterly about the hotel lunch line. "Somebody obviously doesn't understand how you make a sandwich," they groused. I had gone through the same line and, yeah, the condiments were at the end, and I went back and forth a bit, but I didn't get what the big deal was.

The next day, they complained louder and longer, and one of them took me to the line:

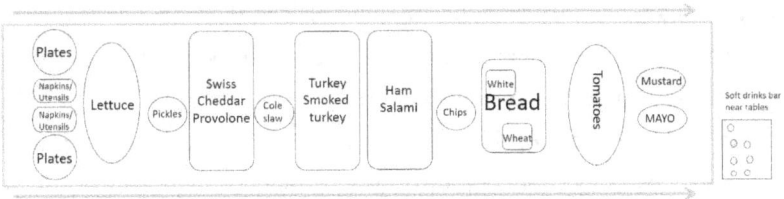

"See," he said, "you have to run all over the place to make a sandwich." Well, I <u>did</u> see and I sought out the hotel banquet manager, René, after class.

"It's set up that way to make it easier to replenish," René told me through clenched teeth. "They're not supposed to make their sandwiches in line. They're supposed to pick up the fixings and make their sandwiches at the table."

The next day, hoping to head off complaints, I shared René's rationale and got hooted out of the classroom. "Typical that they'd build the line for the supplier and not the customer." "Don't they realize you only give us forty-five minutes for lunch?" "Building it at the table makes a mess and wastes food, and I don't want to do that at the table; I want to talk to people."

I spoke to René. "Next, do you want to tell the cook how to cook?" she asked. I demurred.

So imagine my surprise when the next week, in the same hotel, the sandwich line looked like this:

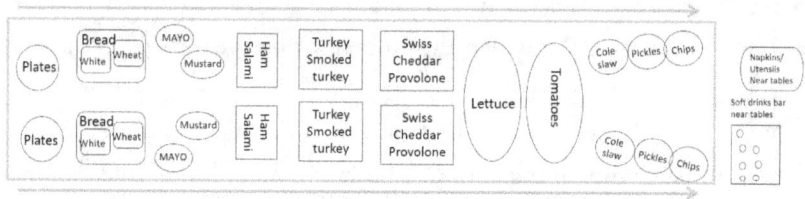

The class had no complaints. After class, I went to thank René for responding to our feedback. She was off that day, and the assistant banquet manager was Raoul.

"I set up the line like an assembly line," Raoul informed me. "René thinks the line is a lunch meat warehouse that you pick your ingredients from, but I always want to build _my_ sandwich in the line. She also measures time in line, and I measure time in the lunch room, which, I think, is the way the guest would measure it."

I was in that hotel a lot. René always set up the line her way and frustrated the class. Raoul set it up his way, and there were no complaints. I learned the impact of process. As a result of this experience and others that followed, I surmised these principles for teaching process focus:

1. **Legitimize task focus.** It isn't wrong; it's just used for simple or ad hoc, mostly individual work. Process focus works better for routine but interconnected work where efficient flow between people or tasks is critical.

2. **Experience a process as a customer.** Maybe the lunch line, maybe two Starbucks that do things differently, maybe something from the client's company.

3. **Reflect.** Talk about the impact on the customer, the measurements, where to start and stop cycle time, and the inputs. Relate it to the existing business.

4. **Hands-on.** Try improving a process. Reflect. Try improving another.

5. **Keep it simple**. For many companies, process means bureaucracy because those who implement process thinking try to codify every tiny step. The complexity overwhelms people and slows everything down.

Process focus can be taught, but it takes practice and feedback, and more practice. The payoffs, however, can be tremendous.

CHAPTER 8

TIPS FOR LEADING INNOVATION AND CONTINUOUS IMPROVEMENT

A sk anyone what they think is the most critical success factor in a company's drive to be innovative or to continuously improve, and, without hesitation, the answer is some variation on leadership: "Can't do anything without the leaders."

True, of course, but not particularly helpful.

Senior executives are just people who have risen to a level where they inspire as much fear as respect. Underlings carefully craft what they say around them. As a result, senior executives rarely get leadership how-to manuals or helpful feedback.

Innovation and improvement have many similarities. Both require a systematic process that is rigorously followed. Both use divergent thinking techniques like brainstorming to come up with ideas, as well as convergent thinking tools like the plus/minus charts that help decide which ideas to implement. Innovation often has a long time horizon (new product development may take five years), while continuous improvement is often more immediate (reduce the cycle time by three days this month). Both methodologies have unique languages and require knowledge and skill development. Both require an innate understanding of the voice of the customer – the person for whom you are innovating or improving.

In companies that I helped implement continuous improvement or innovation, most senior executives truly wanted to be supportive of the effort. Often, they put a person they trusted in charge of the initiative. Sometimes that person was at too low a level, or had too many other things on his or her plate, which proved to be problematic. But just as often, this was a dedicated and competent mid-level executive who took the job seriously.

Therein lies the first tip for leaders:

You can't completely delegate change. No matter how competent the person running continuous improvement or innovation, the leader still has responsibilities. If the person to whom you delegate is really good, he or she will act as your coach, making sure you know where your contribution is needed, but that coaching relationship will be a lot easier if you initiate it.

Some other tips for leaders:

Pick one methodology. Continuous Improvement has a variety of brands - Lean, Six Sigma, Process Improvement, Re-engineering, etc. Innovation has its own panoply of methodologies - Human Centered Design, Rapid Results, Agile, etc. Being able to pick and choose different parts of different methodologies is an advanced concept, a little like spin in bowling – "Alan, quit trying to curve the ball delivery and concentrate on hitting the pins."

Learn the language. Every methodology has its own language. The process is defined by the language, and you will avoid confusion if you learn it. When you misuse the innovation or improvement language, you may seem comically unintelligent to your people, but, more importantly, you definitely will appear uncommitted to the process.

Learn the process by doing a project. Project size doesn't matter. What is important is that you have examples to talk about. Leading by example is the most powerful form of leadership.

Create the right metrics. Metrics drive behavior. Good high-level metrics for innovation include the revenue from new products or markets not in the portfolio two years ago. Improvement metrics are cost reductions or revenue increases from improvement projects. It is important that all metrics be audited (perhaps by finance) to avoid double-counting. Reward results that are due to the improvement and actually drop to the bottom line. Track the savings <u>before</u> you spend the money on something else.

Emphasize the delta. As I trained in innovation and continuous improvement, I often told participants that I could predict success by how executives talk about numbers. If the executive mentioned one solitary number, 15 percent ROI or $1.2 million in revenue, I knew that it boded ill for success. However, if that executive mentioned that number in comparison to another number, 15 percent ROI this quarter from 12 percent last quarter, or $1.2 million in sales compared to XYZ competitor at $750,000, that showed an interest in improved performance or the tracked value of innovation. Innovation and improvement are comparative, and trends are important.

Connect business priorities to innovation or improvement projects. This is a leader's job. What are you trying to get done strategically? What will require improvement over current performance? What will require new products, marketing approaches, or business models? Sponsor the improvement projects or innovation initiatives to get you there. I saw far too many "move the supply closet" type projects waste valuable resources while strategic priorities languished. I heard leaders complain about the time suck of coaching project work: "When do I get to do <u>my</u> job?" That was usually a sign that their coaching projects didn't match their priorities. **Reward learning.** I don't mean the number of people trained, but rather what people are learning and sharing from projects. I saw companies reward translation of improvement projects from one division to another and lessons learned from a high-profile failure. Find a way to reward real learning because avoiding someone else's mistakes is a sign of higher intelligence. This is a practice-makes-perfect game, but it accelerates only if you share the learning.

Be visible. Kick off or close training sessions, attend lunch-and-learn sessions, run project-sharing sessions, and hold a town hall on the subject. Carry the innovation or improvement flag.

Look for symbolic acts that communicate that this is important. Who gets hired and promoted? Who has access to you? How do you react when a big innovation or improvement project fails? ("OK, so what did we learn from this?" <u>not</u> "YOU DID WHAT?!") Share the credit for your project. Promote the results of a small project that made a big difference to your peers and even to shareholders. A leader can't do it all, and shouldn't do it all, but they can invest their passion wisely.

View your leadership as a process. How are you innovating? Improving? Learning? Performing? (In that order.)

The pressure can be crushing. I often told executives, "Cut yourself a little slack. Join the parade. You can still lead from the middle. Be open about what you are learning."

CHANGE CHALLENGE AHEAD

A s you think about change, here are two caveats. The word "caveat" is Latin and translates literally to "Beware." Archaeologists have found *Cave Canem* (Beware of the Dog) signs on volcanic ash-buried buildings in Pompeii, and consumer activists warn of unscrupulous marketers and scam artists with the phrase *caveat emptor* (buyer beware). Here are two *Cave Mutatio* (Beware of Change) warnings.

CHAPTER 9

THINKING BEYOND THE SILVER BULLET

I heard clients facing a change say, "We don't expect a silver bullet, but..."

What they were really saying was, "I know we probably need to change substantially. . . and this easy solution isn't likely to change everything, but we should at least try it."

The term "silver bullet" comes from folklore about werewolves, supposedly mortally allergic to silver. Silver bullets eliminate werewolves like Raid does cockroaches. Monster killers always carried silver bullets, Dean and Sam Winchester of the television series *Supernatural*, or Van Helsing (vampire killer of multiple movies), Silver Bullets-R-Us.

In business, the silver bullet is a simple but sure-fire solution to a complex and/or chronic problem. The problem goes away <u>completely</u>. It is a kind of magical thinking that avoids the hard work and discipline of change.

Why would any company use a silver bullet? Perhaps it faces an intractable problem like the need for a turnaround, or the CEO just wants to spice things up a little.

Here are three examples of silver bullet thinking, all of which should be avoided:

- **I know, I know:** Jumping to a solution before understanding the root cause
- **The bright shiny thing:** Change by the latest fad
- **Switching horses:** Trying yet another methodology when the "going gets tough"

I know, I know: jumping to solutions

In process improvement, a well-written problem statement makes everyone want to solve the problem. We humans frequently describe ourselves as problem-solvers when we really are solution-finders. All too often, we hear a problem that sounds like one we have seen before, and we say, "I know, I know," and blurt out the solution to that problem for this one.

Sometimes these silver bullet solutions even work, which reinforces our tendency to jump to the solution before understanding the root cause of the problem. However, when the silver bullet fails, we typically suggest a different silver bullet, not realizing that the failure was due to a lack of understanding of the problem. This leads to stops and starts in improvement, as well as in strategy, innovation, and acquisition integration. People tend to fix symptoms, but miss the underlying problem. It's all because we fall in love with our silver bullet.

The bright shiny thing: changing by fad

"Here comes the flavor of the month."

When this was how I was greeted by the frontline, I recognized it as change fatigue. Many companies overuse consultants, and many managers are always looking for the next shiny new thing. To be fair, consultants too often have invented bright, shiny new service offerings and sold them as must-haves. Recognize these?

Re-Engineering	Economic Value Added	Balanced Scorecard
Lean	Six Sigma	Management by Objectives
MBWA (Management by wandering around)	Innovation	Agile software development
Rapid Application Development	Matrix Management	Theory Z
Delayering	**Empowerment**	Self-managed work teams

All these methodologies have merit. They also all have their own jargon, deployment plan, key performance indicators (KPIs), and critical success factors (CSFs). Sometimes they require reorganizing and giving people new job titles, assessment criteria, evaluation, and even certification. They voraciously consume an organization's resources for a promised ideal gain.

As in investing, if something sounds too good to be true, it probably is.

Each of these methodologies can improve business performance, but "less is more" is relevant. If a company used one or two per year, it would achieve little and confuse its workforce.

And the workforce isn't fooled. I've heard frontline people cynically undermine a new manager's introduction of a new initiative by saying, complete with air quotes, "He's 'new.' He just needs a 'quick fix' to 'declare victory' before moving on to his next job. Wait it out. This too, shall pass."

Switching horses: not toughing it out

Most methodologies require disciplined implementation. Discipline and hard work aren't compatible with a belief in silver bullets.

Switching horses mid-stream is a common phenomenon. Sometimes it's the result of a bid for power during change. "If I suggest a new methodology, I get to lead it, not you." It arises when results are slow in coming, perhaps due to poor problem definition, which means we have to start over. Or it may mean we're not measuring the right things or executing the plan well.

So what happens is that midway through implementation, just when the first difficulties appear, someone says, "You know, this is just the problem that [Insert different methodology here] is intended to solve. " In other words, "This one is hard. Let's try a new silver bullet."

I suspect that looking for silver bullets and achieving consistent results are negatively correlated. Change is hard perhaps those leading it might practice the mantra:

There are no Silver Bullets. Stick with it. Persistence is the only thing that pays off.

CHAPTER 10

MAKING CHANGE STICK

"We have told the analysts that we expect to grow revenues from 8 to 9 percent per year and to grow earnings by 15 percent per year.

To do that, we must identify new product ideas and launch two new products a year **and** drive efficiency by leveraging scale through standardization, and getting better and better at what we do every day, every month, every year."

I was in the audience of a divisional chief executive's town hall. He was making the compelling case for change, which supported the work I was doing in innovation and improvement processes. He was speaking confidently, making the points that the leadership team had agreed upon in our last meeting.

He paused briefly for breath or effect. Suddenly, he was challenged from the floor by a young engineer, who stood and said petulantly, "But isn't it difficult for a large company to show that kind of growth? Small entrepreneurial startups perhaps, but surely not a company our size?"

(*Oh, no,* I thought.) This executive had a reputation for getting derailed easily. There was an uncomfortable moment of silence. Some shifted audibly in their chairs. Then Andy responded. "I would challenge your thesis. A small startup does not have the R&D department or supply chain efficiency opportunities that we do."

He continued, "*The limiter is not scale; it's culture.* The minute we come up with a new idea or a better, faster, cheaper way of doing things, our 'that'll never work' or 'we've always done it this way' culture just absorbs our growth energy and *sucks the life out of it.* We have to *change that*!"

Applause broke out. About half the audience stood. What Andy said had resonated.

Making change happen is hard. Insights about the need to change are not enough. It requires changing mindsets and decision frameworks that we have developed over time. Even if we internalize the need to change, taking consistent action is tough to do. Breaking old habits is hard. Even if our actions lead to early results, backsliding is all too easy.

This executive had put his finger on the most challenging part of change: making it stick.

How does an individual or a company make change stick? Talk about the change, measure it, and track it. And then talk about it some more.

Talk about it

One of the most successful personal changes I've ever made wasn't even my idea, really. Well, maybe it was my idea, but I might never have acted on it without an external push. One Saturday night when I was twenty-six years old, I was at a dinner party with Kirsten, my wife at the time, at the house of our friends Steve and Roberta. It was after dinner. We were sitting on their living room floor playing Risk. We had most certainly been imbibing, and we were all smoking cigarettes. I think I started the conversation with, "We really *should* quit smoking. We all know how bad it is for us." Steve and Roberta joined in, and soon we were all engaged in what can only be described as a self-punishing whine, filled with the words "should," "ought to," "hard," "try," and "can't."

Thinking about it now, in the paradigm of Think-Talk-Act, I was stuck in the second stage. Suddenly, Kirsten jumped up, grabbed all our cigarettes, tore them up, and threw them in the garbage on top of the discarded leftover spaghetti with red sauce.

"There," she said. "We can stop moaning now; we've quit smoking."

My recollection is that the evening ended soon after that. I think somebody "accidentally" kicked the Risk board. But we all agreed that we had quit smoking.

At the time, I was a booking agent, a telephone sales job. We were allowed to smoke at our desks, and I did. I lit up my first Marlboro as my feet hit the floor in the morning and snubbed out my last as I turned off the light to go to sleep. I smoked three-and-a-half packs of Marlboros a day. (Everyone else at that party smoked less than a pack a day.)

Two weeks later, Steve, Roberta, and Kirsten were smoking again. (All have long since quit.) I haven't had a cigarette in over fifty years.

What happened? Starting Sunday morning, I told absolutely everyone I knew that I'd quit smoking. I did this quite consciously. I wanted to ensure that if I tried and failed, I would be terminally embarrassed. Embarrassment, humiliation, and not finishing what I start all touch my emotions deeply. I don't know why–something in my upbringing, I suppose - but I knew that about myself at twenty-six. I was making it impossible to backslide. Like Cortez burning his ships off the coast of Mexico as his soldiers battled Montezuma, I was ensuring commitment, creating a compelling need to change.

As previously discussed, I used a simple model of change:

- **Insight:** Start with internalizing the reasons why change is necessary and beneficial to individuals and the company, and **why you can't go back.**

- **Action:** Plan what to do and what results you expect, and when.
- **Results:** Measure and track everything. If you're off-track, re-plan; get back on track.

Making change stick starts in the insight phase. Talk about the benefits of the vision in a way that connects with people emotionally. So in the opening example above, Andy's "We have told the analysts. . ." doesn't really cut it. That may touch executives, but it's unlikely to move production workers. Most especially, talk emotionally about the impossibility of continuing to do things in the old way. In change jargon, this is often referred to as the "burning platform." (I found that image to work well everywhere except the offshore oil production business. To those guys, the concept of a burning platform is really scary.)

The best burning platform speech I ever heard was at British Airways, during its 1983-1987 transformation from a nationalized company to a publicly-traded one. It was couched in a story about how Prime Minister Thatcher told British Airways executives of her plan for privatization. The story was rich in detail, describing the paneling in the conference room, presumably at Heathrow, and included the new chairman, John King, and the new Chief Executive, Colin Marshall, fresh from Hertz. "On Colin's first day. . . he didn't even know where the Gents was yet." The storyteller usually imitated Margaret Thatcher's posh Tory accent and high, somewhat squeaky voice.

> "I will sell you. Rest assured of that," she said. "I can sell you off in little pieces, routes, planes, and ramp vehicles – one piece at a time, if need be. Or we can sell the company's stock to the public, and you can become a proper company. It's your choice, gentlemen, really."

I have come to believe that this account is apocryphal; it never actually happened. The story just summarized the compelling case for change so well that it was repeated hundreds, if not thousands, of times. During my work at BA, I heard people claim to have been at the meeting or to have seen a video of the meeting. I personally heard the story so many times that I thought I must have seen the video. I don't think one exists.

Veracity of that story aside, British Airways went from being the least profitable airline in the world to the most profitable in four years. They went from having the worst customer service in the industry to the best in the same period.

This happened early in my career, and for a long time, I looked for other clients to make a similar change. I've realized that most turnaround companies will never have the deep pockets of the British government to invest, nor will they have the Iron Lady as their burning platform.

However, all companies can make a compelling case for change and tell everyone about it. Encouraging the whole company to have this conversation helps people internalize the "why" of the change and adds to "stickiness."

Measure and track the change

"What is measured gets done" is a corporate truism. Unfortunately, there are so many metrics in most organizations now that the numbers have become meaningless. But a few simple metrics, made visible to everyone, are very powerful. I remember that BA correlated its customer surveys to an existing airline industry customer service metric. The numbers were talked about in every meeting. I also remember the profit tree that was taught in the "How BA Makes Money" course, and how the revenue-cost-profit tree numbers were monitored weekly and discussed at every Monday morning staff meeting.

In more recent years, Dr. Richard Taylor and I did a lot of Continuous Improvement training together. He talked about the dashboards and control plans that are feedback mechanisms to let you know you are on track. Ric always emphasized measuring and tracking the inputs to the process, the leading indicators, rather than waiting for the outputs or lagging indicators.

Talk about it some more

Key Performance Indicators (KPIs), dashboards, process documentation, and control plans are the "hard" side of sustaining change. There is a softer side as well. Leaders need to orchestrate conversations with individuals, small groups, and occasionally large group events like town halls, results fairs, and multi-group after-action reviews. These are two-way communications that not only tell and retell the reasons for the change, but also allow leaders to listen to the difficulties, troubleshoot solutions, celebrate successes, and learn from failures.

Of course, you can overdo the celebration by declaring victory before a change has delivered measurable results, or by rewarding everyone indiscriminately. But a realistic celebration builds enthusiasm and cements newly learned habits.

And, of course, in your conversations, you have to avoid self-sabotage. I've learned that my joke "I'm very good at losing weight. I've lost the same twenty pounds five times in the last fifteen years" isn't helping me get thinner. Nor does "our culture doesn't really support process" help with continuous improvement.

Thanks to consultants like me, there are many words for corporate change: transformation, innovation, turnaround, improvement, alignment, integration. These words don't communicate what is most important: ***companies change when the people in them change.*** Tools to help make change stick all involve engaging people, helping them to do more of some things, less of others, and/or to do some things differently. Change is all about the people.

In the early 1990s, I read about a paint company executive who was quitting after failing to overcome cultural inertia in the company he was trying to turn around.

> I feel like I have just spent two years sitting atop a giant marshmallow. Every time I kicked it, it absorbed my impact and then slowly reformed to the way it was.

The article went on to present a different point of view. Lee Iacocca, fresh from turning around Chrysler, commented:

> I sympathize with his frustration, but also I clearly see his error. The way you change the shape of a marshmallow isn't by kicking it from on top; it's by heating it up from below.

Making change stick is the result of talking about it, measuring it, and tracking it. But perhaps, most importantly, it comes about by "heating it up from below."

TRAITS AND VALUES

I'm not exactly sure when I began thinking about leadership in the context of business. Perhaps it was when I read Abraham Zaleznik's 1977 *Harvard Business Review* article "Managers and Leaders: Are They Different?" as part of my Organization Behavior class at the London Business School.

Or perhaps it was when I contemplated the difference between two consulting projects, both conducted with LBS students. At the first, a UK commercial vehicle manufacturer, the CEO took an active role in the project, rolled up his sleeves and puzzled through the data. At the second, a transmission maker, the executive held the student team at arm's length.

A year later, I learned that the first CEO had implemented our recommendations, and the second firm had taken no action. In fact, the report was still on a shelf, literally gathering dust.

I noted that there was something about leadership engagement that was an indicator of successful change.

I started to read a lot about leadership and leading change.

Let's be honest. Most books about change leadership focus on CEOs of large corporations who changed everything. Sometimes these are books by the executives themselves (or a ghostwriter who interviewed them).

Then there are books by historians about a particular innovator who changed the world. If these books are written after the death of the innovator, we often learn that this individual may have changed the world, but he or she wasn't a very nice person. They were miserable to co-workers and family.

I don't want to disparage these books. I learned a lot from them. I also learned from the values of leaders I encountered in my life or read about.

Over time, I developed a point of view about leadership:

- Leadership is different from management.
- Often, a leader and a manager are the same person acting in different ways under different circumstances, which isn't easy.
- Change leaders are not just at the top, but distributed throughout the organization.
- The best leaders lead by example, knowing you can't delegate change. They show up. They talk the talk. They walk the talk.

I began to see examples of leadership values everywhere, beginning with my Boy Scout troop leader. I thought about an old boss with a rough-hewn integrity who demonstrated that he cared for people; I thought about a client who was nobody's idea of a charismatic leader, but for whom people would go through fire because of his passion and support for his people.

I thought about a storytelling shoeshine man who told me to stand on my own two feet and adapt, and other leaders in situations in which they excelled or slipped up. I thought about trust, integrity, self-reliance, constancy, and care, even when no one is watching.

What follows are some stories of people and situations that provided me with insights and shaped my views of leadership values.

CHAPTER 11

THE BASIC TRAITS FOR LEADING A CHANGE

There is nothing more difficult to take in hand, more perilous to conduct, or more uncertain in its success, than to take the lead in the introduction of a new order of things because the innovator has for enemies all those who have prospered under the old order, and lukewarm defenders in those who might do well under the new.
— Niccolò Machiavelli

The Prince

Leading a change is difficult. Machiavelli made the point that change has no natural constituency. People resist change because they fear loss. They fear the unknown, or they refuse your change because they don't feel they have a choice, and people must choose to change. Yes, I sold everything I ever owned and moved across the Atlantic to get a graduate degree, but I chose to do that.

It is tough to get change started; inertia is a powerful force. It is also tough to keep a change moving. With every failure, people will want to go back to the old ways. ***The leaders must keep things moving forward.***

In my observation of many change leaders in both the public and private sectors, the following traits have appeared again and again.

Vision and visionary communications

Change leaders paint a picture of the future state of the organization so that people want to go there. These visionary messages are rich with sensory images and emotional appeals and create a sense of urgency. The vision of these leaders is grounded in the possible but steeped in the future pride of having achieved what many thought unlikely.

Trust

Most people will not blindly follow. The leader's words and actions must convince followers that the leader understands their needs and will act in their best interests. A history of empathy, honesty, and dependability builds the trust necessary to lead people. Consistency between words and actions – always doing what you say you will do - is trustworthy behavior. Transparency, i.e., sharing information and the reasons for decisions, communicates trust that others will use this information well. Giving trust engenders trust; it is empowering.

Empathy and gratitude

People follow a leader who understands them and what they're going through. Empathy, or "feeling with" (as opposed to sympathy, "feeling for"), is a characteristic of good leaders.

One of the first indicators of empathy is gratitude. A leader who thanks people for "bearing with us in these difficult times" or "for understanding that we don't have all the answers yet" is demonstrating empathy by being grateful for the contribution of followers.

Gratitude is more than just saying thank you for your service. It is understanding what that service costs and deeply appreciating it.

Empowerment

No change happens by a leader's actions alone. The entire organization must move as one. The leader's task is to motivate action and then *to let go.*

Often, discussions of empowerment involve an assumption that people fear change. As previously mentioned, people fear loss, and the unknown causes them to assume loss.

But people overcome fear of the unknown all the time, to move sometimes across the ocean or between countries. They get married and start families. The difference is that they **choose** those changes. Those changes are my changes. What I may fear is the loss connected with your change.

Leaders empower others to change by explaining circumstances and empowering choice.

Exemplary actions

Teddy Roosevelt said, "He who leads the parade must not flinch." The leader is an example to followers. This doesn't mean that the leader must have all the answers or be instantly decisive; the leader can take whatever input or discussion is required to determine or alter the appropriate course. But once the course is clear, the leader must *act* without hesitation and actively reward others for the same behavior.

Tough mindedness

Sometimes in a change, leaders must make hard decisions. Perhaps some people cannot be coaxed or led to the new organization. Perhaps the cost of a needed new facility must come from layoffs or cuts in other areas. Perhaps longer hours are demanded that cannot be paid for within existing budgets.

Change leaders don't shrink from tough decisions. They examine all options and are empathetic and humane, but they do not sacrifice the good of the many embodied in the new organization.

Does every leader need all of these traits? Trust, empathy, and gratitude seem more like tickets to admission. Let's say that the Guiding Coalition, to use John Kotter's words, must contain all these traits, but individuals may have different strengths.

CHAPTER 12

FIRST GLIMPSE OF SERVANT LEADERSHIP: ED HOXIE

At my mother's funeral, I started my eulogy saying, "Hi, I'm Alan Culler, Nan's son, and I was a Campfire Girl." I went on to describe how my sisters were both active in Campfire Girls, and Mom was a Campfire Leader, and we didn't have money for a babysitter, so I went to Campfire Girl meetings until I was six or seven.

Then came Cub Scouts. I remember being extra proud of that blue uniform and yellow neck scarf with the bright brass clasp embossed with a wolf. I don't remember much about Cub Scouts, except always having to wash Elmer's glue off my uniform and finishing the pledge with "and to obey the Pack Law." I don't think I knew what the Pack Law was, but it had to do with wolves, which I thought was really neat.

I stayed in Cub Scouts till I was eleven and could hardly wait to join Boy Scouts.

Boy Scouts were no longer a neighborhood thing. There were boys in Troop 119 from all over town. We met in the basement of the Congregationalist Church in the center, next to the green.

Fifty or sixty eleven-to-fifteen-year-old boys are a management challenge. The organization structure was a tad military. Scout Master Mr.
Hoxie had the Dad Council. We called them by Dad and their last name
- Dad O'Brien, Dad Hagman, etc. I know that Mr. Hoxie's first name
was Ed because the Dads used first names, but he was always Mr. Hoxie
to us boys.

The boys were organized into platoons of ten with one boy named as
platoon leader. The first leadership tasks for platoon leaders were getting
their groups quiet for announcements and maintaining order during fire
drills. When an adult asked, a platoon leader simply raised his right hand
with the three fingers used for the scout salute to quiet his platoon. It
took a while at first, but we all shut up. The first ones to notice elbowed
their noisy platoon mates in the ribs to be quiet.

We lined up by platoons. We practiced marching because we marched
in parades on Patriots Day (April 19) and the Fourth of July. (Cub Scouts
marched in the Patriots Day parade, too, but you can imagine what that
was like.)

At every weekly meeting, there was the "presenting of the colors," recit-
ing the Pledge of Allegiance, and singing "My Country 'Tis of Thee." We
also played games, tug of war, Red Rover, a kickball version of baseball,
and dodgeball.

There were activities on weekends, as well as day hikes and overnight
hikes in spring, summer, fall, and winter (yep, sleeping in your sleeping bag outside on a pine bough bed in two feet of snow in the White
Mountains of New Hampshire). Sometimes fathers went along. My dad
declined the honor of attending the Eskimo hike.

Ed Hoxie was an interesting man. He wore what I'd describe today as
techie-retro glasses, black plastic top of the frame and ear-pieces, wide
U-shaped lenses held by chrome metal rims and nose band. Hoxie
smoked a pipe when we were outside and wore a Scottish tam, black with
a red and white checked band. Troop 119 ultimately had over one hun-

dred boys in it (Baby Boom generation), and he knew everyone by name and usually something about them to start a conversation. He was a little older than most of the Troop 119 dads, not as old as my dad, who'd had me at age forty-four, but almost.

He was not tall, maybe 5'8" or less. He had a quiet presence. The dads on the Dad Council did most of the day-to-day management of the boys. Hoxie chaired the council and floated around, having one-on-one conversations with individual boys, giving a word of encouragement here and there. During breaks in the action, you'd see him talking with a small group of boys.

We always announced the boys who achieved a rank or got a merit badge. When that happened, the dad in charge of your platoon sent you up to the front to shake Mr. Hoxie's hand. When I got my cooking merit badge, he said:

"Alan, I'm not sure I believe this; I saw how you cooked bacon and eggs on the Eskimo. If your mother had served you that you might not have eaten it, but it says here you made a stew and bread over a campfire, didn't burn it, and it was actually pretty good. Everybody can improve. Let's hear it for Alan."

There was some laughter at my expense, but the encouragement and the applause felt shirt-button-popping good.

Hoxie was a quiet man. He rarely raised his voice. Most of the other dads did the discipline, breaking up the push fights that always happened with boys that age. Once, there was a bad fight brewing in which pushing had moved to fists raised and punches swung. Boys had circled around to cheer on one or the other combatant.

Suddenly, Mr. Hoxie was in the middle of the circle. No one saw him come in. In his low voice, he called each boy's name. First one dropped his hands. The other boy wasn't ready to stop fighting and reflexively started to push Mr. Hoxie away when he lightly reached out to touch his shoulder. The collective gasp from the ring of boys quickly made the boy drop his hands and mumble, "Sorry, Mr. Hoxie."

He took both boys away for a talk. We thought they'd get thrown out. "Naw, he just had both of us explain what the beef was, and we had to listen to each other without interrupting. It sounded like a dumb fight when you said it out loud. Then he made us shake."

Ed Hoxie played a six-string flattop guitar, performing and having sing-alongs at campfires at Jamborees and camping trips. I still remember that he introduced me to the songs of Tom Lehrer, especially Lehrer's "Hunting Song":

"There are ten stuffed heads in my trophy room right now, two game wardens, seven hunters, and a pure-bred Guernsey cow."

I didn't realize it then, but Ed Hoxie was my first glimpse of a servant leader. He cared for people and encouraged them. I still remember when I made first class rank. Publicly, he joked that I'd come a long way from Tenderfoot and shook my hand. I was promoted to platoon leader. My big task was to keep people lined up and quiet for fire drills.

Hoxie made more of the role, talking about the responsibility for safety and the first eyes on a problem with any of the boys. He encouraged me not to yell, but to be a role model:

"People don't follow your voice prints, they follow your footprints. . . and don't be afraid to ask for help. . .

You can do anything alone except build character."

This was more than sixty years ago. While I've said these words in leadership training dozens, scores, maybe a hundred times, I still remember the man whose dark brown eyes were locked on mine when I heard them for the first time. Servant leader, Boy Scout Troop 119 Scoutmaster Mr. Ed Hoxie.

CHAPTER 13.

FAIRNESS

L eaders wrestle with fairness all the time. Do we believe that workers should share in profits at the same rate as financiers or shareholders? Not in most of the companies where I have worked.

We say we believe that two people who do the same work should be
paid equally. Of course, we often fail at that standard. In the United
States, women are often paid less than men. People of color are often
paid less than white people.

Ability isn't shared equally, some would say, so why should remunera-
tion be equally distributed? Fairness is about relative contribution.

This is the argument for sports and entertainment star salaries, for sales
vs. production worker salaries, and for 300/1 ratios CEO vs. the lowest-paid worker. We forget that no one on a team, in a movie, or in a
business does work entirely on his or her own. Other people make it
possible for a company to grow, a sales quota to be exceeded, a team to
win, or a movie to do well at the box office.

In some places, seniority is rewarded. If I have worked here longer than
you, I am presumed to be better at my job and am worth more. Or perhaps we are rewarding loyalty. Is loyalty a component of fairness?

"He has a family to support!" This is need-based fairness. It justified
paying men more than women for the same work. With so many women
working, does anyone try this excuse now?

Fairness, at least pay equity, should be understood as an often subjective evaluation. What someone's contribution is, the work that they do, their need, or their loyalty, is often colored by how much we like or identify with the person. We rationalize unfairness away.

More fairness phrases:

"First come, first served" is something we've come to expect at a deli, but accept that restaurant walk-ins may be second to those with advance reservations. Should it apply to workers' start dates, seniority, as some believe?

"To the victor belong the spoils." This is a concept we accept in politics, war, and increasingly in economics. But is it fair? It is an extension of might makes right. There are vast inequities in basics like food and housing around the world because some countries won the economic game. There are vast inequities in opportunity because some people have advantages handed down from their parents and ancestors.

"They're the job creators," say those defending the riches of billionaires. It's true that some people have more money than they could spend in ten lifetimes, while others struggle with sustenance and shelter. How I feel about three or five hundred to one income ratios depends upon the one; if the one has "enough," then I am more sanguine about the excess than if the one is hungry and homeless.

What's a fair deal?

Fairness in price and in pay relies on perceived value given and received.

Transactions are often seen as fair or not, based on whether the parties agree on value. Often, our idea of fairness involves reciprocity.

"One good turn deserves another" is a phrase that expresses the expectation of reciprocity. Or some say, "You scratch my back, I'll scratch yours," although that often describes a reciprocal arrangement that implies kickbacks and corruption. Even interpersonal interactions are often viewed as transactional, give and take. "He takes and takes, but never gives anything back." There is reciprocity in a change effort as well, but if the transactional balance shifts to one side it may be hard for the other side to get beyond that.

Fairness in change

Leaders often puzzle through fairness when things change. Who gets the ax in layoffs? Who leads a new product division? Who opens a new geographic territory? How do you staff or choose IT systems in a merger? What do you tell people, and when, as you plan through change?

Perceived fairness involves trust. People must trust that leaders will make the right decision <u>and</u> that the process will be fair. This means accepting all appropriate input and communicating as needed.

W. Chan Kim and Renée Mauborgne, professors at INSEAD and co-authors of *Blue Ocean Strategy*, wrote an article in the January 2003 *Harvard Business Review* called "Fair Process: Managing in the Knowledge Economy."

In the article, they show that people, especially knowledge workers, expect to be involved in the process of decisions that affect them. They demonstrate that even if people approve of the outcome of a decision, they may resist if they believe that the process was not fair and visible.

Kim and Mauborgne suggest three actions:

- Engagement, gathering input from people for decisions that affect them
- Explanation, explaining the factors considered in making a decision
- Expectation clarity, explicitly conveying actions that the decision requires of people

Transparency is now a buzzword in business and politics. People want to know what is going on. The simple truth is that not every stage of a decision can be completely transparent. Companies want to protect sensitive strategic information. Governments want to protect national security. But if business or government keeps secrets that affect people's lives outside of such risks, trust erodes.

Mergers make people nervous. They know that layoffs or material job changes may result. One of the best post-merger integration leaders I ever saw understood this. He took several actions:

- He publicly committed to communicate "what we know when we know it."
- He created a rumor hotline where people could anonymously record a rumor they heard, and there would be a public response within twenty-four hours.
- He committed to gathering input and explaining any hiring or job change decisions to those affected.
- He committed to severance and outsourcing for displaced persons who could not be redeployed.

This leader stuck to these commitments. While some people lost their jobs and others' jobs changed radically, there were no lawsuits, no work stoppages, nor strikes from the unions, and the integration of the two companies happened on schedule. One laid-off manager later told me, "I didn't like it, but the company treated me fairly. They helped me find another job, and I didn't suffer too much in the process."

As a young consultant, I worked behind a grizzled old management consultant twenty years my senior. In a meeting with a CEO his age, he advised the CEO to communicate more and explain his reasons for his decisions. The CEO took umbrage.

"This isn't a democracy!" he fumed.

The Old Hand smiled and spoke softly. "It is true that a business is not a democracy, but it still requires the consent of the governed."

The CEO's gray eyes widened at first, then he looked at his desk and breathed in through flared nostrils and out through puffed lips.

"That's fair," he said. Then the two discussed a communication plan as I took notes.

So life isn't fair, but people can be, and leaders should strive for a visible fair process.

CHAPTER 14

INTEGRITY AND CARE: SAM DAME

I t was 1976. I was working as a booking agent at a speakers' agency in Boston. It was a telephone sales job in the entertainment industry. The business was in its infancy in the 1970s; speakers were paid $500-$2000. Ralph Nader raised his fee to $3000 and became the most expensive speaker on the circuit. Now, politicians and executives earn hundreds of thousands of dollars per speech.

It was a fun job in a dynamic industry, but I wasn't happy. After almost five years, I didn't feel respected. The owner of the agency seemed to block my attempts to connect with customers and went out of his way to humiliate me in front of my colleagues, clients, and customers. I was ready for a change.

The contract that I signed upon joining had a non-compete clause, and the CEO was notoriously litigious, but I wasn't worried. The contract had expired three years before, I reasoned in my twenty-nine-year-old naïveté. I talked to a colleague about starting an agency, but he wanted to move to Colorado to get beyond the range of the non-compete. I had just bought a house and had an infant daughter. That move was just too overwhelming.

There was one other agency in Boston, Lordly & Dame. I knew people there. My first boss, Phil, had joined after a brief stint in Pittsburgh in his own agency (just beyond the range of the non-compete). I met with Phil and his boss, Dave, at a conference. Dave said he wanted to hire me, but would have to talk with Sam, the owner of Lordly & Dame.

I don't remember when I first met Sam Dame, but I remember my first day at Lordly & Dame. I arrived for work at 8:00 a.m. in the little building at 51 Church St. in Boston's Bay Village that L&D owned. They put me in an office with no windows and pecan paneling that covered the interior of the entire building.

It was a foregone conclusion that there would be an injunction served very soon, but I was optimistic. I started organizing my office, getting ready to make phone calls to the colleges in my new territory, the West Coast. (My old territory had been the Northeast, and the prevailing legal defense strategy was "if he isn't working with the same customers, the non-compete isn't valid.")

Sam Dame greeted me sometime in the morning. He was about five feet six with a little pot belly – not bad for someone in his sixties. He had white hair, smoked cigars, and looked like a grandfatherish, twinkly-eyed gnome. He reached up, squeezed my shoulder, and told me not to worry about my former boss. "Bobby will sue," he said. "That asshole always sues. But my brother-in-law David will handle the case, and he doesn't charge me. You'll be fine." My office was right next to Sam's, and he left me and went back into his office.

A little later that morning, I heard Sam on the phone. "Whaddya mean? You PROMISED me you'd do this!" The soft-spoken grandfather sounded very upset. "I DON'T CARE HOW MUCH THEY ARE PAYING YOU. YOU COMMITTED TO <u>ME</u>!" I heard the phone receiver slam down.

I admit that in my fragile state, I was sure the conflict had something to do with me. Perhaps his brother-in-law wasn't going to take the case. I heard Sam dialing the phone. It sounded like he was punching the desk.

"SCUMBAG!" I heard him scream into the phone and then slam the handset into the desk phone again. BANG. I couldn't imagine the phone wasn't broken. I wondered what I'd gotten myself into.

Sam stomped out of his office and into mine. "Damn Victor! Argentine pianist. I had him booked into the Balsams for the summer. He's cancelling me. I can't believe it. This bozo was nothing till I started booking him in the White Mountains." He stormed out of my office again.

Periodically during that morning and early afternoon, I listened to Sam vent to Victor on the phone. "Victor SLIMEBUCKET!" "Victor SCUZZBALL!" His screams were always punctuated by slamming the phone down. This was Boston, and Sam did have a strong New England accent, so it came out more like "Vicktah, ya SkaahmBaahg!"

It became funny. My favorite was: "Hello, Victor. Every morning I get up and look at myself in the mirror and I say, 'Sam Dame, you are an honest man.' Whaddyou say? Good morning SCUMBAG?" It was a unique first day of work.

At 3:15 p.m., an officer of the court arrived with an injunction. I wasn't allowed to work at Lordly & Dame until the suit was resolved, if ever. I hadn't received my last paycheck or my last month's commission checks from my previous employer. Panic started in my throat, but moved quickly to my stomach. As I read and re-read the injunction notice, my lower extremities began to go numb.

Sam walked into my office, grandfatherly once more. He squeezed my shoulder again and said, "It's OK, son. I told you he was an asshole. You go home now and talk with your wife, and meet me at David's office in the morning. We'll work on this there. And tomorrow night, Corinne and I would like to take you and Kirsten out to dinner. If you can't get a sitter, just bring the baby. Now go home. You'll beat the traffic. And don't worry, you'll get your paycheck on Friday for the week, like we said. That asshole will hold up your money as long as he can, but we'll cover you. You're probably short of cash. Take this." He handed me three $50 bills, which I tried to decline, and he stuffed them in my shirt pocket. "Don't want that baby to go hungry. See you tomorrow morning."

I packed up and went home. It was a hard night for us young parents, kids really, worrying, worrying, and worrying some more, no matter that Sam had told us not to. The next morning, I went to the offices of David Kaplan, Sam's brother-in-law, and now my attorney. David explained the way things would go and set me to work writing my side of the story in an affidavit.

I worked all day, and that night Kirsten and I went to dinner with Sam and Corinne at an Italian restaurant in Boston's North End. I think my parents babysat Tegan. I don't remember the restaurant or what we had for dinner. I do remember that early in the meal, Sam leaned across the table, took both mine and Kirsten's hands, and said,

> Alan, I want you to know that we will pay you for as long as this takes (and Bobby is an asshole so he'll try to drag it out) but we will pay you for as long as it takes. And we won't lose, believe me, I've beaten that asshole before and we won't lose, but if we do and we can't find you a job in some other part of L&D, we will pay you until you find another job.

The care that Sam exuded was palpable. I don't remember anything else about the evening, but I can still feel Kirsten's and my collective sigh of relief.

The case took eighty-one days to resolve, with many angry, elated, and desolate moments along the way. At one low point, Sam took me out to lunch and then to a Boston clothing factory that made clothes for Brooks Brothers. Sam bought me a blue blazer. It was nicer than anything I'd owned to that point. Sam thought it was pretty funny that I called it my "rich kid's blazer."

In the end, the judge thought that my working in an entirely different territory was a resolution enough for the non-compete clause. I began to work in earnest at L&D.

There were lots of Sam Dame stories that floated around L&D, especially how he called the phone company every month and said, "Where's my bill?" (Phones were the most significant expense for the agency, often over $10,000 a month.) "Will you send me my bill, so I can pay it while I have the money?!"

There were stories about the summer when an IRS audit took too long, and an exasperated Sam turned on the heat and smoked his cigar until the agents gave up. "They were never going to find anything anyway," he said. "If there's a question, I always decide in their favor."

In the three years I spent at Lordly & Dame, I started up the West Coast and put in place a performing arts division, as well as a business meeting division. It was a great team atmosphere.

Few things drove Sam to the level of anger I heard him express to Victor on my first day. But once I saw him challenge someone for avoiding a tough discussion with a client, refusing to take a call, and telling a secretary to take a message. "You face up to your problems and don't FLUFF IT OFF TO SOMEONE ELSE TO LIE FOR YOU!"

Another time, an agent, a larger-than-life character, was clowning around, holding court after closing a big sale. "The whole secret to this business is integrity," he said. "And once you learn to fake that, you've got it made." We all started to laugh.

Suddenly, the laughs died, chilled by an icy wind. Sam Dame had joined our group.

"For cryin' out loud, Sam, it's just a joke."

"I know it's a joke, Phil. I just don't understand why you think it's funny."

Sam would always resolve conflicts and dilemmas by asking the question, "What's the right thing to do?" Or "How will you feel when you look at yourself in the mirror tomorrow?"

Sam might seem an unusual example of leadership, but his prevailing values - doing the right thing, caring about others, being true to your word, and facing up to problems - pervaded the agency. He and his partner, Dave, led L&D to be a fair, honest, and fun place to work.

Sam Dame passed away in 2009. In three short years, he taught me that to be true to what I believed was the right thing to do. For the most part I've succeeded, but on those mornings when I know I've fallen short, I wince when I look in the mirror and swear I can hear Sam's voice say, *"Good morning, Scumbag."*

CHAPTER 15.

GIVING AUTONOMY: "DO WHATCHA GOTTA DO"

My time at Lordly & Dame included not just Sam Dame but also his partner, Dave.

David Lacamera, aka "Big Dave," was a year older than me, a little taller, and weighed in at about two hundred fifty pounds. His manner was friendly and gentle; he spoke slowly and quietly in a field characterized by loud motor mouths.

When I met Sam Dame, he let me know that this was a formality insisted on by David. "If David wants to hire you, then that's OK with me. Lectures is his business and he runs it."

I was assigned the West Coast, which was a startup for L&D. I soon discovered that there were no established customer lists with phone numbers. I also found that L&D had no direct mail program like my previous agency.

I made phone calls, lots of phone calls, something Big Dave described as "burning the phones," but I longed to have some incoming phone calls. I asked Dave if I could start a simple direct mail program. "It won't cost much. I'll get the addresses and stuff envelopes. I'll print mimeo sheets for the mailers, and I've found a template we can use for the addresses so Kate will only have to type 'em once."

"Do whatcha gotta do."

"Really? I can give you an accounting of all expenses. . ."

"Alan, do whatcha gotta do. You try it out. If it works, great. If not, try something else."

It worked. I mailed. The phones rang. The West Coast territory grew quickly. My sales didn't rival New York, but they were quite respectable, sooner than expected.

I suggested that we might produce a brochure and mail it nationally.

Some agents objected. "I don't think people respond to direct mail. I think they want to have a personal phone call," said Bill, who mostly sold poets and authors to English departments.

"I'm not so sure that's true, Bill," said Dave. "I see the results Alan is having out West, and I think we should try it for the rest of the country." I thanked David for backing my suggestion.

"Alan, I didn't hire you to do things the way we always have done. Of course, I want your ideas, and this one is a no-brainer. I mean it's already working."

We tried a national mailing. Phones rang. Sales went up.

Over the next three years, I came up with ideas, and David encouraged me to try them. His answer was always the same.

"Alan, do whatcha gotta do."

On one of the little start-up enterprises I attempted, I challenged him. "David, this is likely to require more money than anything else I've tried. Lordly & Dame has never done anything like this. You've never done anything like this. 'Do whatcha gotta do' may not be appropriate."

Dave scowled. He didn't look angry often, but he was clearly frustrated with me.

"Alan. Why would I hire you to do stuff we've always done? I didn't hire you to implement my ideas. I'm not the only one who has ideas. So far, you haven't done anything stupid, so why wouldn't I trust you to take a shot at something you think will work? I appreciate you asking and that you think things through before you ask, but don't give me a hard time about letting you do what you think is important to grow this business. Do whatcha gotta do."

I've worked many places since L&D. There have been a few times when a leader gave me the kind of autonomy that Big Dave Lacamera did, but it definitely wasn't the norm. I went to work for myself twice, seeking autonomy, and of my thirty-seven years in consulting, twenty-three were spent working for myself.

I am motivated by autonomy. Perhaps Dave knew that instinctively, or perhaps that was just the kind of leader he was. He ran a fun place to work, and we all felt part of a team, but we were in sales, so while we measured ourselves by what we sold individually, the collective work product we had was the growth and reputation of the firm. Somehow, we shared that as a team.

In my management-leadership taxonomy (managers get the work done and develop people in a steady state; leaders communicate direction and attract followers in abnormal circumstances), Dave Lacamera demonstrated his management skill by encouraging me to think for myself. The autonomy he gave the whole team left me with a willingness to follow him. So perhaps Big Dave was that rare breed – a manager AND leader.

Managers develop their people, not just to get today's work done, but for the future. That requires autonomy, the giving of which attracts followers - an accountability of leadership. The buzzword is "empowerment," and, yes, people need to feel empowered to do work or to change, but then you have to trust that they know what they are doing and respect their ability to do what needs to be done.

> **A leader is best when people barely know he exists.**
> **When his work is done, his aim fulfilled, people say,**
> **We did it ourselves.**
> **— Lao Tzu**

CHAPTER 16

SELF-RELIANCE AND RESPECT: ED MACGREGOR

I have always loved hearing people's stories. Perhaps this began when I was a boy; my father was a great storyteller for whom a book wasn't necessary, and the truth was always a relative term. He also spoke to nearly everyone he met. "Krajcik – Kray-check, is that how you say it, Paul? Is that a Polish name? Oh, Slovak. Did your people come from Czechoslovakia, then? When?" He'd be off on a discussion of the person's background, which I later realized was why he was so good at remembering names.

So I learned from my father to listen to people's stories. Some of the conversations I've had over the years have stuck with me. One was with Ed MacGregor.

I was in my late twenties when I first met Ed. It was before I even thought of becoming a consultant. I was a booking agent for speakers on college campuses and business meetings and represented Dick Gregory, Ralph Nader, H. Ross Perot, Erica Jong, Margaret Mead and many others less famous as well. I had just moved from an agency in suburban Boston to one downtown. I wore three-piece suits to work because I had just read John Molloy's book *Dress for Success,* much to the amusement of the rock music agents down the hall at Lordly & Dame. "Here comes 'Mr. Dress-for-Success.' We're more comfortable with 'success-through-mess.'"

One day - I don't remember when - I walked across the Boston Public Garden to the Ritz Carlton Hotel, not the one on Avery Street, where it is today, but the 1927 grand dame building on the corner of Newberry and Arlington Streets, which is now the Taj Hotel. Lunching at the Ritz was entering another world. Customer service was an almost spiritual experience; I felt like a king.

Wandering around the lobby, I walked down the steps into the basement and was intrigued to find a biscuit-colored marble throne that was the Ritz shoe shine stand. Off to the side in a white shirt, open at his size nineteen neck, and black pants protected by a navy-blue apron stood Ed MacGregor, who shined the shoes of Ritz Carlton guests. Ed had a stack of shoes that housekeeping brought to him each morning, but the walk-in customer took priority. Ed elegantly gestured to the marble throne despite his dinner-plate-sized hands. "Shine, sir?" And so began a weekly fifteen-to twenty-minute mini-vacation while I listened to Ed's stories and he made my Florsheim toecaps gleam like black chrome.

Ed was about six feet five and probably weighed about two hundred seventy-five pounds. He wasn't fat, just solid like a refrigerator or a safe. He was bald, and what little white hair he did have around his ears was buzz-cut short. He had longer hair in his ample ears than my mustache sported at that point. For such an imposing man, he was incredibly soft spoken. I found myself leaning in just to be sure I understood what he was saying.

I was twenty-eight; Ed was at least sixty-five, maybe seventy or more. I think I asked him if he had always done this work.

"Oh, Good Lord! No! This is my second career."

"What was your first?" I asked.

"Engineer."

"Oh - mechanical, civil, electrical?"

"Trains," he said softly. And so began the conversation.

He started working on trains as a youngster in 1919 and worked his way up to engineer. "Yeah, they gave me some courses, but most of what I learned, I learned from the school of hard knocks, when an engineer or a fireman would try to hammer something into rocks they said were in my head. I did get certified, though, had to."

He told me the details of locomotives. He had learned on steam trains ("noisy and dirty – you never got your face clean") and had seen the transition to diesel ("like a big truck, really – just as noisy as steam, cleaner, that is until somethin' broke down, oil's as hard to get off your hands as coal-soot is off your face.")

Ed had started with the Great Northern Railway, which competed with the Northern Pacific line and the Chicago, Milwaukee, and St. Paul line. On March 2, 1970, the three lines were merged into Burlington Northern. "I think they used my pension to fund the merger or at least some executive's golden handshake," he said with a chuckle. "So now I get to shine your shoes, young Mr. Alan."

Ed wasn't bitter. His life circumstances were "just the way it is."

My all-time favorite story was when he talked about the Great White Way.

"It was an electric train, extra-rail in some places, overhead connection in some others. We ran freight and some passengers from Minneapolis all the way to Seattle in the 1920s, powered entirely by small-scale hydro from mountain streams. It was so quiet; we'd come up upon rabbits and deer and had to blow the horn. They never heard us coming. We'd blow the horn, and they'd scamper off the tracks and just stand there looking as we went by. It was magic."

"It was powered by hydroelectric power?"

"Yep. A small wheel-based unit would fit in a stream. It didn't raise the temperature of the water enough to hurt the fish. It was only about the size of your briefcase. They had hundreds of them, I don't know, maybe thousands."

"What happened to that technology?"

"It went away in the Depression, no way to make money on it unless you can do it on a mass scale, and people are lazy. They like it when some big corporation generates power for <u>everybody</u>."

One day in the wintertime, I hadn't been to see Ed for a long while. My shoes were showing the effects of a Boston winter and my youthful disdain for galoshes and overshoes.

"Ed, I'm sorry. I've been busy. I haven't had the time to get here. Can you bring 'em back?"

Ed looked disgusted. He stared at the white salt lines on the leather uppers, the slush-mud caked along the soles, and growled, "Ya know, Alan, you can do this stuff <u>yourself</u>."

What was suddenly clear to me was that I was hiring Ed and not respecting his labor. I was making his job harder and assuming he would just fix things.

Ed brought my ruined shoes back to pretty good condition, considering. I went to see him after that despite my embarrassment. I never let my shoes get in that condition again.

I told this story in leadership workshops because self-reliance is a virtue that leads people to succeed in difficult or uncertain times, in times of change. Also, doing work yourself will lead you to respect the work that others do for you.

Leaders who came up through the ranks, who did the work that they were now managing others to do, instinctively understood Ed's advice about self-reliance. Leaders who had been parachuted in because of a degree or a certification earned somewhere else, heard in Ed's story, to not become dependent on someone else to do real work. Change requires real work and respect for those who do it, or as Ed MacGregor put it,

"Ya know, you can do this stuff <u>yourself</u>."

CHAPTER 17.

FIRST THINGS FIRST: PRIORITIZATION AND FOCUS

I t was July 28, 1979, a hazy, humid Saturday in West Medford, Massachusetts. I was sweeping the floors of 34 Wyman Street, a thirteen-room yellow shingle, 1890s Queen Anne Victorian. As I went from room to room, I'd occasionally put down the dustpan or broom and go downstairs to get a screwdriver or a hammer to make a home repair I'd been meaning to attend to for months or years. I'd sweep, tighten a door knob, pick up some dirt and dust, screw down a window latch, get a new garbage bag for the dust, take off some obsolete window hardware, and clean the smudges off the mirror in the bathroom where I was washing off the dustpan.

This flurry of harried activity was actually the culmination of more than a year of a focused campaign. After nine years as a successful booking agent for lecturers and performing artists, I had decided to go to business school. I was thirty-one, a bit old for such an adventure, and I'd reasoned that if I was going to make this worth it, I should go to a really good business school. I researched and applied to eight schools with all that entailed - GMATs, essays, and recommendations. I got into five of them, much to the surprise of my friends and (I think) the mother of my two small children. Ultimately, I turned down Harvard and accepted the London Business School's offer. We sold everything we owned, including 34 Wyman Street, and prepared to move across the Atlantic.

My wife had gone to visit her mother in Kentucky, not being especially happy to give up that house. I had closed the sale the previous day and now was imitating Mr. Clean, getting the house broom-clean to turn over to my neighbor Jock, who had bought the manse for more than list. I tore around the house, interrupting one task to start another, half-finishing that one before beginning another.

My mother, Nan Culler, arrived to help. She followed me from room to room, asking what she could do. I was at a loss to offer any direction or even to think of anything she could do.

Nan was an amazing woman. She had gone back to work as a math teacher when I was eight. Sometime later, a church member asked her if she would be willing to try something new, and so she became a computer programmer in 1956. I still remember the tour of the three-story former shoe factory in Lawrence, Massachusetts, where she and others at Raytheon worked on the space program. I can hear her telling me about looking for bugs, literally looking through rows of vacuum tubes for the places where a cockroach had crawled across two contact points, shorting out a part of the program. She was ultimately on the team that programmed the operating system for the IBM 360.

When I bought this house, I was nervous about the payments. My mother had calmly asked my mortgage amount and rate, and taxes, and then spit out my monthly payment to the penny. She had calculated thirty-year compound interest in her head with a smile and said, "Don't worry. You can afford it."

Back at the house, Nan quietly observed my hysteria for about ten minutes and then said, "Alan, STOP!" She was a quiet woman, rarely raising her voice, but she did know how to get my attention. I stopped.

"Alan, what is the <u>one</u> thing that you need to do? What is the one thing that you cannot get on the plane tonight without doing?"

"I dunno, Mom. I guess . . . pack?"

She had that astonished look on her face – the one that said, "How can someone so smart be so dumb?" She set her lower jaw forward, half-smiled with her look of benevolent-determination-that-will-not-be-denied, and said, "Alan Cay Culler, give me that broom, put your tools away, and *go pack!*"

It was a very successful intervention. I packed. I turned the keys over to Jock, who was renovating almost everything in the house anyway. I made my flight, moved to London, got an MBA, and began a lifetime career in consulting.

In later years, some of my work involved helping those who were unfocused and stuck on what and how to prioritize. Often my help was as simple as asking my mother's question, "What is the <u>one</u> thing . . . ?"

Sometimes I used this question with others (and, if I'm honest, with myself) to help move from insight to action, to start the change-ball rolling, or to impose a chronological order on a series of tasks. Even now, it still helps me to know where to start with my page-long To-Do list so I can at least cross something off – even if I have to write something new on the list that I've already done just to have the "It's-all-about-the-checkmark" gratification.

Often, however, helping someone prioritize or focus is much more complex.

I saw this when:

- a leadership team wanted to do <u>all</u> the possible strategies that they had brainstormed, or when
- An innovation team couldn't choose which product to prototype, or when
- A continuous improvement team couldn't decide what problem

to tackle or which solution to pick – the dead-easy one or the one with the highest impact.

It turned out that the inability to prioritize and focus was one of the largest leadership problems I encountered in my entire consulting career. If leadership is about ensuring direction (leading toward or away), how can we do that if we are unclear about what is most important? If leadership is also about getting others to follow us – to become leaders in their own right – how can they do that without a focus?

But lack of prioritization is a very human failing. We all get stuck not knowing where to put our focus from time to time. Because it happens to me so often, I've tried to examine why. Let's go back to my summer of 1979 cleaning frenzy. One reason I was so unfocused was that I was overwhelmed by options. I'd go into a room and see something that needed doing and then just do it. I hadn't set a context for what I was doing, and, without a context, every task was equally important and should be done immediately, with disastrous results.

The context for my tasks was that I was turning over the house to the new owner that day and flying off to start a new life. Context for the leadership team struggling with strategic options should be the vision and purpose of the organization, what customers know about you, and what they expect from you.

Context for a continuous improvement team that is choosing solutions rests in the question: What problem are we trying to solve? It leads to the evaluation of each solution, most effectively with a tool like the Prioritization Criteria Matrix.

Causes	Criteria				Total	Weighted total
	No. 1/ Weight	No. 2/ Weight	No. 3 Weight	No. 4/ Weight		
1						
2						
3						
4						
5						

The Criteria Matrix might also be useful for the innovation team in choosing what to prototype. These folks, however, often have difficulty in prioritizing because there are just too many unknowns.

For me, in 1979, the unknowns were paralyzing. Would I find an apartment? Would I succeed at business school? If I did, could I actually get hired by a consulting firm? Would Jock reject the house if a doorknob fell off?

For the innovation team, the unknowns may be just as paralyzing. Prototyping is expensive. New technologies often don't work as expected. For this team, the answer may be in reducing unknowns by prototyping component parts.

On that hazy, humid day in July many years ago, what was really going on with me afflicts many who have trouble prioritizing. In addition to all the unknowns, there were many unspoken and conflicting emotions wrapped up in my decision. I wanted to turn over the house in the best possible condition to my neighbor and friend Jock. I felt guilty that I hadn't maintained the house like I should have, and there were many repairs that I had put off. I had mixed emotions about selling the house, where we had put our heart and soul into renovating, and which my wife loved. I entertained second and third thoughts about my chosen path and career change at a time when the decision was made and my plane was (almost literally) waiting.

When working with leadership groups, these unspoken thoughts, opinions, and emotions were often what bogged down prioritization. Underlying discussion about how to make a decision or who will make it was unresolved conflict and unspoken disagreement. Sometimes it was my job to ensure that the unspoken was voiced so that the group could move to action and focus on getting results.

Sometimes that's as simple as pointing out that a decision has already been made, to let go of your ambivalence, quit revisiting the decision, and take action ("Go pack!"). Truthfully, it was rarely that simple in my clients' lives, nor was it in my own. But when I'm flummoxed, I think of Nan Culler's question:

Alan, what is the one thing you need to do?

CHAPTER 18.

BUILDING OR REBUILDING TRUST

"Well, Alan, I guess we just can't trust you anymore."

When I was sixteen, I had a Massachusetts pumpkin license, which meant that for my first year as a driver, I was allowed to be on the road from 6 a.m. to midnight. After midnight, like Cinderella's carriage, my license turned into a pumpkin.

In a February snowstorm, I totaled the 1963 Pontiac Tempest with the slant four engine and "four on the floor," black with red bucket seats that I had talked my father into buying. When I arrived home later that night - well after midnight - my father, once assured that I was okay, said, "Put your car on the road." So I registered the '53 Dodge I had been taking apart and putting back together since I was fourteen, while my father wrestled with the insurance company until he could buy another car.

I do remember feeling bad about destroying the family car, but we used the Dodge until we eventually got another one. Then my car was still on the road, school was out, and I was liberated. One night, an hour after my license curfew, I tried to sneak into the house very quietly.

I have no memory of where I went that night or who I was with. I do vividly remember my mother on the living room couch in her blue flowered housecoat as I opened the door, saying:

"Well, Alan, I guess we just can't trust you anymore."

Even writing this in my seventies, twenty years after she passed away, I still suck air in through my teeth while my intestines drop to my knees.

Trust is emotional.

We hear a lot these days about voters not trusting politicians or government, or institutions. We hear about consumers not trusting companies, or the media, or the information available on the Internet.

But I go back to that air-sucking, gut-dropping moment, that first time when someone said, "I don't trust you."

What was behind that? I didn't keep a commitment. I violated a law. Mostly, I realized that someone who cared about me was hurt or disappointed because I acted inconsiderately and unpredictably.

Trust is the foundation of the leadership contract.

Most people will follow a leader they can trust. Trust is an emotional bond between leader and follower that allows them to act together, not just to act in concert, but to act **as one.**

However, as with other emotions, when we try to explain trust cognitively, we are reduced to aphorisms:

"Trust is like ice, difficult to form, easily shattered, and once broken, even more difficult to form again."

"Trust is a bank account, which after many deposits can forgive the odd withdrawal, but once overdrawn, is closed, to be reopened only with onerous terms."

These aphorisms provide little instruction about what to do when trust is broken. In fact, the very emotional nature of trust is a barrier to making the change in behavior necessary to repair a serious trust problem. Complicating this is another emotion. When we hear "I don't trust you," we are often left with guilt. Trust-guilt is not a pleasant emotion. As in my accident story, it may originate in the remembered pain of broken trust. Trust-guilt isn't helpful in teaching us how to rebuild trust.

Trust-guilt also may come from an incomplete definition of trust.

Trust is underpinned by honesty and integrity, but that's not all. Remember that people say things like "his intentions are good, but you can't really rely on him." They also say things like "the road to hell is paved with good intentions." So intentions do count for something if people know what your intentions are. That means you have to tell them your intentions. So, transparency is also a factor.

So is track record. We are back to the bank account analogy. If you have made significant deposits, i.e., done what you promised several times, then you might be forgiven a slip-up every now and then.

The Trust Formula

When I was at Gemini Consulting, I was introduced to the Trust Formula*+ as a way of understanding trust and how to rebuild your trust "credit rating" after a significant "withdrawal" or breach of trust.

$$T = \frac{I \times C}{R} \qquad \text{Trust} = \frac{\text{Intimacy} \times \text{Credibility}}{\text{Risk}}$$

The assumption of the formula is that trust is mutual; one-sided trust doesn't last long. Then the formula says trust is a function of:

- **Intimacy** – how well the parties know each other. This can be friendship, but it needn't be. Most important for trust is knowledge of intentions, judgment, and decision-making. This is one part of the path to predictability.

- **Credibility** is another part of the path to predictability. Credibility may come from credentials, but your degrees don't tell your whole story. Mostly, credibility comes from demonstrated competence. We ask for references when hiring someone because we are looking for proof that the person can do what he or she says. A leader's credibility is about a track record in delivering the kind of results he or she promises.

- **Risk** - trust between parties is dependent on the risk involved in trusting. Because risk is in the denominator of the formula, the greater the risk, the harder it is to trust. Prove this to yourself: on your first day at a new job, a coworker tells you he forgot his wallet and asks you for five dollars for lunch. You may or may not fund his meal depending on whether you knew him before and whether you believe him. Now, imagine how you would react if he were to ask for $50,000 to start a new business.

Gemini Consulting taught the trust formula as a way to build trust with a client or rebuild trust after a breach. They suggested actions for each part of the formula:

Intimacy actions: If you determine that the other person doesn't know you well or vice versa, exchange backgrounds, talk about values and decision processes, and share a meal.

Credibility actions: If the parties are unsure whether to trust each other due to:

- A track record of poor **information** sharing, then create a transparent communication process. Always make sure that the information you give is **timely, accurate, and framed in a way that it can be easily received and understood.**

- A question about **judgment,** then create transparent decision-making processes with clear roles and responsibilities. If the trust breach is a "where-did-that-come-from?" then stop, revisit the decision and criteria, and create processes to avoid blindsiding the other party in the future.

- A question of **execution,** i.e., concern that either party will not do what they say, create a schedule to verify interim progress, and a rule that if any commitment looks like it will be difficult, then both parties will discuss contingency plans.

Risk actions: If the risk of trust is great for either party (loss of job or status, financial loss, safety risk), find ways to prevent the risk from happening or mitigate it if it occurs.

Rebuilding trust is not like building it in the first place. We often say that we grow to trust someone by getting to know them. Rebuilding trust is not just like a reacquaintance, though confronting the problem directly and talking it out will always help. But ultimately, the trustees (both parties-- trust problems are rarely one-sided) will have to agree to *behave in a way that leads others to trust them.*

Here are a few suggestions for practicing behaviors that lead to trust:

- **Listen with respect.** As noted, trust is emotional.
- **Show empathy and a willingness to understand.** Behaving in the other person's best interest requires that one ask thoughtful questions and listen with obvious interest.
- **Share your intentions.** Don't imagine, however, that your seemingly good intentions will ameliorate negative results.
- **Accept responsibility.** Own your actions and your mistakes.
- **Improve.** Solve problems, right wrongs, prevent and mitigate risks.
- *PERSEVERE.* Being genuine in your intent to rebuild trust will go a long way. In the words of Lao Tzu:

Trust first; Trust is in the giving.

Note 1: I asked Gemini Consulting alumni colleagues about the origins of the trust formula. Many attributed it to the founder, the late David Teiger, whom I unfortunately never met but who is canonized by Gemini people. Some attributed it to Cavas Gobhai, who was a part of Synectics, Inc., the Cambridge, Massachusetts, creative problem-solving firm started by Bill Gordon and George Prince (now Synecticsworld).

Note 2: I believe that the Trust Formula predates the Trust Equation, which was described in *The Trusted Advisor,* written by David Maister, Charles Green, and Robert Galford and published in 2001. This was presented as a way for consultants to become trusted advisors to senior clients. The major differences are the addition of Reliability (a credibility of execution variable) to the numerator and the change of risk to self-orientation in the denominator. The addition of reliability does add some specificity to the numerator. The model is presented as a self-evaluation for consultants, and later by Green and Galford for leaders. It is therefore less of a model for both parties to resolve differences, and the elimination of risk may preclude attention to this important variable.

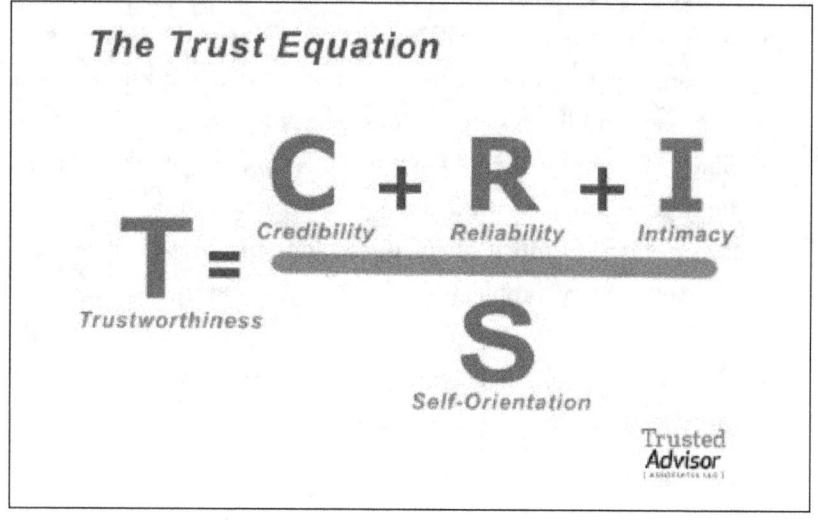

CHAPTER 19

"IT'S JUST BUSINESS" IS NOT A LEADERSHIP VALUE

"It's just business, Alan. Don't take it personally."

It was twenty years ago. My client, a founding CEO, was informing me that he had rejected my advice on a merger he was contemplating. He was prepared to ignore the people issues I had uncovered in due diligence and instead follow the investment banker's counsel: "You can deal with the <u>soft stuff</u> later. Let's get this deal done!"

I never had a clear, bright line between my business and personal point of view. I followed my passion, and my work reflected who I was. I once explained as much to this client, and he said, "Wow. You must be miserable a lot of the time. I keep my beliefs, likes, and dislikes completely separate from what I do to make money."

I was privately horrified, but held my peace. I find this sentiment to be quite common in business.

Peter Block, a teacher and colleague in the field of organizational development, once said in a training session that I attended:

<u>Business.</u> It's such an interesting word. As a noun, there is a lot to like about it —"we do business together" – something a bit more than a transaction, a relationship, or "getting down to business" – taking action on what's really important.

But when business is used as an adjective, something unfortunate happens. Take "it's a <u>business decision</u>" – that means "we know we're screwing you, but the money made us do it."

"It's just business" is all too frequently used to justify taking short-term profit-focused action in the face of known long-term damage to the firm, its customers, employees, or the community at large. It can be a license to ignore possible unintended consequences. "It's just business" can also rationalize ignoring a solution when that solution is inconvenient in terms of time or money.

I once sold off-the-shelf training programs in Pittsburgh. A large bank, our client, had acquired a large Philadelphia bank. Integration wasn't going well because the Philadelphia bank had been told that this was a merger of equals, while the acquiring CEO truly believed it was an acquisition or, more precisely, a conquest. I observed him explode in a meeting of the two firms' leaders: "When I said that we'd pick the best IT systems, I meant <u>OUR SYSTEMS!</u>"

The training manager called my boss and me in to discuss using one of our training programs with the integration team. The program taught how to get things done when you don't have direct authority. The training manager was interested, but I kept asking questions when I should have been closing the sale. The training manager began to see that this training program would be window dressing at best and might throw gasoline on a smoldering fire.

We left the meeting. My boss was livid. "You actually talked yourself out of a sale!" she said.

"It wouldn't solve the problem," I responded, just a tad too defensively.

"Alan, this is business. Not everything works. It probably wouldn't hurt."

"But what if it did?"

"That isn't your problem. And we would have had a $15,000 sale."

At the time, the steel industry in Pittsburgh was dying (though we didn't know it), and my training sales were declining. I later left that firm and went to work for a consulting firm that actually wanted to find true solutions to problems. It turned out to be a good move.

I continued over the next thirty years to do business according to what I believed was right. When I worked for large consulting firms, this approach sometimes created conflict. However, working for myself and with colleagues, those conflicts were substantially less.

Recently, I read Bruce Springsteen's autobiography *Born to Run*. Bruce's first manager, Mike Appel, signed him to an onerous contract that (according to Bruce) essentially made him Mike's employee. After Bruce's first hit album began to earn money, the contract came up for renewal. There was a lot of money on the table, but Bruce was, according to the terms of the contract, entitled to very little of it. Bruce objected. Mike made re-signing with him for five years a condition of paying Bruce more money, saying Bruce might be a one-hit wonder.

Bruce left Mike Appel because Mike made the business decision of taking most of the money today rather than demonstrating his belief in Bruce for the long term. Bruce then signed with Jon Landau because of Jon's passion and heart. To date, Bruce has made over twenty more albums, plus boxed sets.

Most of my work was with large publicly held companies. Some were often driven to do the wrong things for employees, customers, or the community in order to maximize shareholder value. Other executives I knew kept these constituencies in mind. My best projects were working for those kinds of leaders.

Along the way, I became interested in B-corporations, or Benefit Corporations, which define their business concept as a force for good. Some give a portion of profits away to charity; others have a long track record providing employee benefits like onsite child care. They structure their business to provide real value to customers, employees, and the community. Shareholders do well by doing good.

I suspect that the leaders of B-corporations see no virtue in separating their business from their personal values. Certainly, treating business as an arena where amoral behavior is justified - "It's just business" - is a non-starter and not what they would consider a leadership value.

Like B-corporations, my point of view about business leadership includes not just attracting followers and making change, but delivering value as perceived by all those affected by the change.

CHAPTER 20

PASSION AND FORGIVENESS: VINCE PELLEGRINO

V ince Pellegrino, an oil company executive, a client, a friend, passed away in 2014, and it hit me hard. He died of ALS, amyotrophic lateral sclerosis, commonly known as Lou Gehrig's disease. It's a tough way to go, and while Vince wasn't as young as Lou Gehrig, he was eight years younger than me, way too young to die.

My heart still goes out to Mary, Vince's wife, whom he called his MVP, and to his children. It is so hard to lose a loved one.

Vince worked for thirty years as an operator for a major in the upstream oil business (getting the crude oil out of the ground). He was a compact man (five-seven, one hundred fifty-five pounds) with a passion for safety and efficiency. He was an out-of-the-box thinker. He could be very intense.

Vince was also an introvert. He hated it when people would finish his sentences because he was thinking about something so hard that he had trouble getting the words out. But he cared deeply about improving the company he worked for most of his career.

I owe Vince the business model of the last four years of my career. He hired me and twenty other consultants, independents, and those from small firms, to help him build an internal consulting group to implement two common processes: a planning process that tied together strategic and operational plans; and a production efficiency process to recapture the "phantom oil field" composed of unplanned lost production.

He hired one hundred internal process coaches and formed a large team to learn from each other and to deliver results. That is what I later formed Results-Alliance to do. Vince mastered what it takes to manage a network of knowledge workers. He sponsored extensive training programs, had annual meetings where he brought his team together with clients, and founded a Project Management Office (PMO) to keep it all running. Those two processes have morphed somewhat, but they still exist at the firm years later.

Vince could be very demanding. People didn't always agree with him. I had my share of disagreements with Vince. Once at a PMO meeting I facilitated, he and I ended up standing toe-to-toe, screaming at each other. I am a good leadership team facilitator and teach others that facilitating is being the frictionless conduit of information. But in this case, I totally lost it. I was completely unprofessional.

The next morning, I showed up at Vince's office at 5:30 in the morning. (Like a lot of operations guys, Vince always started early.) I had my company computer and my badge to turn in, sure that I had irretrievably stepped over the line.

Vince smiled and said, "Alan, you don't get to take **all** the blame for our fight. I was there too, and I'm not turning my computer and badge in, so I don't expect you to. Besides, I think we still have work to do together." Passion balanced by forgiveness and the ability to admit one's mistakes – Vince Pellegrino was the very definition of a great leader.

CHAPTER 21.

LEARNING FROM GENGHIS

"I am the Scourge of God! If you had not committed great sins, God would not have sent a punishment like me among you."

So bellowed Genghis Khan from horseback outside the sacred Mosque of Bukhara, moments before he ordered the wealthy town elders to surrender gold and jewels, razed their homes and slaughtered them, leaving peasants "scattered to the winds to tell the tale of the horror they witnessed here."

Not a very nice guy.

My first wife described my political transformation, after going to the London Business school when Margaret Thatcher was Prime Minister:

"Alan went from Ché Guevara to somewhere to the right of Genghis Khan."

Most people don't think of Genghis Khan as a positive model of leadership. Perhaps he isn't. He was a conqueror, driven only by territorial acquisition and theft. He was often merciless to his enemies. Genghis Khan has been held up as the archetypal barbarian throughout much of history.

Voltaire described him as "this destructive tyrant . . . bred to arms and practiced in the trade of blood . . . who lays the fertile fields of Asia to waste."

Karl Marx blamed the Tsars cruelty on him "The bloody mire of Mongolian slavery forms the cradle of Muscovy" (principality around Moscow).

The writer in a 1990 article in *The Economist* railed: "Unlike other conquerors, he brought no ideology, no Napoleonic Code, no Roman Law. His simple fanatical aim was to amass huge areas of territory...Genghis' empire, if that's what it was, fell to pieces after his death...."

Is there anything good about Genghis Khan? Is there anything we might learn from him? After all he is so revered in Mongolia as the founder of the nation that the Soviets tried to erase his memory. He passed laws enforcing religious freedom and granted tax exemption for places of worship. Some historians give the Mongol conquest credit for opening East-West trade; the Silk Road was Mongol-made and maintained. He created the first global postal service. His descendants ran the Yuan Dynasty in China (Kublai Khan), the Golden Horde in Russia, the Moghul Empire in India, and the Ilkhanate in Persia and Iraq.

He still isn't talked about as a nice guy, but I was encouraged to discover some things he might teach us.

In 1990, I was working for a propeller aircraft manufacturer in Northern Ireland. I interviewed many people in preparation for the offsite where the CEO intended to win everyone over to an integration plan with the Canadian jet manufacturer acquiring them..

Virtually everyone described my client as " a really warm supportive guy, who can also be Genghis Khan." Evidently he had an explosive temper and angry verbal sharpness that people described as "Mongol beheadings." I was very nervous about the feedback session.

He laughed. "Yeah, I know. I'm working on that. Hey, let's have some fun with this. I bet old Genghis was nicer to his people than he was to his enemies."

I did some research and wrote a whitepaper, and an exercise for the group to decide what they could learn from Genghis. I was surprised to learn that Temujen, Genghis Khan, was an extraordinary leader.

A hunted outcast on the steppe from the age of ten until the age of seventeen, he rose in four short years to be elected Genghis Khan (rightful ruler) of the Mongols. After defeat and desolation two years later, he rose to be Khan again and later to be Emperor of the Steppes and the World Conqueror. In twenty-five years he amassed territory that stretched from the China Sea to the gates of Vienna, from Moscow to South India. His descendants ran the Golden horde in Moscow, the Mughal empire in India, the Ilkhanate in Persia and Iraq, and the Yuan dynasty (Kublai Khan) in China that opened trade with Europe (Marco Polo).

The Mongols before Temujen's rise were a collection of nomadic tribes: Tatars, Merkit, Kerait, Naiman, and hundreds more. He took these scavenging, raiding clans, struggling for survival in a forbidding land of extreme hot and cold, and turned them into one of the greatest armies the world has ever known. The gigantic scale and speed of these Mongol operations were incredible in an age before firearms, mechanized transport and modern communication.

He inspired extraordinary loyalty, even among former enemies, through two-way trust. He divided booty equally. If a soldier was injured Genghis might personally carry his share to his tent. If a soldier was killed, the booty share was transported to his first wife.

Genghis Khan was illiterate. I was shocked to learn that he travelled with Uighur scribes. They wrote propaganda that exaggerated his massacres to soften up the next enemy. Many towns surrendered without a fight. The scribes also recorded the *Secret History of the Mongols,* only recently translated, and "Bilik and Yasa, the leadership maxims and laws of Genghis Khan," which was the title of the whitepaper.

The Great Yasa (laws), a few examples:

- Love one another;
- Respect wise men of all peoples;
- Do not steal;
- Share all food to be eaten; never eat in front of another lest you offer to divide your meal.

- Never eat offered food before he who offers it first partakes;
- Consider all sects as one and do not distinguish one from the other. Nor interfere with a man who speaks with his God if he keeps the Khan's law;
- Whoever becomes bankrupt thrice is put to death after the third time;

Genghis Khan's Maxims of Leadership (Bilik), examples:

- Mongols shall not give their nobles laudatory names like other nations. He who sits on the throne shall be called Khan, and swear his allegiance to the Great Khan. (Khan was an elected position.)
- Ambassadors, emissaries, and messengers, whether of the Khan or his enemies, are protected under the Khan's law.
- At the council speak your mind without fear of reproach, but when the wine is poured the council has ended. Debate no more.
- Any word on which three well-informed men are agreed may be spoken anywhere; otherwise by no means speak them;
- In council or when accepting a man into your service speak last.
- When meeting a stranger or a friend, no matter what your troubles, inquire first after the other's circumstances. Interest creates friendships.

Learning from Genghis

Genghis killed about forty million people. I don't glorify his brutal warlord behavior. However, Genghis Khan did create an organization with several admirable characteristics:

- **A sense of identity.** They became Mongols, not a collection of clans. The word "Horde," which originally meant "camp with corral for horses," became synonymous with thundering blitzkrieg cavalry.
- **Discipline and cohesion.** They trained in maneuvers relentlessly until they "moved as one man."

- **Absolute reward.** These Mongols were guaranteed an equal share of plunder, which the Khan might personally deliver to them if they were wounded.
- **Absolute accountability.** Clear expectations and punishment were the norm. Merit promotion was given for loyalty, honesty, and excellent performance. Death was ordered for deceit, lack of discipline, disobedience, and gluttony.

Since I wrote "Bilik and Yasa" much additional research on Genghis Khan has emerged. Anthropologist Jack Weatherford published several books starting with, *Genghis Khan and the Making of the Modern World* (2005). In this book Dr. Weatherford describes Temujen's mastery of logistics and infrastructure. The Khan invented siege engines, rapidly built bridges and canals to transport troops and supplies. Weatherford lays out the internationalism of Genghis Khan, including his respect for alliances, diplomacy, and trade and his esteem for philosophy and his protection of religious freedom.

In *The Secret History of the Mongol Queens: How the Daughters of Genghis Khan Rescued His Empire* (2010), Dr. Weatherford shows the crucial role that women played in the Mongol Empire, and, while I doubt the Khan was a feminist, he evidently valued the expertise of his wives.

So maybe, even in a negative example like Genghis, there are lessons for leaders to learn.

CHAPTER 22.

BRUUUUUUCE!

S everal years ago, I read Bruce Springsteen's autobiography *Born to Run*. The book was a gift from my eldest daughter, Tegan, and I confess that when I got it, I smiled to her face but secretly dreaded reading 500 pages of rock star navel-gazing. I could not have been more wrong. The book was very engaging, and in its aftermath, I looked at Springsteen's lyrics and really listened to his music for the first time. To my delight, Bruce's song lyrics have the same pithy, emotional flavor as his writing.

I did know of Bruce, of course, but was never a Bruce fan. Oh sure, when "Born to Run" comes on the radio and I'm alone in my car, I bellow out the chorus *"TRAMPS LIKE US. . ."* But I never heard lyrics of his other hits, and I certainly never went looking at his singer-songwriter material on the early albums.

In short, I've recognized that Bruce was not only a leader in his field, but "the Boss" was the band leader of the E Street Band, a group that has stayed together for more than fifty years. Perhaps Bruce could teach us something about leadership.

Passion rules

On signing with Jon Landau as a manager, Bruce says, "It's not just business, it's personal. When you came to work with me, I had to be assured you'd bring your heart. Heart closed the deal."

Doing what you love is a privilege.

I was always grateful to do work that I loved, but Bruce describes the privilege well:

> Friend, there's a reason they don't call it "working," it's called PLAYING! I've left enough sweat on stages around the world to fill at least one of the seven seas; I've driven myself and my band to the limits and over the edge for more than forty years. We continue to do so, but it's still "playing." It's a life-giving, joyful, sweat-drenched, muscle-aching, voice-blowing, mind-clearing, exhausting, soul-invigorating, cathartic pleasure and privilege every night.

Hopefully, leaders are doing what they love themselves, and they can attract followers by making work fun.

Who you work with is almost as important as the work you do

> 1+1=3. . .The primary math of the real world is one plus one equals two. . . But artists, musicians, con men, poets, mystics, and such are paid to turn the math on its head, to rub two sticks together and bring forth fire. Everybody performs this alchemy somewhere in their life, but it's hard to hold onto and easy to forget. . . .
>
> If we didn't play together, the E Street Band would probably not know one another. We wouldn't be in a room together. But we do . . . we do play together. And that, my friends, is where miracles occur . . . old and new miracles. And those you are with in the presence of miracles, you never forget.

How many leaders can say that the work of their team is where miracles occur, and would the team agree?

Use what you have; never stop improving.

> About my voice. First of all, I don't have much of one. I have a barman's power, range, and durability, but I don't have a lot of tonal beauty or finesse. . . I need all my skills to communicate deeply. . . I've got to write, arrange, play, perform, and yes, sing

to the best of my ability. . . .

I was teased endlessly in the Castiles and dismissed as a vocalist . . . I was content to work on my guitar skills. . . Then I got to where I could carry a melody . . . my next band, Earth, I became a full-fledged playing and singing front man. . . .

I thought I was getting pretty good. . . The sound that came back off that tape . . . was truly demoralizing. . . .

So I figured if I didn't have a voice, I was going to really need to learn to write, perform, and to use that voice to its fullest ability.

Don't be defined only by the work you do on the road

Bruce uses a fair amount of ink describing growing up in Freehold, New Jersey, and the burning desire to get out. He talks about overcoming his demons and coming to terms with just *being home*:

Laurel Canyon . . . my small cottage . . . my first home I've ever owned. . . amid butterflies and bougainvillea . . . I want out . . . now. . . Once inside, I immediately start thinking about leaving. . . this lovely little home wants me to stay . . . and I don't stay. . . That's for everyone else, I go... There is no tour to hide behind, no music to "save" me. I'm face up against the wall.

I know a lot of business leaders who succeed because what they do is their whole life. Their families (if they have them) suffer, and eventually, the mono-dimensionality of their lives interferes with their ability to attract and connect with followers.

A colleague of mine used to describe himself as the Dalmatian - the dog - first one on the fire truck whenever a client had a fire. As a consultant, my work was usually done on the client site. In my life, I had periods where I traveled five to six days a week, working ten- to fourteen-hour days on the road. I was addicted to my own adrenaline in the way Bruce describes. It made relaxing and having reasonable relationships with loved ones tough. Like Bruce, I worked hard to overcome being defined solely by my performance on the road, and over time, I even had some success relaxing. And my avocations enriched my work.

Of course, my task was a lot easier; I never had thousands of fans screaming **"BRUUUUUCE!"**

CHAPTER 23.

IS PATIENCE REALLY A VIRTUE?

T he first time I met Will, I remember thinking, *Now here is a guy who looks like a CEO.* Will was straight from Central Casting. He was a little older than I was at the time, late forties maybe. He was taller than me, maybe six-one, and trim and wore an expensive medium-gray small-herringbone suit, tailored so you noticed that he worked out. Will's hair was black with just the right amount of silver at the temples. His teeth were toothpaste-ad perfect, bright white, and straight, and his jaw muscles looked like he chewed rawhide as a hobby. He had a warm smile, but when his gray-blue eyes locked on yours, there was a chill in the air.

Will was the division head for major project finance at a money center bank where I conducted leadership training. Participants formed change teams during the training and then presented their progress monthly over the next ninety days.

The project finance team missed what they promised at the mid-point. Will exploded.

When I lose my temper, I turn into a sputtering fool who cannot put a sentence together; Will was one of those people whose verbal acuity sharpens with anger. He eviscerated the team.

After the team left, I suggested he might be more patient. Will did not take my suggestion well.

"BE PATIENT?! THE WORLD WAS NOT <u>BUILT</u> BY PATIENT PEOPLE!" Will bellowed at me, red-faced, and stormed out.

I was still a little rattled when Bob arrived to hear the progress report from his team.

"I see you've met Vesuvius," Bob joked. Will had a reputation for volcanic eruption. Later, his temper derailed him from the CEO track, but his team delivered at the next meeting.

Reflecting on patience

I can think of many examples to support Will's "great men ain't patient" case. Andrew Carnegie and his partner Henry Clay Frick built the Pittsburgh steel industry, but they weren't patient men (as learned by the Homestead Works strikers in 1892). Henry Ford, founder of the Ford Motor Company and force behind the adoption of the assembly line, was known for many things, but patience wasn't among them. Steve Jobs of Apple, Jeff Bezos of Amazon, Elon Musk of Tesla - all have each been called many things, but the soul of patience not so much.

There are stories of each of these men losing their tempers. They each set extremely high standards and frequently belittled people who didn't meet them. Of course, these business tycoons offered being part of something extraordinary in exchange for putting up with their impatience with delay or underperformance.

So…could Will have been right?

Patience and perseverance

Contrary to what many people think, Thomas Alva Edison did not invent the light bulb. People had been burning filaments under glass since the late 1700s. There were several patents for incandescent lights by 1870. Edison may be given cultural credit because he commercialized the light bulb, and actually made a profit selling them.

Edison tried many different filaments in his search for the right one. In

1879, he hit on carbonized bamboo, which burned with an eerie orange light and lasted for a long time. When I visited his home in Fort Myers, Florida, in the 1970s, the docent told our tour group that the chandeliers with twenty 20-watt bulbs were "installed when the house was built almost a hundred years ago, but Mr. Edison went on to experiment with almost three hundred filaments after that."

"Why?" I blurted out. Others on the tour laughed. "There is no money in a lightbulb that lasts for a hundred years," she smiled.

Edison was a press hound. He was always giving interviews. Once in the middle of his perfect filament quest, he bragged that he had examined over two hundred different filament materials.

"Why don't you give up?" The reporter asked.

"Give up? NO! I now know two hundred ways NOT to make a light bulb."

He was persistent, but was Thomas Edison patient? If you read about his relationship with Nikola Tesla or his battle with George Westinghouse about direct current (DC) versus alternating current (AC), patient might not be the word that comes to mind. Uber-competitive maybe, but patient, probably not.

Anyone who starts a business, trains for an athletic event, or engages in invention, innovation, or improvement knows that gains come from multiple iterations, a process that requires patience, persistence, and perseverance.

Patient managers? Patient leaders?

Managers get the work done and develop people. How could you educate, train, and create growth opportunities without patience?

Leaders work in abnormal circumstances. They provide direction and attract followers. These circumstances aren't always opportunities for patience.

"OK, ladies and gentlemen, there is a fifty-foot tsunami approaching and we need to get to higher ground. I know that some of you take longer to process risk than others, and we want to allow time for you to become comfortable with action in this situation. Some of you run faster than others, and that is totally OK. Take your time and move at your own pace, but if you are both a slow processor and a slow runner, you may have a PROBLEM!"

In urgent timeline situations, leaders might be forgiven for a lack of patience.

In most organizations these days, the manager who manages the day-to-day and the leader who leads change are the same person. Perhaps using patience to develop people can also build the commitment to follow a leader and make change. Change requires persistence and perseverance, and not a small amount of patience.

What a manager-leader shouldn't be patient about

A while after Will's explosion, but before the next team presentation, he and I had a conversation.

Will said, "There is just absolutely no way **I** would ever make a group presentation to my boss where I was telling him for the first time that I wasn't meeting a commitment. They should have given me a heads-up. I mean, Andy [Will's boss] wasn't in the room, but he could have been. It is the ultimate sign of disrespect."

Once again, Will had a point. It didn't excuse his anger, his explosion, nor his over-the-top dressing down of the team, and I told him so, but he wasn't wrong about what the team should have done. Some of his impatience was justified.

I often talk about three critical elements of trust in business:

1. Share accurate information in a timely way to those who need it. Protect confidentiality.

2. Be as transparent as possible about decision-making so people can understand your judgment.

3. Do what you say you are going to do (and if you can't, see number 1).

So don't be patient with violations of trust. Constructively confront them as soon as possible.

What a manager-leader should be patient about

People process information differently, learn at different rates, and commit to action differently. So as far as possible without hindering business commitments or placing undue hardship on customers or other team members, be patient with those differences. Help when asked and when you can help, do it patiently.

Be patient with yourself

This is the opposite of Will's issue. Will was too patient with his own flaws. He knew his anger was a problem, but never apologized, and apparently didn't work on it until he was fired a few years after we worked together. He was more patient with himself than he was with others.

Many people, not just me, are much more patient with others than they are with themselves. They cut others a break for being slow learners or failing to change behavior, but constantly beat themselves up for doing those very things.

So . . . these are words of advice to myself . . . if they work for you too, so much the better:

Persist . . . Persevere . . . Don't give up . . . But be aware, there is little virtue in beating your head against a brick wall you could easily walk around, between struggling to learn something when you could easily hire someone who already knows how to do it.

But if you've committed to learn something, to do something, to solve some problem, **Be Patient**. Stop comparing yourself to others, and instead compare yourself to your own milestones that you met this week, last week, or last decade. If you're frustrated, step away for a while. Remember Murphy's Law:

Nothing is as easy as it looks. Everything takes longer than it should. And in every field of endeavor, everything that can go wrong

<u>will</u> go wrong, at the worst possible moment.

And, by the way, just knowing about Murphy's Law does NOT mean that it won't apply.

Be patient.

CHAPTER 24.

TAKING A STAND

I grew up in Lexington, Massachusetts, home of the first battle of the Revolutionary War. Most people outside of Massachusetts learn this as the Battle of Lexington and Concord. People in Lexington and Concord, however, refer to them as two battles because they occurred about six miles apart. Each town has its own Minuteman statue; Lexington's is on the left and Concord's is on the right above. Both skirmishes were resistance to General Thomas Gage sending Redcoats to destroy weapons stockpiled at a farm in Concord. At Lexington, Colonel John Parker of the Lexington Minutemen allegedly said,

> Stand your ground. Do not fire unless fired upon, but if they mean to have a war, let it begin here.

Then an unknown person fired a shot, later immortalized by Ralph Waldo Emerson in his "Concord Hymn" as the "shot heard 'round the world." Minutemen lost badly in Lexington, but routed the British in Concord and then conducted guerrilla warfare from behind every stone wall and tree all the way back to Boston.

The story of the Battle of Lexington and Colonel Parker's stand was told over and over in my youth. Of course, reinforcing this story were the town parades every April 19th and the omnipresent statue on the Lexington Green as well as the preserved belfry; the fact that I attended William Diamond Junior High (Parker's assembly drummer) helped as well. Suffice it to say I grew up in the shadow of a leader who took a stand.

Later, I spent my work life talking to business leaders. I facilitated leadership workshops, helped leadership teams come to public agreement on strategy, and/or served as a sounding board for an individual leader. Wherever I was I heard leaders tell stories to describe themselves and what they stood for. I realized that the best leaders communicated with stories. "Here I stand" is a powerful leadership story.

At one point, I facilitated a leadership workshop in the oil production industry. Leaders in this industry work in a high-hazard arena. If they mess up, they mess up the environment or worse - people get hurt and sometimes die.

One particular leader, Zeke, told a story about safety. He began:

"I tell everyone who works with me. . . focus on the three Ps.

- People – make sure everyone goes home safe to their families.
- Pipes and pumps – make sure you take care of the kit – it both keeps people safe and makes money for us.
- Profit - if you take care of the people and the kit, the profit part is easier. You just have to be sure that you spend when you need to spend in order to pump oil safely."

Zeke went on to tell a story that emphasized his stand. This story had a huge impact on everyone at the workshop; people still talked about "People, Pipes, Profit" at the end of the week. I repeated it at other workshops and it always hit home because it is simple, easy to remember and makes an emotional connection. Zeke's clarity about what was important to him caused others to think deeply about what they valued.

I thanked Zeke because he made me think, too.

What do I stand for? What's important to me?

- **Helping People** - I believe that individuals and groups fare best when they learn and grow. A lot of my work helped others gain insight about what they need to learn and act on in order to achieve what they want to achieve.

- **Achieving Results** – I was most often hired as a consultant to deliver a certain result. In many cases, what I ended up doing was installing an improvement process, be it Lean Six Sigma, innovation in products and services, or new ways to connect with customers. I always focused on the measurable outcome.

- **Maintaining Balance** – This is something I struggle with in my own life and saw others struggle with as well: balance between people and results, work and family, and work and play (recreation is re-creation). I believe we don't live in an either/or world, but a both/and world. And so I still strive for balance, and encourage others to as well.

Thanks again, Zeke.

What is important to you as a leader? What is the simple way you frame those values? What stories do you tell to describe your stand?

CHAPTER 25

LEADERSHIP IS WHAT YOU DO

" People follow your footprints, not your voice prints. "
I first heard this in Boy Scouts, and years later still remember this leadership aphorism. I have heard leadership trainers use it; I may have even used it myself.

It's important for leaders to speak simply and to ask good questions. I believe these are important leadership skills, but perhaps more important are leadership *actions*, what a leader actually *does*.

Sometimes lives depend upon leadership, e.g., in safety response, and other emergency situations. In change, people require clear direction and the ability to get people to follow your actions. Below are some ways to help others to follow.

Lead visibly

When I was consulting, I told leaders to vote with your feet, i.e., demonstrate what is important to you by what you attend. I recommended that they show up at training programs that they sponsored, for example. This was in line with the advice of Dr. Edgar Schein, who described organizational culture as the "long shadow of the behavior of leaders." People need leaders to be predictable and consistent in what they systematically pay attention to and do.

Be confident

Sometimes being unflappable in the face of chaos is enough to get people to follow you. "If you can keep your head when all around you are losing theirs. . ." goes the Rudyard Kipling poem, *If*, that graces Hallmark graduation cards.

On the morning of September 11, 2001, I was on the fifth floor of an office building on Park Avenue South and 28[h] Street in New York City. I was working for a small McKinsey spinoff consulting firm. I was the second oldest person in the firm, but I was stunned silent by the fall of the twin towers. One of the founding partners, Marc, was confident and caring.

"First, call your family," Marc said. "Let them know you are OK. Then, we are going to shelter in place until we figure out what is going on."

During the next four hours, as we watched the news on the Internet and television, Marc circulated in the office, talking to each person. He appeared calm and listened to each person's concerns. About 1:30 p.m., we all left to walk to our various homes.

Like Rudy Giuliani and George W. Bush later in the day, Marc's confidence made us all feel better. I later had major policy disagreements with Marc, but they never eclipsed my gratitude for his calm demeanor on that awful morning. I would have followed him anywhere.

Demonstrate that you care

Marc was calm and confident and connected on the things we were concerned about – reassuring our families, and being safe ourselves.

The best leaders I followed have been the ones who spoke directly to my interests, to the things I was concerned about. They took my side in disagreements with the company, or, at the very least, let me know that they understood why I was upset. These leaders may have ultimately convinced me to accept a decision that was difficult, but they first acted out of empathy.

Implement the simplest solution quickly

"Plug the leak." "Stop the bleeding." "Get everyone to safety."

Quick action and first-things-first are what leaders do. They concentrate on simple solutions.

On September 11th, we needed news. We had a TV, but it was used only for watching training videos. There was no antenna. I sprang into action and scoured the place for a wire coat hanger, hoping to MacGyver the problem. I finally found one and arrived at the conference room to find everyone huddled around the operating television. Someone had gone to Radio Shack across the street and bought an antenna. Simple actions are always the best.

Make connections between followers

In my later chapter about climbing Mt. Rainier, I describe the team leadership lessons I learned. The last lesson, Feel the Ropes, is about holding the rope both in front and behind us to be certain that our rope teammates were okay. Emphasizing connections between followers is critically important.

No leader can connect with every follower all the time. Creating connections between followers becomes the glue to keep everyone moving in the same direction.

My Rainier summit attempt was long before Facebook, Twitter, and Instagram became the glue of the Arab Spring and grassroots political campaigns. We have more tools to do this now, but the principles are the same. Invite your followers to connect with each other. Help them see how they share interests. Help them to feel the ropes.

Purpose

Perhaps the most important action for a leader is purpose, the vision or direction you hope to instill in followers. We lead toward something or away from something.

There's a story set in the Middle East that is important to Judaism, Christianity and Islam. As the story goes, an infant was saved from bondage when his mother put him in a basket made of rushes and placed it into the river. The daughter of the king found the baby and raised him as a prince. Later, Moses learned of his ancestry and led Hebrews away from slavery and toward the land of milk and honey.

When first fleeing, Moses' people were quite motivated to get away from Pharaoh, who was perhaps the ultimate burning platform of change. What kept these nomads wandering in the desert for forty years was the vision of a place where they could settle down and their unstressed goats could eat sweet grass and give enough milk for the tribe as well as their kids. The people could build hives and raise bees for honey. Life would be sweet and nourishing.

Purpose and vision, described in sensory-rich, emotionally appealing terms, attract followers. But it is more than what the leader says about purpose. It is how he or she lives it day-to-day. It is the footprints left to follow.

CHANGE LEVERS

To be honest, I've always been uncomfortable with the term "change levers," which denotes a mechanical model of organizations. An organization is a collection of people and the structures, policies, processes and systems that guide people's actions. It is much more organic and even emotional than a mechanical model implies.

I use the term levers in the sense of a tool to move a seemingly immoveable object. It hearkens back to Archimedes who said, "Give me a lever long enough and a fulcrum on which to place it and I shall move the world."

Most levers in business are processes or structures that a leader can use to start, accelerate, or enhance change. It is worth remembering, however, that the mechanism a lever turns on is people, with all their messy emotions and unpredictable responses.

"Change levers" also implies a direct relationship between acting on something and change. "Pull this lever and change happens." Or "if you find that the change is getting a bit too chaotic turn this dial back to '6' and that should calm things down." Of course, nothing could be further from the truth. It is possible that a leader can change organization structure, train people, and communicate frequently, and people might still behave in the same old way.

Leaders must familiarize themselves with all the change levers: strategy, metrics, organization design, communication, and training. Then decide **what problem are you trying to solve?**

If people don't see that the old way of doing things isn't working anymore, then some combination of visionary communications and strategy might be the place to start. If you start there, you will have to explain the threat, the why, and the case for change, with a focus on the future, what we are moving toward. The pull of vision-led outweighs the push of threat-driven change.

If the way you have organized accountabilities is out of synch with what the business now requires, perhaps a new organization combined with some new metrics would communicate what is important and re-align accountabilities.

If lack of competence, knowledge and skill contribute to the problem, consider a learning intervention.

Change is the leader's responsibility; it isn't something you can delegate completely. That is not to say you should do this alone. You will need allies, a group across functions and levels who understand the why and are enthusiastic about making the change. These leaders may come from your existing management team, but often they are outsiders, people who are respected for their competency but perhaps viewed as difficult due to their consistent – but valuable - challenges to popular opinion. You may decide to work with a consultant to help you, but if you do, plan to be involved in specifying the problem to be solved and the approach to solving it.

What follows are brief descriptions of change levers. Books have been written on them, some of which I reference for further research. Deciding which to use is an act of change leadership.

CHAPTER 26

THE VISION THING

Vision may be the most over-used word in leadership literature. Entrepreneurs are called visionaries because they see the promise of a new technology or an unmet customer need. Political leaders who capture our better selves in words are described as having a bold vision.

In my lifetime, John Kennedy was the first political leader viewed as visionary. "Ask not what your country can do for you; ask what you can do for your country," expressed the greatest generation's value of service. "The torch has been passed to a new generation of Americans" inspired Baby Boomers like me in 1961 to want to contribute.

Martin Luther King Jr.'s "I have a dream" speech touched me too. I still believe in the "day when all of God's children, Black men and white men, Jews and Gentiles, Protestants and Catholics, will be able to join hands and sing in the words of the old Negro spiritual: Free at last. Free at last. Thank God almighty, we are free at last."

A vision has the power to focus people, capture their imagination, and pull them forward.

Not all see the value of vision, however. When George H. W. Bush was asked what his vision was for America, he derided it as "the *vision* thing."

That's the thing about the vision thing; it seems unsubstantial to many.

Likewise, when Lou Gerstner arrived to turn around IBM in 1993 and he was asked the same question, he said, "The last thing IBM needs right now is a vision."

IBM had just lost $8 billion. It was subdividing into individual divisions that competed with each other. It was buying into the "mainframes are dead, PCs will rule the world" mythology, but it was still its old arrogant "We're Big Blue!" self. The company hadn't acknowledged that it was broken. There was no compelling case for change. You can't offer someone a new destination if they see no reason to leave home.

This way out, follow me

A vision is the end state of change, the direction in pictures.

By this point in the book, you know that I boil down leadership to actions in an abnormal environment like war, or emergencies or change. A leader has two accountabilities: provide direction and attract followers.

I liken leaders to the fireman who enters the burning building and shouts, "The building is on fire! **This way out,** people, follow me!" If the fire is close to your rear end, any opening to **out** doesn't require much vision.

If the change is more complex, if the case for change is clear but the path forward is not, a vision will both engage and guide followers.

What is a vision?

A vision is a clear and inspiring picture of the future state. Vision statements are often written with emotionally evocative and sensory rich language:

Nike: *To bring inspiration and innovation to every athlete in the world (2022)*

Honda: *Serve people worldwide with the "joy of expanding their life's potential" (2022)*

Tesla: *To create the most compelling car company of the 21st century by driving the world's transition to electric vehicles*

Apple: *To make a contribution to the world by making tools for the mind that advance humankind (1980)*

Patagonia: *To use all its resources to defend life on earth*

Visions evolve over time. Honda's 1970 vision was "Destroy Yamaha;" In the 1960s Nike's wanted to "Crush Adidas."

Vision, mission, and values

There is a lot of confusion about these words, and in common usage, they do overlap a lot. Here is what I used as definitions:

- A vision is a destination; it can change if you reach it. It should pull you forward.
- A mission is your reason for being, your purpose, your Why.
- Values are the principles that guide you day to day.

Clearly there are overlaps and difference in terms. Patagonia's vision statement above is not a destination. Despite what they call it, I think it is their mission. Both Yamaha and Adidas still exist so Honda and Nike didn't achieve their visions; instead their visions changed.

Prerequisites for a vision

The case for change

A vision may explain why we need to change. I have seen a vision built as a series of From-To statements:

From	To
Commodity pricing death spiral	Solid differentiation (no competition)
No money to invest in good ideas	Abundant money to invest in good ideas
A declining company people want to leave	A growth company people want to join

It is really about offering a positive view of the outcome after the change. "The world's favourite airline" was British Airways vision post-privatization. It carried the primary goal of customer service and implied the second goal of profit, because if customers chose BA as their favorite airline, planes would fly full and profit would follow.

Hope

Often leaders seeking to compel change evoke fear. But people will not change if they are frozen with fear or drowning in despair. "Everything we've ever been or done is worthless and destroyed," results in "Oh, man, what's the use?" Have you ever tried to lose weight when you are depressed? "It's hopeless. Guess I'll just finish this pint of ice cream."

The best leaders evoke pride in what was, what can't be taken away, what will not change. Then they offer the excitement of a new beginning.

Reduce resistance

"We fear change," said Garth Algar, Wayne Campbell's sidekick in the movie *Wayne's World*. This phrase is repeated a lot by Mike Myers and Dana Carvey in their *Saturday Night Live* skits that turned into this movie. I don't know why they said this so often, but maybe because it nails the absurdity of reluctance or resistance to change.

As discussed, the fear may be of the unknown - loss of a job, power, pay, the currency that their skill affords, relationships. The leader must provide information as quickly as possible. Showing where the perception of loss doesn't meet reality and demonstrating how the vision offsets real loss when it does exist often dissolves reluctance.

People also may resist change that they perceive as being done to them. They feel that you're taking away their autonomy and input. They don't resist all change; they resist your change. (My anti-authority, counter-dependent self knows a lot about this.) The only antidote for this is choice; help people see the future and *choose* to change.

So before introducing a vision, a leader must:

- Make a compelling case for why things cannot stay the way they are,
- Offer pride for what was, hope that everything won't change, and belief in the ability of followers to make the change.
- Provide enough detail about the change so followers see that the gains compensate for the losses, and
- Give them a choice to commit to the change.

How to build a vision

Building a vision often entails visualization techniques in which you envision the details of the path as well as the outcome in your "mind's eye." Visualization techniques have been used in sports for a long time. I ran my first marathon through neighborhoods in the Boston area that I knew very well, and so visualizing my race was easy. My second race in Washington D.C. didn't go as well, in part because I didn't know and couldn't visualize the course. Some leadership groups find guided visualization helpful. Some don't.

A fellow consultant expressed frustration with the way some process consultants helped groups of leaders build a vision. "I can't attend another of these 'Imagine you are floating on a pink cloud' sessions," he fumed. He went on to create a process he called Vision Engineering, where the group examined trends affecting their business and evaluated the interrelationship between those trends and the likely speed of evolution. From this analysis he created future scenarios and the success path for each of them. The group then brainstormed a name for both the scenario and its success path.

I used the Vision Engineering process several times. Because the group had done the thinking together, the words they came up with or their vision had special meaning. However, communicating the vision to the rest of the organization was a challenge. "You kinda had to be there" did not lead to effective communication. Successful leadership groups learned to explain a little of the process along with the scenario names and visionary words.

Short-term vision is better

Become what by when? Most people can focus on a change for a few months. Those inside organizations can hold on to a five-year vision, but only if there are interim milestones to reinforce progress. The vision that is perpetual, always looking to the future, is great if there are improvements and successes along the way.

Words are just words

There were times in my long consulting career when I facilitated a vision off-site and it became clear, either during the off-site or most often afterwards, that all the pretty wordsmithing was B.S. This group of leaders could not or would not live up to their awe-inspiring prose. Why set a goal you can't or won't achieve? Because you think the vision thing is expected of you?

A vision is a great change lever if it represents the emotional commitment of those leading change. The power of vision is to turn good intentions into emotion-grabbing commitment. If you are the leader, the vision must speak to <u>your</u> emotion first and make <u>you</u> want to commit to it. If it does that it may also reach others and drive your shared commitment forward.

CHAPTER 27.

STRATEGY: IT'S THE THOUGHT THAT COUNTS

A strategy is a **plan** to achieve an **objective** in the face of **competition.**

A strategic plan is therefore a clarification of the objective, perhaps including measures of success (new sales, new customers, market share, operating costs, production time, hiring time, staff retention, profit, share price, etc.).

Then the strategic plan is what we are aiming to do and why. It is a collection of decisions, actions we **will take** and actions we **will not take.**

In addition to **what** we are going to do and **why**, the strategic plan will include **how** we will do it, step by step or otherwise detailed actions, perhaps with some measures or milestones to tell us if we are on track. Then the plan will define who will do what by when (accountabilities and schedule) and at what cost (budget). These detailed planning tasks are often left till later in the planning process or placed into the category called implementation. In my experience strategic planners who fail to consider implementation issues at the front end sometimes produce unrealistic plans that need substantial revision later on.

The place where a strategy differs from any standard plan is the phrase at the end of the definition - in the face of competition. In many cases, a new strategy is a response to a competitor.

For example, a company that has repeatedly lost sales to a competitor on price may utilize continuous improvement to reduce costs. Or a company may work to innovate a new game-changing technology or service process to change the competitive playing field.

If a business is repeatedly caught flat-footed by competitor actions, it may need to create a separate function of environmental scanning and competitive intelligence. (No, I am not suggesting corporate espionage, just monitoring what is going on in your industry.)

Often when facilitating leadership groups at strategy off-sites I used this quote by Dwight D. Eisenhower.

In planning for battle, I have always found that plans are useless, but planning is indispensable.

"Huh?"you may say. "That makes **no sense**. Plans are useless but planning is not? Which is it?"

What Eisenhower is saying is that the plan itself isn't what's important. No battle ever went according to a plan. What's important is the _process_ of planning, the thought that goes into anticipating the enemy's movements, and considering its advantages and disadvantages. That thinking allows the general to act and react during the battle and not slavishly follow a plan.

To me, this concept is critical for business strategy. It's not about the report, or deck or pristine strategy left behind by the strategy consultant. Rather, it's all about who did the thinking, the client or the consultant. Client thinking bodes success; consultant thinking rarely does.

It's the thought that counts.

Strategic thinking

When you hear someone called a strategic thinker, often that's just code for smart. Here are some attributes of strategic thinking that most everyone can master.

Strategic thinking is data-based, so gather and analyze information about customers, competitors, and anyone who influences a market.

Look for what your company is uniquely qualified to do. If your processes are inefficient and your technology is out of date, competing as a low-cost producer might not be for you.

Look for patterns. Often the best strategies come from trends that are unspoken or others have missed. For example, growing Internet use led to a new iPhone feature in 2005. Now we all search everything on our phones.

Look for what is missing or different. Are there trends in another market that might apply? The Italian espresso café that Howard Shultz, then a manager at a Seattle coffee roaster, observed in Milan in 1982 became Starbucks.

Monitor technology that will change the game. Netflix is an excellent example. Its DVDs in the mail offering killed the Blockbuster video stores, and it was among the first entrants into streaming and independent production.

Anticipate moves by other players. A strategy is a dynamic plan that must respond to or even anticipate competitors, suppliers, regulators, etc. When Mark Zuckerberg founded Facebook, MySpace was the dominant provider of friend/connection news sharing. Facebook started out as a closed network, available only to university students. Facebook made itself seem too niche for MySpace to bother with until it was too late. On the other hand, small producer RC Cola introduced diet and caffeine-free colas only to have their innovations copied by Coke and Pepsi.

The Ansoff Matrix*

Products

	Existing	New
New (Markets)	**Market Development**	**Product/Market Diversification**
Existing (Markets)	**Product/Market Penetration**	**Product Development**

* Adapted from *Strategies for Diversification*, H. Igor Ansoff, Harvard Business Review 1957

Frameworks

It is impossible to discuss strategy without addressing frameworks because business academia and strategy consultants promote frameworks as the core of strategic thinking. Frameworks are useful to structure the thinking of analysis and also to communicate the frame, the why of the new strategy.

Historically, a 2x2 matrix has been used to choose which product/market combinations are relevant. The Ansoff matrix helped to decide which strategies to pursue.

The Boston Box, named for the Boston Consulting Group (BCG) that first promoted its use, is helpful in deciding which strategic opportunities to pursue.

Dr. Michael Porter at the Harvard Business School created the Five Forces model to explain the dynamics of competition in an industry (seen below in a media company's analysis of their market).

This framework is especially good at ensuring that all parts of the industry are considered in a drive for differentiation.

The Boston Box

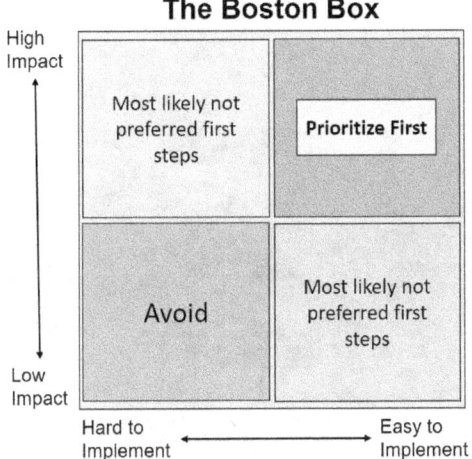

Drs. W. Chan Kim and Renée Mauborgne published a different set of frameworks in *Blue Ocean Strategy.* Their focus was changing to compete in a place where no competitor was competing, or "blue ocean." To do that Kim and Mauborgne encouraged companies to examine all potential drivers of value and to innovate a new value curve by four actions - reduce, eliminate, create, or raise (see the Four Actions Framework). Kim and Mauborgne describe this process as value innovation, but the use of the four actions model follows significant customer and industry analysis.

Frameworks can be useful in strategic analysis, with these caveats:

- Not everyone naturally thinks in frameworks and so all frameworks need explanation.
- Even people who naturally think this way may resist a completed analytical framework they were not a part of populating.

Michael Porter's Five Forces Shows the Context for Media Company's Strategy

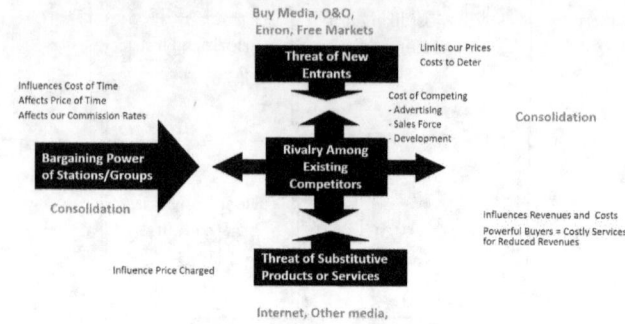

Planning

There is really nothing mystical about a strategic plan. It is what are you going to do and why. It defines the specific actions you will take and <u>not</u> take to deliver increased revenue, profit or both. It probably will have some complexity, as you may make decisions in:

- Product or service design. There are three elements of design:
    - ○ hardware – a physical product or the physical components of a service.,
    - ○ software – we tend to think of this word in computer terms, but is anything that instructs how to use the product or service, or
    - ○ service – and personalized connection to the customer.

  Each element is an opportunity to differentiate.
- Marketing (price, place, promotion).
- Operations (make vs. buy, quantity, quality, timeliness).

The plan will also include resources, schedule and budget, i.e., who will do what by when and at what cost. It may also include some contingency plans if something doesn't work as expected.

The Four Actions Framework

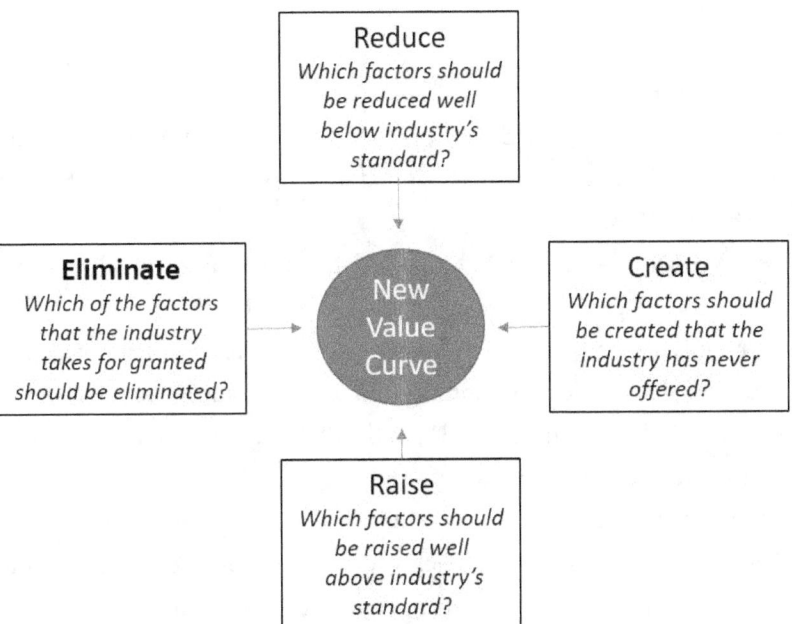

Source *Blue Ocean Strategy* W. Chan Kim, Renée Mauborgne, 2005 Harvard Business Review Press

Who plans?

Do executives formulate strategy and operations managers execute it? Or do strategy consultants formulate strategy, present the deck to the C-suite executives and operations managers execute it?

Separating strategy formulation from implementation is always problematic. Understanding gets lost in the hand-off between planners and implementers.

But you can't bring the whole company to the offsite. As a consultant running strategic planning offsites I advised clients to invite an extended leadership team comprised of key functional or departmental managers critical to implementation. To keep strategy refreshed, I advised clients to set up an ongoing process with a strategic planning forum, a discussion group whose membership included a rotating cadre of opinion leaders from across the company.

Implementation

Brigadier General David Sarnoff, who was in the Allied High Command for the European theatre during and after World War II, said in his role as CEO of RCA,

A "B" quality plan executed in an "A" quality fashion will always beat an "A" quality plan executed in a "B" quality fashion.

A plan is just a plan and nothing happens until it is implemented. The quality of that implementation depends on having implementers at the planning table to think through the detail and anticipate how different parts of the plan may interact.

The process that a group of leaders goes through to create strategy enables these leaders to react quickly to events on the ground. In a world of increasing volatility, uncertainty, complexity, and ambiguity (VUCA), this ability to react strategically is a differentiator.

CHAPTER 28

METRICS AND MEASUREMENT SYSTEMS

M etrics and measurement are important in a change effort. How else would you know you had changed?

However, metrics and measurement also drive behavior.

I was once at a call center for a healthcare insurance company. The firm had an excellent reputation for customer service, one of the highest in their industry, but costs in the call center were increasing. Average call handle time was increasing. The firm needed more staff. Someone decided that customer service representatives (CSRs) were too chatty.

To address this perceived problem, the management added a two-sided digital clock display to the CSR computer screen. One clock gave the day's average call handle time; the second clock was the elapsed time on the current call.

Average call handle time went down, but management noticed an increase in mid-call disconnects. The leadership assumed a technical problem, but IT found nothing. After some analysis and discreet observation, they discovered CSRs were disconnecting calls mid-call in order to meet that day's average call time. The management disciplined the problem

CSRs, but the problem persisted.

Further analysis of the problem discovered that the reason average call handle time had gone up in the first place was that the firm had introduced a new Medicare Advantage (MA) plan, which was quite successful. The plan was complex with many coverage options, and CSRs were explaining the options to seniors.

"When the clocks showed up," said one CSR, "we all figured we were being measured on call handle time. If I got one of the MA calls, I dumped it while I was talking so it looked like a technical disconnect."

Be careful what you measure and how.

What are metrics and measurement?

Some definitions:

- **Metrics**: Also called measures, indicators, or key performance indicators (KPIs), metrics can be numbers (continuous data like average call handle time) or attributes (discrete data like color, pass/ fail, on/off, yes/no, etc.). Continuous data is better for showing trends and improvement. Discrete data can be quantified, e.g., percentage passed, but to track improvement, you will need more data to establish validity.

- **Measurement**: This is the process of defining how we measure with precision and accuracy every time. The measurement process requires that both the metric and the measurement process are very specific.

Metrics

In my work with British Airways, we used two basic kinds of metrics:

- **Results metrics**, like the customer service ranking done by JD Power Associates. Between 1984 and 1987 BA went from worst to best on this metric.

- **Process metrics,** like queue wait time at the ticket counter at Heathrow. This was one of a suite of process metrics used to gauge customer perception of BA's service. From analysis of these metrics, the airline created a peak staffing protocol and a role called Queue Combers, who talked to people in line to be sure they expedited passengers whose flight time was imminent.

Results metrics measure what you want to achieve; process metrics tell you whether you are on track to achieve it . . . or not.

Which measures?

There is a lot of criticism of corporations for being too focused on financial measures, like shareholder value as measured by share price and dividend.

In 1992, Robert S. Kaplan, a professor at the Harvard Business School, and David P. Norton, founder of The Palladium Group consulting firm, published an article in the *Harvard Business Review* called "The Balanced Scorecard - Measures that Drive Performance." Kaplan and Norton turned this into a book in 1996, *The Balanced Scorecard: Translating Strategy Into Action.*

The premise of this book is relatively simple. Instead of only financial measures, a company should measure across four perspectives: financial, customer, internal operations, and innovation and learning. Kaplan and Norton went to great lengths to describe how each of these perspectives should be linked so that, for example, when customers said they wanted "product customization and low price," operations wasn't hamstrung trying to provide flexible manufacturing and long production runs. The measures must be linked and where necessary traded off against each other – or "balanced."

The concept is a good one but, in my experience, more leaders acquired the language than studied the methodology, let alone implement it in a disciplined way.

In 1987, Art Schneiderman of Analog Devices coined the term "Key Performance Indicators" or KPIs. Schneiderman had in mind a few metrics that showed how an organization or operating process was performing. He didn't intend that every operating process metric should end up in a corporate scorecard or that employees should be held accountable for scores of metrics, some obsolete or conflicting. But that happened in a lot of companies.

So be careful with metrics, and especially with using too many KPIs, as the method of driving change. More is NOT better. I worked for a client once who had a rule, "if you add a KPI you have to take one away." It led them to an annual project to rationalize metrics. The project always asked for input from everyone in the company and the response was often overwhelming. Their output was one of three possibilities: stop the metric; keep the metric and explain why; or modify the metric to make it less onerous, e.g., reduce frequency.

Participation in metric design worked. Performance increased and employee climate improved.

Measurement process

If you are going to use a metric to drive change, people must trust how you are gathering and calculating the data. For example, if you want to track the percentage of company revenue from new products, a common innovation metric, do line extensions count? What about color changes?

These days a lot of companies use customer surveys. Perhaps this started in 2003 when Fredrick Reichheld created the Net Promoter Score to answer the question, "How do you measure customer delight?" Reichheld posited that asking, "How likely are you to recommend?" was a proxy measure for customer delight. Proxy measures are often based upon correlation analysis, but can be based upon simple observation. "When this happens, I also notice that this happens."

It is a good proxy, but now most of us are sick of surveys and fewer people answer them. So what is the relevance of those who do answer to your customer base as a whole? What research must you do in order to base your change results upon this proxy measure?

The bottom line

The "bottom line" has now morphed into meaning the "last word," but it originally meant net profit. Everyone thought holding people accountable for profit was a good idea. However, profit as a metric is fuzzy. Do you draw the bottom line above uncontrollable costs like amortization? What about allocated corporate overheads?

Metrics must be:

- **Carefully defined** – It must be absolutely clear what you mean and why you chose this metric to demonstrate your company has changed, improved, innovated, or integrated.

- **Consistently measured** – The process must be done in such a way that it can be demonstrated to be accurate e.g., a consistent relationship to an accepted external standard, like JD Power's service ranking. The process must also be precise, that is repeatable every time, and reproducible regardless who is measuring.

- **Thoroughly thought through** –Think about conflicts with other measures, tradeoffs between different metrics, and unintended consequences of chosen metrics. It helps to have a pessimist on the review team, the glass-half-empty-guy who frequently says, "Let's consider the worst case scenario." Remember the clock screen displays in the health insurance call center? Where was the worst case scenario guy when they were evaluating the idea of installing the clocks? The simple question, "What if the CSRs disconnect long calls?" would have been helpful. Metrics can be powerful tools to help drive change, but remember that metrics drive behavior. People focus on what they are being measured on, especially if some part of their compensation is attached to that metric. What you measure is what you will get.

CHAPTER 29.

LEADERS SHOULD LEARN ORGANIZATION DESIGN

"Competitors are eating our lunch. Disruptive technologies are destroying our business model. We can't figure out how to manage these darn millennial workers. We must need a new organization. Call a consultant."

Okay, maybe that conversation never happened, but many leaders use organizational design as their go-to action to make change. It is the single most frequently pulled *change lever* - more than strategy, product-market innovation, operational improvement, and even more than training. The first thing many executives think of in a crisis is reorganization and they often hire an expert to do it. Like most change consultants, I did my share of drawing boxes and wires.

"New CEO? We need a new organization. New strategy? We need a new organization. New processes? We need a new organization. We need to innovate? We need a new organization. We haven't reorganized in eighteen months? We <u>must</u> need a new organization."

Most companies reorganize too much and the end result is confusion and inertia. "If my boss calls . . . get her name." "Don't worry about the new org – just keep your head down. It'll change."

My view of the role of organization in a company is based on two fundamental beliefs:

- **An organization is the mechanism for implementing strategy.** People implement strategy. How groups of people are formed and who reports to whom communicates a great deal about the strategy.
- **The job of an organization is to impart clarity of purpose and accountability.** Changing the formal organization produces two things:
   - It communicates priorities - what's important around here now.
   - It clarifies accountabilities for those priorities.

That's it. That's all a new organization does. Clarity of purpose is not nothing; in fact, it's critical to change. But a new organization is not the only tool a leader has to create clarity of purpose. Accountabilities are also important, but structure is only one of several available performance management tools.

So my first reaction when asked to help design a new organization was to ask why it's necessary. There are, of course, real reasons to reorganize, e.g., changes in business model, post-merger integration, a new market or product line expansion. Then my second reaction was to teach leaders something about organization design. Why? Because if an organization implements strategy, its design is too important to be left entirely to consultants and human resource professionals. **Organization design is a critical leadership capability.**

Here are some of the things leaders should know about designing an organization:

First, stop doing personality-based organizing. "Since we outsourced payroll, Maureen in accounting won't have enough to do, so let's give her the customer call center, too." It's like a giant game of pickup sticks. Instead, design the jobs first, set the hiring specs, and then put the people in roles based upon agreed specifications.

Second, stop doing red-lining. Red-lining is cost-driven organization design, so named for a phenomenon I observed dozens of times. The CFO and trusted advisors go in a room with an organization chart and draw red lines through people's names. Then they calculate salary and benefits costs of those who are left. If the total figure doesn't meet a preset number, they draw more red lines. If it does meet their expectation, they cobble together what's left into an org chart and present it.

To impress the street, some senior executives promise "10 percent cost savings across the board." I've seen consultants win business by promising these blanket figures as well. This automatically leads to red-lining. In the interest of being fair, I saw management cut the staff of an already strapped growth business at the same rate as an over-staffed declining one. The resulting organization structure had no realistic chance of working.

An organization should be designed rationally so you can explain it. How else would you achieve clarity of purpose?

High level design

At a high level, there are two different elements to designing an organization:

- **Vertical** – This is the accountability structure – the boxes and wires – that details who reports to whom. The objective is clarity of purpose and performance accountability for the day-to-day, routine work.

- **Horizontal** – This is the integration structure, sometimes called the "informal organization." It includes shared services and functions like finance and accounting, human resources, processes and systems, networks and forums, as well as growth capabilities like systematic innovation and improvement. The objective of the horizontal organization is unity or alignment – how people work together.

Vertical structure

The major types of vertical organization - functional, product-based, and customer-based - are aligned to strategic business drivers. For businesses driven by:

- **Low cost** - an organization based on function (marketing, finance, operations, etc.) reduces duplication and staff costs.
- **Product innovation** – an organization based on a platform, technology, or product allows people with similar expertise to innovate together.
- **Customer loyalty** – an organization based on industry, geography, or key accounts allows a company to get close to the customer.

This type of pure-form organization often creates a lack of integration, a scenario popularly described as "silos." In silos, people within one function, product or customer group have difficulty communicating across the organization, perhaps because they spend most of their time with others like themselves or because the "my team" mindset is heightened by competition for resources. As mentioned in a previous chapter, I spent much of my career in silo-busting.

The silo-busting solution is cross-department communication. This can be achieved by discussion forums and networks and by shared processes, such as strategic portfolio management, investment, operational budgeting, leadership development, procurement and sourcing policy, etc.

Since the 1970s, most large companies have been structured in some form of matrix organization that juxtaposes two or more drivers. Matrix organizations attempt integration structurally. They create dual (or in some cases, multiple) reporting relationships, the "two boss phenomenon." Accountabilities of each reporting relationship must be agreed or negotiated, e.g., business finance has a solid line to the business head and a dotted line to corporate finance. (Of course, what the dotted/solid lines mean must be specified in detail, like which boss gets priority at year end and which at tax time.) Matrix organizations often compromise the clarity of the pure forms and require that everyone have higher level skills of influence and negotiation.

All vertical structures, and especially the matrix, can get complex when you add in multiple lines of business across international borders. In these environments, carefully planning the horizontal structure is imperative.

Horizontal structure

Horizontal structure communicates and integrates across vertical structures like business units. Horizontal structures can be formal things like all units using the same Human Resource policies or capital budgeting system. Horizontal structures can also be a network of informal relationships: "Hey, call Charley and ask how they do this. Can we share a supply order and get it cheaper?"

When I started my career as a change consultant, the vertical structure was the only thing talked about, even by consultants. In the mid-1980s, General Motors had almost 49 percent of US car and truck sales, 850,000 employees, and the eighth-largest budget in the world, including countries. But the company was cost-challenged because Japanese competition was gaining share with lower-priced vehicles. GM engaged a large consulting firm to reorganize GM in a million-dollar project - a very rare, if not unprecedented figure at the time.

Previously GM was organized into five car divisions and two truck divisions. This organization was created by CEO Alfred Sloan in the 1930s to have "a car for every pocketbook." Car buyers were meant to start out with a Chevrolet, graduate to a Pontiac, Oldsmobile, or Buick and finally end up with a Cadillac. Low-end truck buyers bought Chevrolet trucks, and business buyers bought GMC. Each division had its own design, manufacturing, marketing, and functional services. There was a lot of expensive duplication. Also, over time every marque had expanded offerings; the original pocketbook differentiation had long been lost.

The consulting firm created a new organization with two divisions, BOC (Buick, Oldsmobile, Cadillac) and CPC (Chevrolet, Pontiac,

Commercial - trucks). Each of the two new divisions shared functions for design, manufacturing, marketing and functional services, whereas previously each marque had its own. The new organization allowed plant closures and saved lots of money. It also facilitated the look-alike GM cars of the 1980s, widely credited with the further decline of GM market share.

What the consulting firm apparently failed to consider was interdivisional integration. Previously, the 850,000-person GM organization worked because the guys at the Chevy design and technical center knew their counterparts at the other marques, and picked up the phone to solve problems together. The reorganization blew up the informal horizontal organization that made the place run, and it took several years to straighten out and rebuild.

These days, most organization design models are alignment models, i.e., the McKinsey 7S, the Galbraith Star, and the Burke-Litwin Model of Organization Dynamics. They all make the point that organization structures, systems, and processes should be aligned around purpose and strategy. Now many consultants understand the importance of integration between organizational groups.

Matrix structures are not silver bullet for integration

While the horizontal organization has at least entered the conversation, some organizational designers seem stuck on hard structural solutions and are locked on the matrix as the integration mechanism of choice.

Matrix organizations require dual reporting relationships, e.g., functional managers who report to the local business and the corporate head of their function. A matrix seems a simple way to structure in integration, but it is anything but. Each of those reporting roles need to be documented (see RACI and RAPID below) and matrix structures requires higher level communication and negotiation skills to work this out. This is the part that often gets skipped. I have seen four- and five-way matrices - corporate, local and regional geography, product or platform, and key customer group. No one understands the differing priorities inherent in each reporting relationship, and therefore the matrix structure creates a pressure cooker for confused staff. "Whose permission do I need?"

Some design practitioners emphasize more flexibility such as R&D networks and leadership development forums. Too many organization designers rely on formal constructs like information systems and formal processes to enable information sharing and joint decision making, e.g., strategic planning and capital budgeting processes. (Two processes that are often overlooked are how the organization innovates and how it improves.)

RACI — Example: Building the Toolkit

Activity \ Person	Nick	Karen	Ben	Stephanie	Consultants	Mark	Kendra	Doug
Design the Basic Structure of the Toolkit	A	R		C		I		
Design the Prototype	A	C		R				C
Write the Tools	R, C		A		R			
Collect Input From Consultants	I		A, R					
Program the Prototype	I	C		A, R				C
Screen the Tools	A, R				C			
Test the Toolkit	A	C	R	R	C	C	I	C
Promote and Celebrate Launch of Toolkit	A	R	R	C	C	C	C	C

R = Responsible person
A = Accountable person
C = Consulted person
I = Informed person

Detailed organization design

The reason many reorganizations fail to achieve the intended results is that the work stops too soon. High-level job boxes and integrative processes are necessary, but not sufficient. Ultimately, leadership must prepare detailed job specifications, and assess, assign and, if necessary, train candidates.

Leaders must clearly define roles and responsibilities in their job specifications, and then teams need to agree roles and responsibilities. One option is to use facilitated responsibility charting or RACI, to determine roles:

Responsible, who does the work?

Accountable, who has final say?

Consulted, who must be consulted before the fact?

Informed, who must be informed after the fact?

Further, decision rights need to be agreed. A good tool here is the facilitated decision rights tool RAPID, developed by Bain & Company consultants.

RAPID works like RACI, but clarifies decision roles as opposed to actions.

The acronym stands for the person who is authorized to:

Recommend, usually the person who generates the idea and documents the pros and cons.

Agree, a person at a different function or level who must agree with the decision.

Perform, the person who must carry out the decision.

Input, the person who provides information or materials critical to the decision.

Decide, the single person accountable for the decision.

Both RACI and RAPID are facilitated discussion processes to gain agreement and commitment, not forms to be filled out by a manager, staff person or consultant. And like all aspects of change you have to over-communicate about it. You are changing some people's jobs, and you must re-contract with the entire organization.

You may be thinking, *sheesh – that's a lot of work; it's enough to make my head hurt.*

Yup. So you can see why I think reorganizing because we-haven't-done-it-in-a-while isn't a good idea.

You may hire an architect to help design a building, but you have to be clear about what you need, want and like. As Bauhaus architect Mies Van Der Rohe said, "God is in the details." Organization design is no different. It is a critical leadership change capability.

Key decisions: RAPID methodology

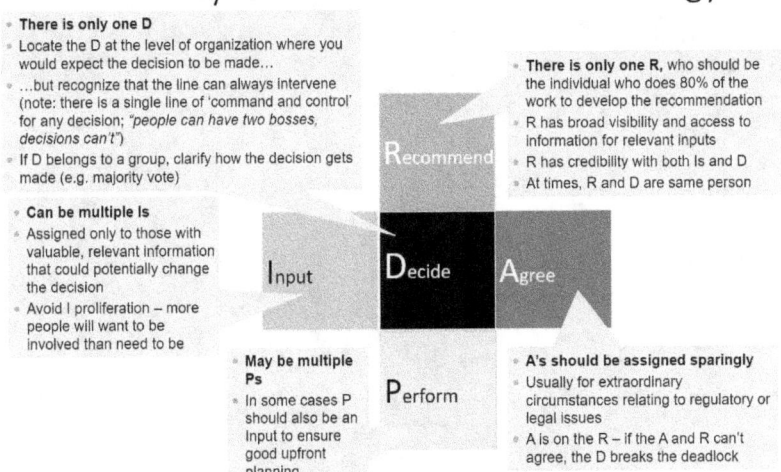

- **There is only one D**
- Locate the D at the level of organization where you would expect the decision to be made...
- ...but recognize that the line can always intervene (note: there is a single line of 'command and control' for any decision; *people can have two bosses, decisions can't*)
- If D belongs to a group, clarify how the decision gets made (e.g. majority vote)

- **Can be multiple Is**
- Assigned only to those with valuable, relevant information that could potentially change the decision
- Avoid I proliferation – more people will want to be involved than need to be

Input

Decide

Agree

Recommend

- **There is only one R,** who should be the individual who does 80% of the work to develop the recommendation
- R has broad visibility and access to information for relevant inputs
- R has credibility with both Is and D
- At times, R and D are same person

- **May be multiple Ps**
- In some cases P should also be an Input to ensure good upfront planning

Perform

- **A's should be assigned sparingly**
- Usually for extraordinary circumstances relating to regulatory or legal issues
- A is on the R – if the A and R can't agree, the D breaks the deadlock

**RAPIDs should reflect what will work in 90% of situations –
Design for the rule, not the exception**

CHAPTER 30.

THE "SOFT STUFF": ORGANIZATION CULTURE AND CLIMATE

What is culture?

I always asked inconvenient open-ended questions like this one to groups of leaders engaged in change. It was a habit that left me vulnerable to workshop humor and cynical or sarcastic comments, often at my expense. In one case, an operations guy, about fifteen years older than me, said, "It's what my wife keeps in those little white plastic tubs in the refrigerator." The entire group laughed and joked for ninety seconds, which felt much longer at the front of the room.

In those days organizational culture was discussed only by industrial psychologists and was almost universally pooh-poohed by people who actually made things. Even Tom Peters and Bob Waterman, whose 1982 book *In Search of Excellence* legitimized culture-driven behavior, talked about common behavioral norms (bias for action, close to the customer, stick to your knitting) and almost never used the word culture.

These days, it's different. It seems like everyone has learned what organizational culture is. It's invisible; it drives behavior. It takes a long time to build and is almost impossible to change.

At one client site, an oil and gas company, people would say, "We are a culture driven by autonomy. We are a loose confederation of 'local energy companies.'" Citing their history, I would remind them that they were that way because twenty years ago their chief executive was on an acquisition spree that built the company to its current size, adding, "The 'local energy company' strategy you quote was a way to focus local management on day-to-day operations during that period, so executives could focus on deal making. It shouldn't justify <u>not</u> following corporate policy today."

People at a respected diversified financial services firm once said, "Our <u>mission</u> is to do <u>whatever</u> <u>it</u> <u>takes</u> to satisfy the customer." This culture led to a scenario where revenue grew at 15 percent (fantastic!) but expenses grew at 25 percent each year (unsustainable). The company began adapting its culture to be more systematic and profitable. "It is in the customer's best interests to move from an ad hoc way of operating to an efficient process-focused way." Not surprisingly there was resistance, excuses, cries of how "process [bureaucracy] is not in our culture."

I should be happy that I worked long enough that the soft stuff finally emerged as important, i.e., It's the people, stupid. But culture victimhood isn't quite what I hoped for. And all this discussion of culture misses an important point.

Culture is a long-term variable. It can be changed over two to five years with focused leadership. The merger of British European Airways (BEA) and British Overseas Airways Corporation (BOAC) occurred in 1974. When my project team arrived in 1983 the merged company still housed completely separate cultures. There were separate Heathrow facilities, systems and even letterheads. The short haul (former BEA) pilots felt that they were treated as second-class citizens compared to the long haul (former BOAC) pilots in a culture that some described as old class differences between World War II fighter and bomber pilots. After our three-year program of facilities co-location, aircraft cross-training, and a single pilot evaluation and scheduling system, a pilot was a BA pilot; there was one British Airways culture.

The late Dr. Edgar Schein was one of the leading academic lights of organizational culture. Dr. Schein described culture as the product of behavior over time. The founder and other leaders' behavior have the greatest impact, but others contribute to the beliefs, norms, and habits that make up the "way we do things here."

Schein Model of Organization Culture

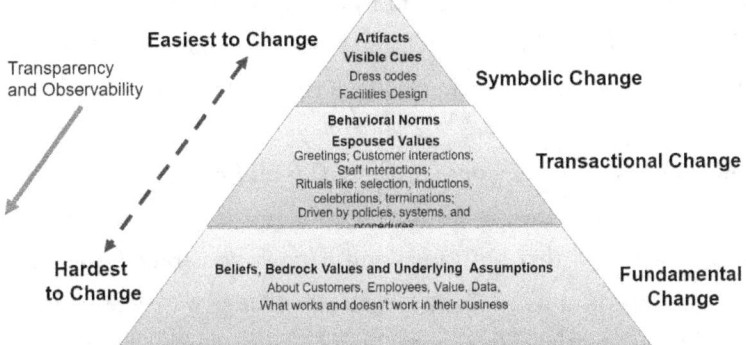

Schein's model of organizational culture is almost universally accepted now, but when it was first published in 1985, it was earth-shattering. He proposed three levels of culture:

- **Artifacts,** the visible cues, how the place looks
- **Espoused values** and behavioral norms, which are easily observable and talked about
- **Underlying assumptions,** bedrock values, and beliefs that define who we are and that everyone agrees upon, but rarely discusses. They are like water to the fish, critical but invisible.

Schein developed the pyramid model above, arranging the three levels by the easiest to change to hardest to change.

IBM is a case in point. The company was built in the late nineteenth century from an amalgamation of tabulating companies, time clock manufacturers, and punch card companies into the Computing Tabulating and Recording Company (CTR). In 1914 Thomas J. Watson joined the firm, became president in 1915, and in 1924 changed the name to International Business Machines.

IBM didn't invent the modern day computer, and in fact Watson was said to believe that there might be a market for one mainframe in the entire world. IBM commercialized the mainframe computer.

It is difficult to overstate the influence of Watson on IBM culture. My mother was a computer programmer in the 1950s, and in the 1960s she was part of the team that programmed the operating system for the IBM 360, the first IBM minicomputer. After a visit to Endicott, NY headquarters she came home with enameled desk signs, "THINK" and "The Customer is King," both famous Watson sayings. She still had them when we cleaned out my parents' house in 1998. (I wish I had saved them.)

The "THINK" sign was Watson's way of creating a professional workforce. He insisted that both men and women wear blue business suits with white shirts and ties. "The Customer is King" was Watson's view of how IBM differentiated its service. Mainframe computers were expensive hardware, but they broke down a lot. When they did, IBM would send a swarm of blue suits, often ten to fifteen people, to fix the problem.

In 1993, the computer industry had changed. Mini-computer producers Digital Equipment Corporation and Wang had taken large segments of IBM's business. IBM introduced the first Personal Computer in 1981, but ultimately outsourced the operating system to Bill Gates and Paul Allen at Microsoft.

IBM still tried to swarm the blue suits to solve customer problems, but margins on smaller computers didn't support that. Big Blue was in trouble. IBM CEO John Ayers' solution was to have each of the businesses set up independent business units. Analysts predicted break up and in 1993, IBM's board fired John Ayers and hired Lou Gerstner.

Gerstner had sneered, "The last thing IBM needs right now is a vision!"

But, of course, he had one. He had been at RJR Nabisco and saw that the only thing that held a disparate conglomerate together was information technology; he'd come from American Express Travel services where IT unified credit cards, travelers cheques, and a high-end travel agency. He saw that systems integration was a service and IBM had service in its DNA. They just hadn't thought about it as a product that people would pay for.

Gerstner killed the Ayers idea of independent business units and began integration. He emphasized services, ultimately including management consulting.

But he didn't start there. Gerstner's first act was to change the dress code to all business casual all the time. IBM was in shock. The IBM dress code had relaxed a little over the years. Nobody measured cuffs anymore. Gray suits seemed to be OK. Some of the crazy techies wore blue shirts with yellow foulard ties, but no suits? No ties? No way! I'm told the salesforce rebelled and were told that if they thought the customer required formal suits they didn't have to adhere to business casual.

The world was also shocked. I had a client in advertising who hated Gerstner, whom he had never met, because he "single-handedly destroyed the professional workplace. We went from IBM blue suits to flip-flops and jeans on Fridays and working from home in pajamas two days a week."

I don't think that was all Lou Gerstner's doing, but he did signal a culture shift at IBM by changing the Attributes, the visible, the symbolic. Over the nine years he was CEO, IBM turned around and Gerstner wrote *Who Says Elephants Can't Dance?*

As Peter Drucker said, "Culture eats strategy for breakfast."

Organizational climate

Organizational climate, on the other hand, is a much shorter-term variable that can be changed by managers in weeks or even days.

Climate is the collective perceptions of people on issues such as goal clarity, quality standards, and collaboration and respect. Climate tends to affect motivation, teamwork, and commitment. There is a huge body of research on organizational climate starting with Kurt Lewin in 1939 showing that climate affects short-term variables like productivity performance and medium-term variables like absenteeism and staff retention. This research also shows that a climate can be changed through management practice independent of organizational culture.

In 1967, George Litwin and Bob Stringer performed a landmark climate experiment. Using Harvard Business School students they set up three manufacturing "companies" with "experimental climates," each based upon American psychologist David McClelland's three motive needs: **Power, Affiliation,** and **Achievement**. Managers were given a one-page brief to describe the way they should manage according to these motive needs. The experiment lasted months and demonstrated the impact of climate on motivation and performance.

In 1985, I wrote a training exercise for the British Airways Seeds Programme (change agent training) based upon the Litwin–Stringer experiment. I wrote three video scripts for three actors playing CEOs who set the tone for each company's climate.

In the simulation participants built paper airplanes. Each production team operated in one of these artificially created climates, and at the end we discussed the three climates and their results.

As with the original Litwin-Stringer experiment with HBS students,

- the Power climate company, Brigadier, started out strong but then imploded.
- The Affiliation climate company, Balance, had trouble getting started, but then came on strong just a little too late in the game.
- The Achievement climate company, Blazer, won hands down. It was a great training exercise and we ran it at several companies over time.

It worked every time. What is still most amazing to me is that on the basis of a few minutes of video we created a marked difference in behavior and results.

I've heard the author Daniel Pink decry the "gap between what science knows and what business does." This gap seems especially true of the research on Organizational Climate.

Shouldn't it be easy to create the climate you want in your business? What gets in the way?

It is true that, as compared to the real world, the experimental climate in a classroom is controlled and intervening variables are limited. There are fewer distractions, fewer opportunities for changing business circumstances, individual differences, and emotions. The soft stuff is hard to do in the real world.

We could do a better job of managing climate by giving more autonomy and by sharing power through transparency and participation. This might close this gap between what science knows and business does, stop complaints that "the culture won't let me," and start effective management of short-term variables like organizational climate that affect motivation and performance. And if you want to change culture, start with the visible attributes first and empower change teams for the rest.

CHAPTER 31

CHANGE TEAMS

"Y ou can't make change without changing yourself, but you can't make change by yourself either."

I heard this at a leadership workshop in some change effort somewhere. I don't remember who said it. But it speaks to John Kotter's guiding coalition, a group of leaders distributed across functions and levels who direct a change.

It also speaks to change teams who research what customers want, design new processes, redesign preventative maintenance, or rationalize and combine overgrown product platforms. These change teams are often cross-functional and cross-level, joined by anyone with knowledge of the process and skill to make change.

Change teams do the nuts and bolts work of change.

What are change teams?

In change efforts, I saw groups of leaders in leadership training choose changes that needed to be made to achieve the vision.

For example, at Managing People First, the leadership program for the top 2000 people at British Airways during the turnaround, I saw groups of leaders redesign passenger loading processes, preventative aircraft maintenance protocol, and travel agent loyalty programs.

General Motor's Leadership Now was a training program for the top

1000 leaders. There was no formal change team component and yet I saw leaders spontaneously form change teams to rationalize car and truck platforms and improve the dealer parts delivery process.

In Continuous Improvement (CI) initiatives, project teams drive improvement. In the best CI initiatives, these teams go through training together and are directed to areas that need improvement. Improvements are tracked and verified by the appropriate senior executives.

In poorly run CI initiatives, groups pick projects at random, double counting of CI results runs rampant, and improvement efforts are often abandoned before results are achieved.

Successful innovation initiatives also include teams with training and project selection processes like CI, but may also have a funding mechanism much like a venture capital fund with stages of seed capital, i.e., mezzanine financing etc. This structure allows more freedom at the idea generation stage, but exerts more control as the firm invests in development of the innovation. As a result, innovation teams are less temporary, behaving more like mini-startups that grow into viable business units over time.

What is a team?

Team may be the most hackneyed word in the business lexicon. It is used as a positive description for any business unit or sometimes the company as a whole. Speaking of the GM team when General Motors was a workforce of 850,000 may have built some pride, but it didn't contribute to operational clarity or performance.

Team behavior, or teamwork, often refers to a spirit of cooperation that many of us felt when playing sports or singing in chorus or acting in school plays. These are pleasant memories and so when we use the word in business, it is a way to share credit for a good result. No one ever says "great teamwork" when you fail. Teamwork, a warm feeling of collaboration, is not the same as a team.

Jon R. Katzenbach and Douglas K. Smith were McKinsey consultants in 1993 when they wrote *The Wisdom of Teams: Creating the High-Performance Organization.* The book largely ignored decades of social science research in small group dynamics and studied teams in business and in the military.

(Full disclosure: from 1999-2003 I worked for Katzenbach Partners, Jon Katzenbach's firm after he left McKinsey, so one might say I am fully indoctrinated in these definitions of teams.)

Katzenbach and Smith defined a team as a performance unit that usually had:

- A small number of members (5-7)
- Complementary skills
- Commitment to meaningful purpose and clear performance goals
- A collective work product (rather than a collection of individual work products)
- An agreed working approach (which often includes a leadership role that rotates according to the skills needed)
- Mutual accountability for results

Further, Katzenbach and Smith differentiated a "real team" from the "single leader work group" or temporary "working group."

Characteristics	Single Leader Work Group	Real Team
Best used when	Time is short, and the leader knows the process and outcome	Work and outcomes aren't known, and there's time to build a team
Run by	The leader	Rotates to those with knowledge
Working approach	Decided by leader	Decided by the team
Accountability	Leader top down	Mutual accountability
Work Products	Mostly individual	Mostly collective

Katzenbach and Smith came back together in 2001 to publish *The Discipline of Teams: A Mindbook-Workbook for Developing Small Group Performance.* This book includes a reiteration of the team definitions along with some helpful warnings about pseudo teams and compromise units. The book also includes research on virtual teams, and compares real teams and single leader work groups.

Perhaps the most important point to take away from the Katzen-bach-Smith framework is that the team is a performance unit. So is the single leader work group.

However, because outcomes and ideal processes in change efforts may be uncertain, the real team, as Katzenbach and Smith described it, has greater applicability. Teams take time to build.

How to build a team

Group dynamics research shows that as people join a group, they first ask questions about the purpose of the group. They then want to know about the other members of the group to determine if they belong.

Think about attending the first meeting of a book club, hobby club, or an adult education class. The group leader describes the purpose of the group, some basics about the group – for example, how often the meetings are held and for how long. Then the leader asks everyone to introduce themselves. If the members already know each other the lead-er might ask each person to describe their skills or a "little known fact" about themselves to deepen the group's knowledge of its members.

The group leader is attending to membership issues: What is this group? Who are these people? Do I belong here? Sometimes in business there is a sponsor who outlines purpose or gives a charter to the group.

What follows are issues of leadership and approach - Who is in charge? How will this group be run? What is my role? Sometimes this can be contentious. If there is disagreement about who leads or how, the conflict must be resolved before the group can get on with the work.

As the work progresses and people get accustomed to working together, behavioral norms are set and finally the group gets on with performing the work. Every group takes time to work together well. We often hear people say things like "it took us a while, but we finally gelled."

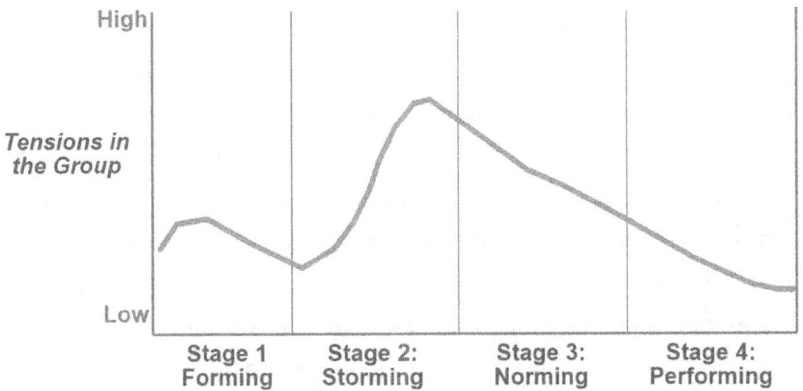

In 1965, Bruce Tuckman, a Princeton PhD working at the Naval Research Institute in Bethesda, Maryland, published "Developmental Sequence in Small Groups" (*Psychological Bulletin* 1965) in which he named the stages in such a catchy way that the names have stuck since:

- *Forming* (pretending to get on or get along with others)
- *Storming* (letting down the politeness barrier and trying to get to the issues, even if tempers flare up)
- *Norming* (getting used to each other and developing trust and productivity)
- *Performing* (working to a common goal on an efficient and cooperative basis)

Tuckman outlined the stages, but also showed how the tensions in the group changed as the group developed. Leadership issues create the most tension and can destroy groups.

In the *Discipline of Teams,* Katzenbach and Smith demonstrated how forming both single-leader groups and real teams was similar in the beginning. Every group needs:

- A clear charter outlining purpose and goals
- Clear communications
- Starting roles and responsibilities
- Measures and processes for accountability

Then the two types of groups diverge. The single leader outlines the working approach and accountabilities. The real team agrees their approach and how and when leadership will emerge. Though Katzenbach and Smith do not refer to Tuckman, they do allude to the length of time and tension required to get to high performance in a real team, and recommend this performance unit should be used when time allows it and purpose requires it.

I contend that many purposes of change teams require the investment in a real team. If you want ongoing high performance, you must invest the time to build it.

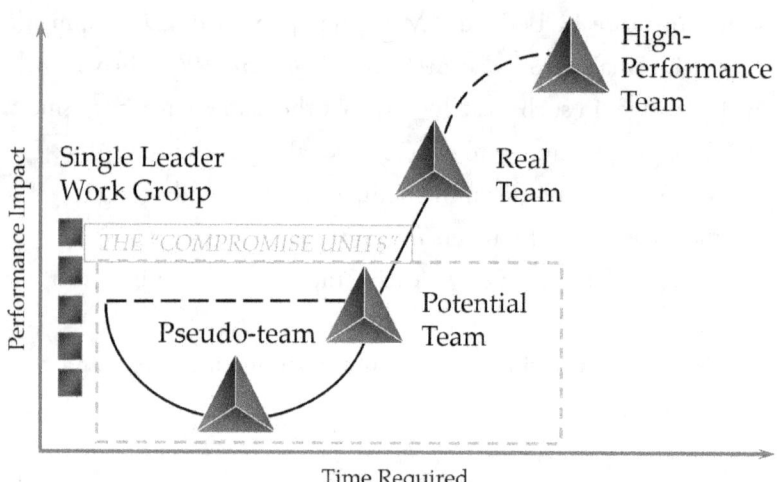

Working with consultants - the client team and the consultant team

Consultants often ask for a team of client resources to help with the change. In my experience it is rare that consultants are asking for a real team. I will admit that even at Katzenbach Partners we misused the term and were, in fact, often looking for a single leader group. I have seen content or expert consultants ask for a team when what they wanted was two or three administrators to schedule appointments and request data.

At Gemini Consulting, where I did large scale re-engineering projects that would ultimately be managed by the client, I saw a variety of approaches. There were often large client teams that we trained to do the work. Sometimes the consultant was the leader. Sometimes a client was the leader. Rarely was the team a real team that mixed both consultant and client resources, but it did happen.

In continuous improvement work I saw a variety of real team and single leader work groups. I saw both clients and consultants lead. In real teams the consultants often served as an external resource to demonstrate a tool.

Team dysfunction – what to do when it's not working?

Here are signs of a change team that is not working:

- Members don't show up for meetings.
- People show up but don't contribute to the discussion.
- Destructive conflict, disrespect, name-calling, and finger-pointing occur.
- There is overly polite meeting behavior, but unproductive meetings (few decisions or agreed actions).
- There are lots of hallway complaints, not brought up in meetings.
- Members run to senior executives with complaints or early results.
- There are missed deliverables or other poor results.

This list is not exhaustive.

Much has been written about group dysfunction. Wilfred Bion from the Tavistock Institute in the United Kingdom identified a key difference between a "work group" (purpose, charter, individual roles and responsibilities, and expected outcomes) and what he called the "basic assumptions group," which were the shared underlying assumptions about the group's culture and character.

Through his research, Bion identified three basic assumption group types:

- The *dependency group* - which owed its existence to someone who would protect the group and its members. This could lead to members communicating behind the scenes with a senior executive or the group leader and not interacting with or doing real work in the group.

- The *fight or flight group* - which believed that the group was under attack. This assumption led to poor inter-group cooperation, and the win-lose atmosphere ultimately destroyed intra-group cohesion, causing members to seek safety outside the group. Leaders sometimes create external "enemies" in an attempt to engender group cohesion, learning too late that only half the group will *fight*; others are in *flight*.

- The *pairing group* - in which two group members assumed superiority of position or ideas. Bion noted that if the group accepted the pair bond then all work went through them. Or if the group did not accept the pair the two group members sat at the sidelines making cynical commentary or otherwise disrupting the work of the group.

These dysfunctions were not mutually exclusive; some groups have more than one.

Bion's solution was to not confront the dysfunctional assumption, but rather to reestablish the primacy of the work group, i.e., get back to real work and revisit purpose, charter, roles and responsibilities.

One of the more widely distributed books in this area is *The Five Dysfunctions of a Team* by Patrick Lencioni, a former Bain consultant. He has written more than ten business books.

Academics criticize *The Five Dysfunctions of a Team* because it is written as a fable and is not research based. The book has been on several best seller lists including the *New York Times*, *Business Week* and the *Wall Street Journal* and has sold more than a million copies.

Lencioni posits five team dysfunctions and possible suggestions for countering them:

- **A lack of trust**, which he describes as an unwillingness to be vulnerable. This creates a difficult environment in which to ask for help, admit weaknesses, or leverage the strengths and complementary skills of the team.

- ○ Begin team formation by having each member share one strength and one weakness.

- **A fear of conflict,** which creates "make nice" norms and an unwillingness to confront tough issues. The false agreement can create destructive two-faced behavior that undermines work toward results.

  - ○ During formation set norms for confrontation.
  - ○ Set a process to argue for and against all ideas.

- **A lack of commitment**, which shows up as absenteeism at meetings, revisiting decisions multiple times and a resulting lack of clarity and results.

  - ○ Be sure that everyone is heard on every decision.
  - ○ Acknowledge disagreement but ask for commitment once heard.

- **A lack of accountability,** which means team members hold each other accountable (not leader-driven accountability). This leads to missed deadlines, poor performance, and resentment from those who do meet commitments.

  - ○ Establish an accountability process agreed at formation.
  - ○ Establish norms for questioning failures, and early warnings of failure to request help.

- **Inattention to results,** which Lencioni describes as the team result, or as Katzenbach and Smith call it the "collective work product." What often happens in dysfunctional teams is that individuals achieve their goals, but the team fails.

  - ○ Lencioni suggests team rewards so that no individual can achieve success unless the team succeeds. This would work in the Katzenbach-Smith real team, but would be less effective in a single leader work group.
  - ○ Emphasize team goals, whether through rewards or rec-

217

ognition, and frequently discuss both the team end goal, milestones and the working approach.

One criticism of Lencioni's model is that he relies upon external processes like strength and weakness exchanges and written norms, rather than the structure of the work itself.

Also many of his suggestions fall under Tuckman's Forming stage of development. While this is critically important, these issues are present in each stage of development. For example, conflict management is the work of the Tuckman Storming stage, but can arise at any time people feel their input is ignored.

For both Bion and Lencioni, the response to group dysfunction is to return to the business of the work group. The response to Wilfred Bion's basic assumption group dysfunctions is to identify them and confront them, but to return to the business of the work group. Similarly, the response to Lencioni's five dysfunctions should be to get back to the work.

Lencioni's organizational development processes (sharing strengths and weaknesses, rotating group facilitation responsibility, public expressions of commitment) are helpful. I have used many of them. But as Katzenbach and Smith said, "real teams are built by doing real work."

CHANGE MANAGEMENT STRUCTURE

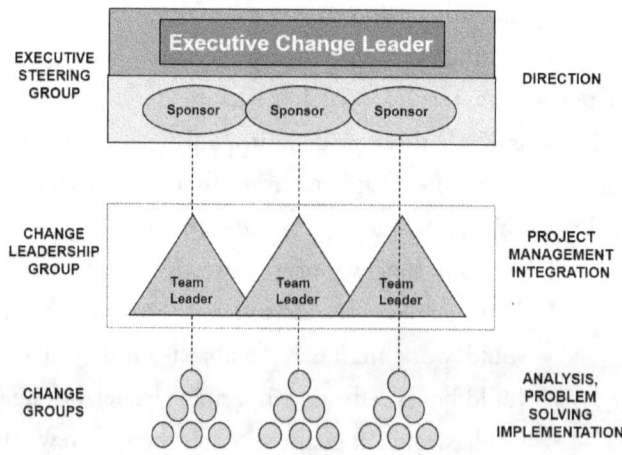

Integration is the challenge of using groups in change

Groups do the actual work of change. They improve processes, innovate new products and services, and streamline procedures.

The challenge is how to integrate the actions of so many different groups. CEOs and other C-suite executives often assume that everyone is on the same page.

In my experience that kind of alignment, even among top leadership groups, is rare and where it exists it is the product of conscious effort and much discussion.

As a consultant on large scale change efforts, I often used an integrating structure to keep the project and its change teams on track.

An example of such a structure is shown at right.

This picture evolved from my work at British Airways and my work in large re-engineering projects at Gemini Consulting. There were weekly meetings of each team, vertical groups of leaders and horizontal team leaders.

At each meeting, each participant gave a brief presentation called the "two-minute drill," outlining:

- Team's achievements for the week
- Current challenges
- Help (resources) needed

These drills were documented, aggregated and communicated literally up, down and sideways. It was cumbersome at first, but alignment and integration were good and any problems in the schedule were quickly visible.

One criticism of Gemini's work was that we took over the client's organization and monopolized the company resources. In some cases, this criticism was justified; often consulting leads set up single leader groups with themselves as the leader. As a result, the client group members felt used and abused and when the project finished the remaining client organization structure felt disempowered. Adding to the void left behind was that many Gemini re-engineering projects achieved cost-savings by a RIF (reduction in force), thus leaving a reduced disempowered group to run new processes.

There were projects, however, that avoided this crisis by effectively building real teams. Stream leads saw themselves as teachers of the methodology and gradually worked themselves out of a job, leaving an intact functioning team when they left. Coincidentally these projects tended to emphasize redeploying people from streamlined processes to do other things. Real teams and redeployment are requirements for effective re-engineering.

The structure you use to manage the change, to align multiple teams' goals and actions, to integrate, and to communicate priorities must ultimately shift into the functioning organization.

It seems Bruce Tuckman realized this, too. In later research, he added a fifth stage of team development: Forming – Storming – Norming – Performing – **Adjourning.** Admittedly, this isn't a perfect rhyme, but it does communicate that change teams do need to plan for transition to steady-state, day-to-day operations.

CHAPTER 32

LESSONS IN TEAM LEADERSHIP FROM MT. RAINIER

D ecade-marking birthdays seem to have a certain effect on me. When I turned forty, I was determined not to repeat the life-altering experience of my thirtieth birthday, after which I chucked my career, sold everything I owned, and moved my family to London for a two-year excursion into poverty while I went to business school. At the forty-year mark, I reasoned I would plan extra-career activities to stimulate my sense of adventure and convince myself I wasn't yet dead. So during my fortieth year I ran the first of two marathons, went up in a hot air balloon, avidly resumed downhill skiing (after a twenty-year hiatus) and made a summit attempt on Mt. Rainier.

Lest you think this flurry of athletic activity indicates some sort of super-jock frame, I should add that I was the typical "weekend warrior" of sport, struggling to keep my weight down and my knees intact simultaneously (a feat that gets harder with every year).

I learned about Rainier from a man with whom I occasionally ran and hiked when I was thirty. Pete turned forty around that same time and brought back pictures of his mid-life encounter with Rainier. Pete's stories and photographs convinced me that someday I'd contact Rainier Mountaineering.

Rainier Mountaineering is a company of "born-to-the-mountain" guys (also women, I was told) who cater to us adventure seekers by offering a one-day mountaineering school and two-day group summit attempt.

The folks at Rainier Mountaineering were very helpful. When I registered by phone they told me what clothes to bring and how to get in shape for the climb (bicycling over running). One thing everyone repeatedly told me, from telephone reservationists to the guides at the school: "This is <u>not</u> an easy hike."

The mountain

Mount Rainier, a 14,410-foot dormant volcano just south of Seattle, is the fifth highest and most extensively glaciated mountain in the continental United States. The Rainier Mountaineering brochure said the mountain "... is demanding and at times relentless; the combination of altitude and cold challenges the climber...." What the brochure curiously omits is the astounding beauty of the mountain.

My first visual encounter was from Sea-Tac Airport. There it was, an enormous snow-cone seemingly suspended in mid-air above a cloud bank. The next day was much clearer. From downtown Seattle the snow-topped peak glistened in the distance and projected extraordinary vistas for the entire three-hour drive. Upon seeing Rainier it is easy to understand the Native American name *Tacoma*, "the mountain that was God."

Entering Rainier National Park, I drove through an evergreen tunnel formed by the six-feet thick, sixty-feet tall firs on either side of the road. As I arrived, first the sunset and then the moon painted the surprise views of the peak in a progressive rainbow, from burning orange to chilling blue light. Finally I arrived at Paradise Lodge, an enormous structure of Alaskan Cedar built in 1917. Though it was dark, I was aware that I was at 6,000 feet, above the tree line, and resolved to get up to see the first reflected sunlight strike the surrounding peaks with the eerie golden light the Swiss call "alpenglow." There is a story in the camaraderie of Paradise Lodge, a camaraderie bathed in wine and firelight, and savored by mountain-hearts following a dream. But this story is about the team leadership found on the mountain itself.

The school

Learning to be a mountaineer in a day was a daunting task.

The guides of Rainier Mountaineering used the school not only to teach climbing and survival techniques we would need on the mountain, but also to weed out those who were not fit. (This "testing" made some nervous, and others of us unreasonably "gung ho.")

At 7:00 a.m. the group convened on a slope near the lodge. The guides had us each share our reasons for making this assault and the conditioning that had brought us there.

Soon we were outfitted with boots, crampons, ice axes, and steadying ski poles, and we walked up to the edge of a small snowfield. It was 70° Fahrenheit; the sky was September blue; the climb was 1,500 feet or so, half of it on paved trail.

We were taught the rest step (for use above 10,000 feet), one step, breathe in and out, next step, breathe in and out. At this altitude it seemed unnecessarily cautious. We later would find the rest step a very useful means of conserving energy at altitude.

We learned to walk with crampons not just on ice (which is easy) but on rock (which isn't easy).

We were taught to walk roped together, holding the ropes in front and behind, leaving slack but still "feeling" the other members of our rope-team.

Most of the day was spent practicing the skill of self-arrest with an ice axe. From a variety of positions each of us had to fall on the glacier. We were instructed to yell "Falling" to alert others of our predicament. We were then left to slide down the glacier until our instructor shouted, "Stop!" (hopefully before we dropped over a 200-foot precipice). We then self-arrested: rapidly turn over, dig the ice axe into the ice and dig into the "anchor position" with our crampons. This technique could save your life and the life of anyone who happened to be roped to you. We were encouraged to take it seriously.

We practiced self-arrest for about five hours, with rare breaks for water and whatever snacks we brought. We practiced self-arrest backwards, forwards, sideways, blindfolded, alone, in pairs, and roped together in five-man teams. (A few of us even thought it was fun.) By final exam time we had practiced this technique with every person in the group from every possible position.

We weren't told that there was a final exam (though Pete told me and now I've told you). The exam was a surprise. While on an endurance hike across the glacial snowfield an instructor simply pushed you over toward the edge. Most everyone in our group passed; a couple of people decided to wash out voluntarily and Bert, a seventy-year-old Australian man who had passed every physical test, was asked to withdraw because his deafness in his right ear slowed his reaction time. (At forty, I felt badly for Bert. I'd have even trusted him to be on my rope team. Now at seventy-plus and wearing hearing aids, I feel his disappointment even more, but Rainier Mountaineering takes no chances, and I respected that.)

The climb: day one

The next day started early. We were to climb to Camp Muir at 10,000 feet.

It was a warm day, 75°; most of us were in shorts. We climbed individually (no ropes yet). We used crampons, and the guides varied the pace, continually checking the stamina of each member of the group. We climbed through the occasional snowfield but mostly climbed on loose shale and over boulders. Our group was now twenty-one, sixteen of us one-day wonder mountaineers and five Rainier Mountaineering guides. The head of this assault was George; the other guides called him Georgo. He was about six feet tall, blond, full of toothy smiles and an easy confidence that would be read as arrogance in a flatland bar. Up there, it was reassuring.

Each of us climbed in the lead position for a while and brought up the rear for a while (more testing, we supposed). We all got used to hearing Georgo's voice from the front: "Coming up to a stream," "We'll rest at the flat space above that outcropping of rock," "Some tricky crevasses in this snowfield, step in the tracks of the person in front of you." Each of us learned to pass on Georgo's instructions to those behind us, even though that day his voice was clearly audible to the back of the line.

The day was beautiful, the air clear, clean, and fresh. A few high cirrus clouds began to lazily drift in. Though "this is not an easy hike" was true so far, it wasn't that difficult either. We arrived at Camp Muir at 4 p.m. We took in the exhilaration of the view of other lesser mountains and other volcanoes like Mt. St. Helens and Mt. Baker.

We cooked our dehydrated food and went to bed, under protest, by 7 p.m. At 12:30 a.m. the guides would wake us so that we could climb to the summit and all the way back down in a day.

The climb: day two

We awoke at 12:30 a.m. to a raging storm of snow and ice. I stumbled to the door of the shelter, looked out at the curtain of stinging whiteness and said to myself, "We ain't going anywhere," and began to get back into my sleeping bag. Just then the door opened wide with a bang. "Listen up! You will need long underwear, wool and waterproof pants, parkas, gloves and masks. Get your headlamps, crampons, and rope harnesses on and be down on the glacier in fifteen minutes!"

At that point, I was thinking that my previous venture of selling everything I owned and moving to England sounded like a cakewalk compared to this, but I found myself following instructions just like everyone else in this hut. Getting down on the glacier was no easy task. The path down was a steep (40°) thirty-five-foot embankment of glacial boulders, most about four feet in diameter and covered with ice and snow from the continuing storm. Miraculously, no one fell.

We milled around on a flat space at the base of a vast white slope. Mostly what I could see were bobbing head-height lights. They looked like a convention of Tinkerbells. The noise of the storm made conversations difficult, but most of us were stunned speechless by the hour and the weather anyway.

Somehow, each guide put together his rope team. Our guide, Paul, roped me into the rear position,"Anchor" it's called, a dubious honor Paul bestowed on me for my enthusiastic practice of self-arrest. "Born to the mountain" I heard him say. Somehow, at that moment, the appellation was neither complimentary nor particularly reassuring.

Suddenly, Paul was in front of us, yelling at what most surely was the top of his voice with every ounce of energy his five-foot-eight frame could muster. "O.K. YOU GUYS, THIS IS IT! GET PSYCHED! GET READY! YOU ARE GOING TO BE CLIMBING IN SOME OF THE MOST DIFFICULT CONDITIONS KNOWN TO MAN. PAY ATTENTION TO WHAT YOU ARE DOING. IF YOU LOSE YOUR FOCUS, YOU COULD DIE! BUT YOU CAN DO THIS. WHATEVER YOU DO TO GET YOURSELF PSYCHED UP - DO IT NOW! ARE YOU READY?!"

Though I was questioning my sanity as I listened, when I opened my mouth, I was screaming, "LET'S GO!"

And so we went.

We walked at an upward diagonal across the snowfield of the first glacier. The snowstorm had blotted out my depth perception and hearing. All I could see was a bobbing string of Christmas tree lights moving ahead of me. I saw no people, not even the person in front of me, just the floating headlamps. But I could "feel" the person ahead of me, hand fixed on the rope. I could feel Bob, the anesthesiologist from Chicago, with whom I had raced down the glacier on my belly till we both heard the call to stop and self-arrest. The feel of Bob on the rope was important, as was his voice echoing back what I knew were Georgo's descriptions of the terrain ahead.

We reached a steep embankment, and Bob echoed back Georgo's instructions: "Climb up the boulders to the ridge. Watch the ice." When I reached the ridge, the Christmas tree lights swayed wildly side to side. "Wind. Get down on your knees," the voice came back. We then climbed down onto the Ingraham Glacier. This was not a snowfield. This was ice.

I turned my headlamp up to my left. What I saw was a sheer wall of ice. I turned my headlamp down to my right, and it disappeared into blackness. We walked on a "path," a track literally cut into the ice with an ice axe, a track only wide enough for me to stand with both feet together, if my ankles were touching.

"Rest step," the voice came back.

Now I understood the importance of the rest step. Despite being in close to the best condition of my adult life, it was darned hard to breathe up there and the climb was steep. We moved slowly, carefully, without mishap, but with a focused stillness that contrasted sharply to the screaming storm.

I followed the floating headlamps, Georgo's relayed messages and the feel of Bob at the other end of the rope to 12,600 feet, where, after a brief pow-wow, our guides turned us around. The mountain that makes its own weather would not relent. We would have to leave the summit for another day.

Paul pulled me aside after the announcement to check that my disappointment was manageable. I was disappointed, of course, but I told him, "I pay you guys to think about my safety. I do what you tell me to do. No problem, really." Paul went on to explain quietly to me that the trip back down to Muir would require the same concentration. I noticed that he took each of the others aside as well.

It was 2:30 a.m. and still snowing. We turned around and inched back down, over three glaciers and two ridges. I don't know what time it was when we got back to Camp Muir. I was beyond tired and slept soundly until awakened at 9:00 a.m. for the climb down.

The climb down from Muir was in 70° sunshine. (Who would have believed it possible a few short hours before?) The climb would have been easy but for the fatigue. The guides kept us in single file with plenty of needed rest stops.

At 5:00 p.m., when we reached Paradise Lodge, I wished I had booked in instead of planning a return to Seattle that night. I don't remember the drive except for one postcard-like picture that I pulled hastily off the road to take. The photo now hangs on my bedroom wall, a field framed with purple spike flowers with a young doe grazing in the middle, oblivious to me, the very blue sky above, and the sunset-bathed presence behind it of the "mountain that was God."

The lessons

I thought very little about leadership while on Rainier. But I had a long flight home and client work to develop the leadership of senior executives immediately upon my return, so I reflected on my experience during that flight. I told this story to these leaders of a large international corporation that had fallen on hard times. These men and women had their own mountain to climb. I told them that I hoped what I had learned on Rainier would be helpful as they joined together in teams to plan the company's renewal.

Here is what I learned:

Team leadership is everyone's responsibility. Each member of my rope team was responsible for the life and success of each one of us and all of us. We learned to climb in all positions so that any one of us could lead if required. So it is in business. Leaders, followers, all members of the team, are responsible equally for the success of individual teammates, the team, and the entire organization.

Fitness and conditioning are critical. Just as the Rainier Mountaineering guides weeded out those unfit for the summit attempt, so leaders in organizations must select the most fit and deselect or develop the unfit. Even so, each of us took responsibility for our own readiness, as team members must in business.

The team leader excites the other team members. Georgo's bravado and easy confidence were infectious. Paul's "GET PSYCHED!" speech worked on Rainier. Business team leaders need more variety and subtlety of exhortation but the concept is the same. "Follow me!"

The team leader shows personal interest in his teammates. Paul's interest in my reactions made me much more receptive to his "we're not out of the woods yet" instruction. Business team leaders must also attend to the emotions of teammates. Emotions affect performance.

"Eyes continually ahead, voice back." The leader of the team must carry the vision of the future and communicate it to all just like Georgo's echoed voice.

Create trust. Being on a forbidding mountain in the dark, blinded by blowing snow and ice, would have been intolerable but for TRUST.

- I trusted myself first - I had learned the skills I needed to know.
- I trusted that the members of my rope team had learned what they needed as well.
- I trusted Rainier Mountaineering, its guides and instructors.

So in business, team leaders must demonstrate that they know what they need to know. The leader must create opportunity for each team member to learn and demonstrate knowledge, skill, and judgment.

"Feel the ropes." Holding the rope before and behind helped us feel connected and supported. Often a business team's connection and supports are less visible. The leader creates opportunities to "feel the ropes." These may be informal get-togethers, celebrations, and recognition of the team by those outside. The team members may have a nickname or wear pins that identify past successes. Or the leader may just take every opportunity to reinforce the group's mutually agreed upon goals. Successful team members are connected and supported, and leaders of successful teams help them "feel the ropes."

Finally, what I learned is:

Lessons of leadership are everywhere, especially within us.

COMMUNICATIONS: INSPIRING ACTION

Most change leaders are good public speakers or learn to be. I have had the opportunity to see many natural public speakers and many others who substantially improve.

Jack Welch was the CEO of General Electric from 1981 to 2001. In retirement, Welch went on the lecture circuit earning over $100,000 per speech. There is a lot of valid criticism of Welch as a CEO, but he learned to speak succinctly and powerfully. As CEO he insisted that division leaders have a one-pager – a single slide from which they described their business performance and strategy.

I did CI training work for GE Capital during the period when GE was emphasizing Six Sigma. They sent me to the Crotonville Leadership Center to observe some training. Seated in the back row of a steep auditorium, I observed a division leader taking suggestions from a group of managers and supervisors.

"WRITE IT DOWN!"

Jack Welch stepped from behind the down spots at the top of the auditorium near my seat. He wasn't shouting but I had no idea he was there. I jumped so much I almost fell off my seat.

He went on to explain what he meant to the leader and the group.

"Bob, I can see that you want to discuss what Paul said, but this isn't the time in the process to do that. By writing Paul's comment down on the flipchart you communicate that you heard him and have recorded his suggestion to discuss and evaluate later."

He then described overall improvement goals of Six Sigma, thanked the group, and expressed confidence in their work.

After he sat down, he turned to me and said quietly, "Sorry I scared the bejeezus out of you. Hi, I'm Jack Welch."

Welch had spoken for a little over three minutes, but by explaining the process and giving his vision for the improvement effort, he left people more informed and enthusiastic.

I was still a little shaken, but introduced myself and why I was there. Later at a cocktail party for the trainees, he remembered my name and introduced me to a small group with the humorous story of our recent encounter.

"Never saw someone jump so high."

Most people in business define communication as a transaction, the transfer of information, when in reality communication is a contract. "I want you to understand this information because I want you to take action."

I often used an advertising campaign as a model to explain how to think about communications during change:

- Determine target audiences and what you want each to do.
- Determine which media will actually reach them (at least three forms of media).
- Craft appropriate messages for each medium and include a call to action.
- Determine frequency of the message in order for someone to remember and be convinced to act (research shows seven to twenty-two repetitions are required).
- Execute communications.

- Monitor reception. This includes website, email, and telephone hotlines (customer service lines or human resource lines for staff). Measure response rates as well as feedback from formal and informal two-way discussions.
- Adjust and continue.

Some clients took this on board. Others sent a mass-distributed memo or email and that was it.

Then I began to coach leaders directly.

- Keep it simple.
- Use personal language, e.g., "partnership" vs. "meshing the gears."
- Balance hard methods (written) with systemic soft (conversations). Combine high tech (like social media) with high touch like town halls and management by walking around.
- Communicate the why of the change as well as the how and when.
- Communicate X 10. As described earlier, change anxiety distorts reception. One way to monitor this: If you are asking yourself whether you are communicating enough, you probably aren't.

A successful change effort isn't all about communications, but some of the most dramatic failures start there:

- Secrecy invites rumor.
- Never say "don't worry" or "nothing will change" or "no one will lose their job" or "if you like your [manager, workstation, system] you'll be able to keep him/her/it."
- When things go wrong, own up quickly. Crafting the perfect communication is less important than maintaining trust.

CHAPTER 33.

BOILING IT DOWN: THE LEADERSHIP ART OF TALKING SIMPLY

"Conceptual reductionist intercourse facilitates adherent adhesion in ongoing dynamism."

Or in other words: In times of change, a leader makes it easier for followers to follow by speaking simply - boiling it down.

Many who write about change say communication is critical. Leading change in organizations is complex. An organization may be changing strategic direction, technology, systems, processes, structure, but the soft people stuff – climate, culture, emotion, behavior - makes it tougher still.

People in the midst of change are easily overwhelmed. To help them, a leader needs to have the skill of boiling the words down to the simplest possible level. For example, an energy technology company had a series of high-profile accidents, some involving fatalities and environmental damage. The company's future was in doubt and it embarked on a complex effort to change systems and technology and communicate a need for vigilance and new behavior. The change program was moving slowly until a middle manager boiled it down. "What we must do," he said, "is to reduce risk and increase value, by operating more <u>systematically</u>." That became shortened further to: **"Risk Down, Value Up - Systematically."**

Those five words captured the imagination of the organization by boiling the change down to a watch phrase, against which all action could be measured. A slogan didn't make the change happen instantaneously, of course, but it added clarity and the change moved more quickly.

Simplicity is not a new concept. Occam's razor, the idea that among competing hypotheses the one with the fewest assumptions (the simplest) is probably correct, has its roots in the thirteenth century. Leonardo Da Vinci was known to say, "Simplicity is the ultimate sophistication." Mies Van Der Rohe, the 1930s Bauhaus designer, stated it elegantly. "Less is more."

In the 1970s, the phrase "K.I.S.S." or "Keep It Simple Stupid" took hold in the popular media. Apparently, this phrase had its origins with a Lockheed aeronautical engineer, Kelly Johnson, who used it to say that military aircraft should be designed with maintenance in mind. Keep it simple because breakdowns usually happen when only the most basic tools are available in the field.

There is a skill to boiling things down. Over the years I have seen some good examples of things said by leaders during change. Often it involved seeing complexity in terms of two or three categories.

Those categories can be about time horizons or context:
- "Keep the doors open today and build the future."
- "Management is about the steady state; leadership is about change. Each of us needs both skills."

The categories can be about different parts of the enterprise:
- "We need to help our suppliers improve so we can build better quality products that delight our customers."
- "Customer Intimacy, Product Leadership, Operational Excellence" (Michael Treacey and Fred Wiersema categories in *The Discipline of Market Leaders*)

Sometimes the categories explain two or more sides of a complex issue:

- Change is about:
    - Insight – understanding the need for change, the vision
    - Action – doing things differently
    - Results – achieving what we intend
    - Learning how to do this again
- Innovate – Integrate – Improve – Iterate
- We improve competence and increase confidence to use the skills.
- What things should we **stop** doing? What things should we do **differently?** And what things should we **start** doing?
- Either/or is often a false choice. How can we think in terms of both/and?

Of course, one can get carried away with simplification:

"There are two kinds of people in the world: Those who divide the world into two kinds of people and those who don't."

Boiling things down incessantly can lead to speaking in slogans. Slogans only work as an exhortation to those who are already on board, i.e., those who have discussed the issues and made the decision for which the slogan is shorthand.

"Boiling it down" isn't a substitute for truly engaging with followers, but striving for simplicity in communications helps a leader to be understood, to connect and move forward with employees on shared goals.

CHAPTER 34

BE CURIOUS: THE LEADERSHIP ART OF GOOD QUESTIONS

"What's your latest obsession?"

The late Dr. Denis Pym, Organizational Behavior Professor at the London Business School, told us eager MBA candidates what a great question this was for engaging conversations.

"I've come to hate cocktail parties," said the impish Dr. Pym. "It's all donors and academics standing around drinking plonk white wine, eating Jarlsberg, and talking about banalities. This question gets you away from the dreadful 'What do you do?' If people quibble about the word 'obsession,' I move on, because talking with dispassionate people is painfully boring. But this question sparks some really interesting conversations. You get to *know* people."

Denis was a bit eccentric, to say the least. He expounded on "the transformation of labour in the post-industrial economy," lived on a Kent farm and told us how he asked corporations to pay him for his consulting in sheep. But he was onto something. Get people to talk about what they are passionate about, and you'll be amazed at how you'll connect with them.

For five years I conducted a leadership workshop for mid-level leaders at an international oil company. The workshop was called training, but its real purpose was to engage managers in solving problems facing the corporation. This group of leaders touched many people and their job was to make daily work happen. As a result, they sometimes felt change _happened to_ them, but for change to happen they had to lead it.

The key accountability of a leader is to attract followers. One idea I shared with these leaders was that leadership is about asking good questions. People choose to follow because you make them feel part of something. People are more likely to feel part of something if they are talking, not you. How do you get people to talk? Ask them a question.

I'm not suggesting the standard managerial question: "Have you considered the impact on this quarter's contribution margin?" In pursuit of accountability some managers ask progressively more detailed questions to test the thoroughness of the work. Sometimes they play Gotcha with subordinates to avoid slipshod thinking. Some managers get far too much enjoyment from this kind of question.

Nor am I talking about the "I'm so smart" question: "Clearly you have built upon the work of Dr. Deming in this customer feedback system, but have you considered the work of Argyris and Schon on double loop learning to avoid coloring feedback by the means used to collect it?"

Nor am I talking about the "I'm the executive and you're not" question: "Do you mean to tell me. . . ?"

No, I'm talking about questions that truly engage, that open a real dialogue from which you learn something. These are questions born of genuine curiosity about what the other person has to say.

First, some questioning basics:

- Open-ended questions begin with What, How, When, Where, and Tell me about. They let the answerer talk.
- Closed-ended questions begin with Do, Did, Will, Have, Is, and

Should. These questions can be answered yes or no or with short responses. They are used to clarify and summarize. When over-used, the dialogue feels like an interrogation.

I think everyone knows this distinction conceptually, but sometimes I find myself asking closed-ended questions unintentionally. The result is somewhat like the *Saturday Night Live* sketch with the late Chris Farley interviewing Paul McCartney:

"Do you remember when you were in the Beatles?"

"Yes, I do."

(long uncomfortable pause)

"That was awesome!"

Clearly, if we want people to talk, we need to ask an open-ended question. "Tell me about your job. What are the critical elements?" "What's working well today?"

In their 1985 book *A Passion for Excellence,* Tom Peters and Nancy Austin introduced the phrase MBWA (Management by Walking Around). Even they called it a "blinding flash of the obvious." The premise was that leaders should get out of their offices and talk to customers, suppliers and their people. Good managers have always done this. Everyone knows it's a good idea, but in these days of the email-instant-messaging-social-media-tsunami it is tougher to do.

When you are walking around, what questions you ask depends on why you are asking.

Some types of leadership questions include:

- **"Getting to know you" questions**: They demonstrate that you are interested in others as people. "Where do you come from?" "How long have you worked here?" "Tell me a little about yourself." "What do you do outside of work?"
- **Questions about the work**: "What's going on today?" "What's working?" "What do you wish worked better?"
- **Questions to find success stories**: "What are you most proud of?" "What around here do you want to make sure we <u>don't</u> change?"

- **Questions to surface work problems or risks:** "What's getting in the way of your work?" "When do you say 'I can't believe we do it this way'?" "What keeps you awake at night?" "How do you ensure we make safe decisions?" "How do you know?"

When making a change, you might use questions to test understanding of why we are changing, or check on progress, or surface problems or things that are getting in the way.

Ask easy questions first, slightly harder questions next, and save the hardest for last. The hardest kind of question, and the one with the biggest payoff, is the open-ended question that calls upon the answerer to:

- **Speculate** about something that is unknown or uncertain. "What level of quality errors do you think would cause a customer to leave?" "What kinds of features would delight a customer to such a degree that she would call all her friends to recommend us?"

- **Compare** two or more unlike things. "How do the problems we are having with delivery compare to something that frustrates you on vacation?" "What is the customer value of our medical device product compared with XYZ pharmaceutical?"

- **Evaluate the impact** of an action or decision over multiple time horizons or groups of people. "What is the difference between the way our suppliers look at this product versus the customer, our people and the regulators?" "If we looked at this change over ten years, or fifty years, would that make any difference in how we look at it now?"

Use high payoff questions sparingly because they take time and thought both to ask and to answer. But use them occasionally. They can take the discussion to a very different level. You will know they are working by the sound of teeth-sucking inhale ("Ooeesh") or nasal-vocal exhaling ("Hmmmnn") followed by "That's a gooooood question. . . ."

There is another requirement in the leadership art of good questions. You have to want to know the answer. What are you genuinely curious about? Ask those questions.

You can't fake curiosity. Memorizing a list of questions that you don't care about will show you to be a caricature of a superficial boss, and not someone who genuinely connects with and attracts followers.

And, of course, you have to listen to the answer and remember it. We've all been in the active listening courses that teach us how to nod, make eye contact, vocally tune in ("Uh-huh") and summarize ("So if I hear what you're saying. . .") But if you're not truly interested and just focused on the behaviors, you come off as phony. So the leadership art of good questions starts with asking *ourselves* some questions:

- "What am I curious about?" "What do I want to know, learn, verify, or think about?"
- "Why would anyone follow me? What's in it for them?"
- "What would surprise me about myself as a leader? About this work, or this change? About those with whom I need to connect to make this happen?"

D.J. De Pree was the founder of Herman Miller, the furniture makers of the Eames chair and the awesome Aeron desk chair. His son, the late Max De Pree, shared one of his father's stories in his book *Leadership is an Art.*

In 1927, the Herman Miller millwright, an excellent mechanic and a long-term employee, died unexpectedly. Mr. De Pree visited the widow and was surprised to learn that the man was a sculptor and a poet. The pastor read some of the millwright's poetry at the funeral, and it was beautiful, and unexpectedly moving.

In his book, Max De Pree asks the questions, "Was this man a millwright who happened to write poetry, or a poet who happened to work as a millwright in a furniture factory? How would I know the answer?"

I urge you to think about this question: *If the millwright was one of my followers, how would I have really known him? What questions would I ask?*

CHAPTER 35

"WHAT?!" LEADERSHIP CHANGE COMMUNICATIONS

I am shocked by what passes for communication inside companies.

Savvy marketing executives mount a sophisticated campaign to introduce a new product to customers. It includes targeted messages with twenty impressions across multiple media, exquisitely timed for maximum cumulative impact. Then they send a two-line email to the customer service centers who will take the orders.

Or a CEO has meeting after meeting with the CEO of an acquired company. They have a detailed plan to roll out the synergies of the merger to the analysts over three calls with dizzying PowerPoint presentations. Then they stand up at an employee Town Hall and say, "Don't worry. Nothing will change."

Somehow executives are more diligent communicating with shareholders, analysts or the market as Investor Relations; with customers as Advertising, and with the community as Public Relations. But they define employee communications as the quarterly newsletter, published by HR, that nobody reads.

Employee communications staff may have the same professional qualifications as the advertising department, but leaders don't think to call them. They just dash off a short memo and blast it out to "All Employees" in an email.

When I studied Organizational Development at Columbia, Dr. Warner Burke said to us aspiring OD consultants:

> I will tell you what to say in your first meeting with any new client. You don't need to do any research, just say, "You have a communication problem in this organization." You will always be right. It is in the nature of organizations to have poor communications. Remember that party game that is called Rumors or Whispers? You know, one person whispers a simple sentence to another at the party and the message is whispered from person to person and at the end of the line everyone laughs at how the message has changed. Organizations are that game on steroids, whispers distorted by thousands of people.

Of course we all thought about our own poorly communicating organizations and laughed, but it was a serious point. In a change, this failure to communicate can make the difference between actually innovating, improving, or integrating an acquisition - or not.

What to do to improve communication

Change your mindset. We define communication to outside constituencies (customers, shareholders) as building commitment. We often have a call to action in our communication to track the receipt and the outcome we hope to accomplish. On the other hand, most of us define communication to coworkers as the transfer of information. In radio terms this is just the broadcast signal transmission. If we measure at all, we track transmission: send email, check; write piece for the newsletter, check. We do not measure the noise the signal must overcome, nor receipt of the message, nor the connection to the decision or action we hope for as a result of the communication.

So the first step in communicating to coworkers during change is to plan what we hope to accomplish with the communication and ask how we would measure that outcome. If we want to build commitment to the change, how would we know that was happening? We might track energy for action among a critical mass of employee opinion leaders, the growth of that critical mass, and an increase in the speed of implementation until we finally have everyone selling the new product or improving with the new process. In short, we get there by treating internal communications just as we would advertising or public relations.

	Message			
	Vision/ Objectives	Project Status	Change Process	Path Forward
Meetings				
Steering Committee	✔	✔	✔	✔
Management One-on-One Meeting	✔	✔	✔	✔
Plant Managers	✔			
Key Communicators	✔	✔	✔	✔
Electronic				
E-Mail				
Voice Mail System (VMS)				
Publications				
Project Newsletter	✔	✔	✔	✔
Special Events				
Letter From Steering Team	✔			✔
Focus Groups	✔	✔		✔
Town Meetings	✔			
Customer Meetings	✔		✔	
Brown Paper Fairs	✔			✔

Create a planned internal communications campaign. Think as if this were an advertising campaign. You would:

- Define and prioritize target audiences

- Define communication needs of each audience
- Determine best media to reach each audience
- Determine optimum frequency of message for each audience
- Plan messages for each audience
- Select media (think multiple impressions and mixed media for each message)
- Execute plan
- Monitor reception
- Adjust and continue

As you think about targeting audiences and defining their needs it quickly becomes apparent that the leadership team needs different information than a customer service rep, just as families have different concerns than suppliers or franchisees have different concerns than unions. You can speak differently to different groups, but you should also discuss what messages must be consistent across groups. Then plan where people get their information. If no one reads anything in the newsletter beyond the first story, put the critical information in the headline, and pick supporting media.

One client during a merger created this matrix to track messages and media.

Frequency: Communicate X 10. During my first large change project, the 1984-1987 British Airways turnaround, I told groups of managers that they should plan to double their normal communications. One day an obviously agitated manager hailed me in the hallway. "Alan, Alan. What you told me about communication is WRONG!"

I stopped, expecting a whine about how he didn't have that kind of time or his people were smarter than that, but he continued.

"That factor is rather more like TEN than two. When people don't know what's going on they simply MAKE IT UP. And what they make up is always worse than the truth."

Research shows that if an audience is distracted, it takes twenty-two repetitions to get through the clutter. I don't know what the right number of "multiple impressions" is; I just know that it is more than anyone expects.

Monitor Reception: Two-way is better. Communication in a change effort should include the opportunity for feedback. This can be simple conversations, a question and answer period at a town hall, or a website that lets employees post questions or rumors they've heard in order to get answers, clarifications or the TRUTH. You should monitor email read receipts, hotline call numbers, and questions posted to adjust communications as needed.

Some guiding principles

- **Strive for transparency.** I understand the need for some secrecy in change. After all, if you know that some people will be displaced or redeployed but you don't know who or how yet, you don't want to stir the pot. I would say only this: People are smarter than you think and a vacuum in the information space is quickly filled by rumors. A leader in a merger I worked on committed to telling people "what we know when we know it." It went a long way to easing minds and keeping people focused.

- **Frame discussions of the change in terms of the impact on key constituencies –customer, employees, shareholders, and the community.** Help your people help others through the change. Keep the language personal, e.g., "supplier partnerships" not "plug and play vendors."

- **Acknowledge the emotional component of change.** People worry. Some worry more than others, of course, but change evokes fears of losing their job, their coworkers, and their comfort level. As a leader, acknowledge that and tell what you are doing to help. "We have counseling available through the Employee Assistance Program," "If you have a question please post it anonymously on the website," etc.

- **Communicate the why of the change and not just the what**

and how. Communicate what success and failure will look like, how you'll measure, what you are sure of and what your assumptions are. If people understand the why they can better help with the how.

- **Communicate X10.**

Change is hard. Changing multiple people is harder still because of the accumulated company values and beliefs (culture) that support the old way of doing things.

A leader has precious few tools to help people change. Communications is a big one. Use it well.

LEARNING

There can be no change without learning.

Think about it. Without some new insight, why would anyone do something differently?

I became a change guy by first being a trainer. In leadership training programs I saw hard-bitten thirty-year managers come to an epiphany of sorts. They'd agree that the world had changed and that the way they managed had an impact on the success of the corporation. One such manager said:

> I have suddenly realized that the success of this huge corporation comes down to me doing something that I may not be entirely comfortable with. But I can do that. And if everyone else does that too we will be a different company, one that I will be proud to be part of again.

Acquiring new knowledge and skill (competency) isn't enough, of course, but it is a start. Companies need to add the organizational and process supports that reinforce newly learned competencies. This builds organizational capability to complete consistent action. But individual learning is where it begins.

In the 1990s, many companies figured this out at the same time. Corporate training took off. My friends who worked in training and development were ecstatic. Finally they were getting noticed.

But many leaders mindlessly delegated change to Training and Development (T&D) departments. Up until that time, T&D supported employee-selected training, a "college catalogue" of available courses. As a result, strategically important leadership or change training just took its place in the catalogue, and C-suite executives paid little attention.

Training also became so popular that it was the go-to solution for every problem. People are coming in late? Train 'em. People are making errors? Train 'em. People are confused about the conflicting priorities, i.e., "we're told to do this, but we're rewarded for doing that." Train 'em some more.

In the 1990s my frustration with this reality became the article "Why Training Doesn't Work" in this section. Later, I became obsessed by the idea that change leaders need to understand all the levers of change – including training.

I also think we all need to understand how we learn.

CHAPTER 36.

HOW TO LEARN

I was a terrible student.

Correction: After the age of about eight, I was a terrible student. I've just read some of my early report cards, going back to Mrs. Green's Nursery School (my mother saved everything). Apparently, I learned to read early, perhaps the product of being the child of a schoolteacher and having two older sisters who enjoyed reading to me almost as much as I enjoyed being read to. Also, apparently, I was "quick and eager to learn - a joy to have in the classroom." When you compare these comments with some from my middle school and high school years, the contrast is stark. "Definitely not working up to his potential."

Somewhere around the third or fourth grade the power differential between parent or teacher and me began to chafe. "Alan has a problem with authority, which if he doesn't learn to manage, will constrain his progress far beyond this class."

I suppose I am still working on this. I still cringe when a friend uses the phrase "Let me help you understand something."

As my career developed, I earned a substantial part of my income as a trainer. It was my job to help others to learn leadership, strategy, innovation, Continuous Improvement methodologies, and organization development. So I spent quite a lot of time puzzling about how to help someone learn.

253

I concluded that it is impossible to teach anybody anything. We can only provide opportunities to learn. Learning, at least for adults, is a <u>choice</u>. We choose to learn because we see value in it; what's in front of us is either interesting or beneficial in some way.

Even rote memorization has its purpose. I can't tell you the number of times that my problem solving in business was helped by memorized times tables or the recognition that 169 is 13^2. Once, when a client said, "Tomorrow," and paused, I continued on with ". . . and tomorrow and tomorrow creeps in this petty pace from day to day till the last syllable of recorded time . . ." Memorizing that speech from Shakespeare's *Macbeth* occasionally created some ice-breaking laughter.

But adults need a <u>reason</u> to learn; we need to see the value. That's why I always introduced training programs or exercises with Purpose, Process, Product – why are you doing this, how will you do it, and what will you have at the end.

So wanting to learn is foundational. Sometimes the connections are obvious, sometimes not. Sometimes we think we don't need to learn; we're already good enough. That's when feedback helps.

I learned to define what I mean by feedback because of an event from a 360-degree feedback event several years ago. I asked the group, "What is feedback?" and the microwave engineer sitting at ten o'clock in the "U" said, "It is the degree of amplitude at which an advanced wave system becomes oscillatory."

A smarter person with greater presence of mind might have recovered more easily than I did that day. So now I just define the word:

"Feedback is information about performance that leads to action to change or to maintain performance." Feedback is a signal that we need to learn something.

A colleague once said to me:

"Alan, if one person tells you you're a horse's rear end, you can call him the same and pretty much forget it. But if <u>three</u> people tell you that, you better start looking for a saddle."

Feedback can come from any number of sources: a one-on-one conversation with a peer, subordinate, coach or manager; a control chart that tells you your process is out of control; low performance on a safety measure such as days away from work; watching a video of your presentation practice; standing on the scale the morning after an ice cream binge; or a loving nudge from your spouse, "The GPS says you're going 80 in a 55 zone. That can't be right, can it?"

The thing about feedback is – you have to want it, actually seek it out. Another colleague often joked, "Whenever anyone asks me if they can give me some feedback, I always say no, 'cause it's always bad news. No one asks permission for the good stuff." It's a joke, but I wonder if it limited the feedback that he got.

These days we rely more and more on technology for feedback – the Fitbit on my wrist, those "Your Speed is" LED displays on village roadways, emails about antivirus software updates or renewals, last call vs. average call time on call center workstation screens. But the key is that you have to want the information and commit to taking action to change or maintain performance.

So first there is the choice to learn, then there is evaluation of the current state of our knowledge or skill on the subject (feedback). Then there is a choice about how much we want to learn or how good we want to get at something.

Some of us have experienced being out with a group of friends that includes a new smartphone owner. An innocuous question arises in the conversation about a celebrity or a TV show or a sports record and instantly said owner is reading from his or her phone the entire Wikipedia page plus several other articles on the subject. Casual inquisitiveness has met graduate-level research – definitely not what was asked for.

In his book *Outliers,* Malcolm Gladwell highlights the research of K. Anders Ericsson, a Swedish psychologist and a professor at Florida State University. Dr. Ericsson's research theorizes that expertise - true world-class performance in sports, the arts, all academic and secular fields - is built by spending 10,000 hours in deliberate and focused practice. It is not enough to practice what one is already good at or enjoys, but to deliberately practice what one is <u>not</u> good at. Long before I knew of this research, I often said that I play <u>at</u> the guitar so that no one ever expected me to be very good. I got my guitar for my thirteenth birthday and have played recreationally on and off for sixty-plus years. My pattern has been to pick up the guitar after not playing for a while, get as good as I was when I was thirteen, and then put it down again. These days I'm trying to get more proficient than I was when I was thirteen and find myself wishing I had invested the hours of deliberate practice that Gladwell describes. Ericsson's research has taught me how to advance – practice that which I am not good at and measure improvement.

So to learn I must want to learn, evaluate what I know or the skill I currently have, study/practice in a deliberate, focused way, and measure my improvement. I should also be prepared to think about <u>how</u> I learn best.

People are different, so it's no surprise that people learn differently. There is no shortage of psychologists and learning theorists to explain these differences, and I won't pretend to know or describe them all, but here are a few that struck a chord with me over the years.

Carl Gustav Jung, the Swiss psychologist, posited that people have two primary mental functions: perceiving (taking in information) and judging (making decisions). Jung's theory was that some people take in information by sensing, step by step in an ordered process using clear sensory inputs, or; they are intuitive and jump around making connections between unrelated facts and unstructured data. Jung also said that people make decisions either by logical ordered processes (thinking) or by comparing options to deeply held emotional values (feeling). I suspect *sensing thinkers* might prefer more structured learning environments than I do; I prefer to immerse myself in many aspects of a subject (with a broad definition of the subject), which is why I had to be careful training some groups – engineers and accountants, for example.

Some people talk about being visual learners, i.e., "I have to see it." I saw others close their eyes to listen when I lectured. (I chose to believe that many of them were <u>not</u> just sleeping or checking their eyelids for holes, but rather taking in information through hearing.) I have a friend who prefers books-on-tape because she can eliminate visual distractions on the page and around the room. Clearly we all take in information differently through our senses. However, I don't agree with proponents of Neuro Linguistic Programming, who say this is the primary way our brains work. Sense preference is a factor to consider, just not the only one.

A quote often attributed to Confucius says, "I hear and I forget, I see and I remember, I do and I understand." This shows that learning may require engaging multiple senses, and some experience as well.

Dr. David Kalb, creator of the Learning Styles Inventory (LSI), theorizes that in order to learn we each pick a comfortable place on two intersecting continua: the *perception continuum,* somewhere between conceptual thinking and pure pragmatic experience; and the *processing continuum,* between watching and reflection and experimentation and testing.

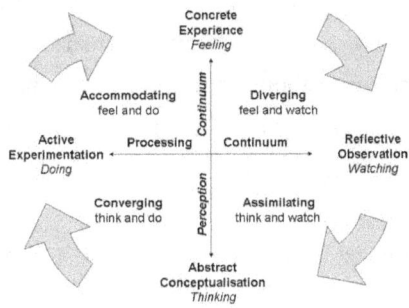

The resulting learning styles model looks like this:
- Diverging learners like to work in group and brainstorm.
- Assimilating learners like books and lectures.
- Converging learners are comfortable in applied disciplines.
- Accommodating learners rely on other people to learn and experiment.

I remember being intrigued by the discussion when I took the LSI. Like a lot of self-report instruments, the discussion and comparisons with others are more educational than the instrument output itself. It is worth thinking about how you learn as well as the why, the what and the how much.

Why am I writing about how to learn? The act of writing solidifies my own learning and since I want to share leadership wisdom, thinking about how it might be received requires some explaining.

Also, my change leadership work always required learning. My clients needed to learn how to innovate, integrate, and improve, and I needed to learn how to best adapt to their needs, issues, and learning styles. Finally, our world changes rapidly – technologically, politically, economically, sociologically, etc. We either learn or get left hopelessly behind.

I'm told that some companies require workers to learn and get certified on their own time in order to be eligible for corporate training. I suppose this is like continuing education credits for accountants, lawyers, teachers and other professionals. I do believe we each need to take responsibility for our own education, but I worry about dictating that from above.

I'm a better learner than I used to be, primarily because I want to learn. I want to learn more about a lot of different things. I want to pass on what I know to my children and grandchildren, my old clients and colleagues and anyone who might read this book. Even in retirement I want to go on learning.

Now if I could only get over this problem with authority!

CHAPTER 37.

LEADERSHIP CHANGE CAPABILITY: TRAINING

Why training?

"The difference between education and training," expounded the lean and craggy British consultant, "is that education is about knowing <u>what to do and why</u> and training is <u>practice</u> actually doing it. If I were to elucidate a bit more, I am quite happy for my daughter to participate in sex education at school, but I believe I would object if she were to get training on the subject."

There are many names for it, education or training, or learning and development (L&D) and my least favorite, "upskilling." While there are nuanced differences in terms, I will use the term training. I present it as a capability that change leaders should master. A capability is the combination of knowledge, skill and supporting processes, both individual and organizational.

I view training as a capability not a lever, despite the fact that it is the second most frequent process that leaders think of when faced with change. (The first is organization design.) Training is also a process that many leaders admit to knowing nothing about and so immediately delegate to HR, L&D, or a consultant, and sometimes ignore completely after that.

As I've said before, **you can't delegate change leadership.** And so I believe leaders should know something about training because it is a powerful process that is often central to change.

Training is used to increase the individual knowledge and skill required to do a job. Unfortunately, training is often overused and misused, like managers who send overloaded people to a time management course, putting them further behind. A quote by instructional design guru Robert Mager crystalized this for me. "If you think someone needs training to do a task, ask yourself, 'If I offered them a million dollars, could they do this?' If they could do it for a million dollars, you don't have a training problem; you have a motivation problem."

Corporations differ widely in how they handle routine training. Some Learning and Development departments have PhD instructional designers and trainers on staff and manage programs that cover every stage of an employee's organizational life. Other corporations buy programs from external suppliers and do a lot less training. Often the only thing these departments have in common is that their budgets are the first to be cut whenever corporate profits fall.

What are the kinds of change training?

For the most part, this chapter is about face-to-face classroom training. Computer-based training is useful for delivering content knowledge and some individual analytical skills, but any knowledge or skill that involves interacting with other people must be practiced with others. People also can learn from the observation and feedback of one-on-one coaching, but training to teach new skills and mobilize people in change is best done in groups of twelve to thirty-six in a classroom setting.

In change there may be new knowledge and skills that are obviously needed, e.g., how to collect data on new metrics, use new analytical software, or learn a new model of selling to address new groups of customers. It could be training in innovation or improvement processes.

But the most frequent type of change training that I saw was leadership training.

Leadership training makes sense. Leaders drive change. They must be clear about the need for and direction of the change (insight and vision). They must engage and attract followers quickly (the guiding coalition and a sense of urgency). They must inspire action and ensure results (change projects and metrics).

Leadership training can also be used to communicate new strategies, priorities and new ways of working as well. It is a vehicle for communicating what is important and building commitment to change.

The design and development of these change-inspired leadership workshops, when they exist, often have one of two significant flaws:

- The **workshop is abdicated** to the training department, which often means there is a disconnect with the strategic urgency of the training. This shows up as leadership training that is a part of the normal routine curriculum, takes a long time to develop and enters a voluntary scheduling apparatus. "We've determined that we can reach 50 percent of the critical population over the next seven years." This doesn't communicate any urgency and probably dooms the change effort.

- The workshop is considered too important for the training department, which means it is **developed by people who know nothing about training.** "It's a series of talking heads over three days, and death by PowerPoint, but we're getting the whole company through in three weeks." This approach may communicate urgency, but is unlikely to teach anybody anything.

Clearly, the best path to developing a leadership workshop is one that draws on training design and development expertise and delivers it in a way that trains a critical mass of leaders quickly to overcome inertia. To avoid total abdication to experts it is useful for leaders to understand a little about training design.

Models of training development

There are two current models of training development that communicate the same message:

It ain't just about what goes on in the classroom.

The first model is the 40-20-40 model, developed by Robert Brinker-hoff of the Rhode Island School of Design. In his 2001 book *High Impact Learning,* he advocates focusing 40 percent of effort on what happens before training – establishing need and readiness; and 40 percent of what happens after participants come back from training – the systems, processes and management that support new knowledge and skills. The other 20 percent of effort and resources should be focused on the design of excellent classroom training.

The second model is the 70-20-10 model, developed through empirical research by Morgan McCall, Michael Lombardo and Robert Eichinger of the Center for Creative Leadership. In this model, leaders learn most by doing; surveys and observation showed that leaders learned 70 percent from a series of challenges that allowed them to fail and try again. They learned 20 percent from tough feedback from colleagues, bosses and mentors. They learned only 10 percent in a classroom. This pattern does make intuitive sense to me, but to apply it in a training plan would require crafting on-the-job learning experiences and monitoring growth. The problem I have with this model is that I heard about 70-20-10 in organizations that treated on-the-job training in haphazard ways and invested nothing in mentoring or feedback. In those organizations, 70-20-10 was favored as a reason to reduce costs by cutting classroom training.

Training design basics

While I have an MBA and additional post grad work in organizational development, I don't have formal training in Instructional Design. I do know PhDs in this field and respect their expertise tremendously. However, after working behind some of the best instructional designers and materials developers in the business, I learned a couple of things.

First there is a (universally accepted) instructional design process known as ADDIE:

The ADDIE process makes sense. First analyze the strategic need and current individual levels of knowledge and competency. Then design specifications, learning objectives and the best flow of learning experiences. Develop written and other audiovisual materials, structured experiences, reflection and planning guides, and job aids according to adult learning principles for different types of learners. Implement (pilot, revise, and rollout) and evaluate whether people found the training valuable, retained the knowledge and practiced the skills. Finally, evaluate whether the training contributed to the business result.

For most instructional designers, the rule of thumb is that design and development take thirty to forty hours for every single hour of classroom delivery. Of course, training can be developed in less time, but the point is that the person in front of the classroom isn't just a glib, walk-on trainer. He or she is supported by well designed and developed materials.

Learning objectives

What I learned from working behind training designers, designing programs myself, developing training materials and delivering training, is that **establishing clear learning objectives is critical.** This goes back to the seminal work of Robert F. Mager, *Making Instruction Work.* You have to ask yourself at the end of each unit and after the completed training program, "What do you want learners to know or do more of, less of, or differently?" (These are learning objectives.) "How will you know they are behaving as expected?" (This sets up evaluation.)

Learning objectives are carefully crafted. Wording is very important. For example, there is a huge difference among learning objectives such as to be able to describe (cognitive awareness tested verbally), to conduct (specific action or skill tested by observation), and to achieve (results based according to a specific metric like return on investment).

The leader's role

My intent isn't to turn leaders into instructional designers but rather for leaders to have intelligent conversations with designers. A leader who knows something about this process can avoid the trap of saying, "I want a five-day custom-designed leadership training program linked to our new strategy to be delivered starting in two weeks."

A leader who knows about training also can avoid abdicating drivers of the change effort to the training department. That leader might actually show up at the training, thus lending credibility to the mobilization of people.

Some companies take the leader's role even one step further. General Electric, for example, experimented with the idea of the leader as teacher. By actually delivering training, the leader sets direction and wins followers. Powerful.

Change isn't easy for people. Learning a new habit is hard. If the leader shows his or her skin in the game it can make a huge difference.

CHAPTER 38

WHY TRAINING DOESN'T WORK

In the 1990s, training became the go-to for all corporate problems. And that was dangerous because it meant spending a lot of money on something that didn't work.

At the time, corporate America spent between $30 and $40 billion a year educating its employees. At least one third of that money, $10 - $15 billion, was wasted, like pushing stacks of $100 bills through a paper shredder.

In 2018, according to *Forbes* magazine, US corporations spent $87 billion on training. In 2023, Statista reported US corporate training expenditure of $101 billion. That's a lot of money in the shredder. Every business leader should be paying attention to that kind of waste.

I based my earlier estimate of training waste on the frequency with which I saw the symptoms of training that doesn't work:

- A corporation enters a downturn and instantly cancels all training.
- The office Neanderthal is sent to interpersonal skills training, and no one notices any difference - except that he is angrier.
- Another co-worker returns from the same seminar and is very nice - for a week.

- A manager berates staff because "nothing is getting done around here" and sends her entire department to a time management course. A month later, the group is further behind schedule.
- Supervisors in a training session repeatedly ask, "Why don't you train *my boss*?"
- The training department is the lowest-paid staff group in the company.
- A senior salesperson argues with a sales trainer: "Look, it's fine for you to be pushing all this teamwork stuff, but I earn my money on commission. I don't get orders, <u>I</u> <u>don't</u> <u>eat.</u>"

The list could go on. In the view of some line managers, training will solve all problems. In the view of others, it never works. Shred, shred, shred. But why might a training program fail?

There are many reasons:

- The training program might be poorly designed.
- The wrong methodologies might be used - too much lecture, for example.
- The instructor might not be competent.
- The facilities might be inadequate.
- The materials might be confusing.

Learning is a complex process. In order for it to occur in a training program, many conditions are necessary. Good design, correct methodology, and excellent instruction, facilities, and materials are all necessary components. However, they are not sufficient to make training work. I believe that when training doesn't work, it most often doesn't work for these two reasons:

- **The need to learn is absent or unclear.** Participants don't understand the reason to learn new knowledge or skills, and so have at best a lukewarm desire to learn, and/or
- **The training is not integrated into the organization.** A British training manager once cynically confided to me, "Our job is purification. We get the toxic fish, purify them, and then put

266

them back into the polluted pond." Without a link to strategy, structure, culture, systems, or management, the training is not reinforced at best, and incongruent at worst.

All too often, line managers don't really understand training and are content to leave it to the experts. Paradoxically, the training professional is often responsible only for the *process* of training (design, development, and delivery) and is therefore hampered from addressing the true causes of training failure and waste.

Clearly, establishing the need to learn and integrating training with the rest of the organization could be either a line or a staff function. Unfortunately, it is frequently lost in the white space in the organization chart. Shred, shred, shred.

Why the need to learn is absent or unclear

Adults choose what they want to learn, and they need information to make that choice.

Children are educated as if they are sponges. Children have no experience base, the theory goes, and so they will simply absorb content if it is repeated enough.

Adults, on the other hand, are problem-centered learners. If an adult perceives that new knowledge or skill will help solve a problem that he or she wants to solve, then he or she will <u>choose</u> to learn.

The keys are **the desire to solve a problem** and the **perception** that new knowledge and skills will help. For example, the office Neanderthal who is sent to interpersonal skills training may not *perceive* a problem or, if he does, may not *want* to solve it. This, then, is first a counseling problem and not a problem solved by training.

There are many ways to help adults perceive their need for new knowledge or skills, but perhaps the best way is to tell them why the skills are necessary.

It may not be solely a training problem.

Training professionals are usually schooled in analyzing performance problems and determining which parts of the problem are caused by a deficiency of knowledge or skill. They are also trained to evaluate individual or group needs compared to competency models and to write objectives for training based upon those needs.

However, what sometimes happens is that someone else decides what the problem is and that the solution is training. The manager who sends her group to time management training may have a work process problem, an organization structure problem, a motivation problem, a staffing problem, or a management problem - or some combination of these problems. In any case, training alone didn't work because a month later, the group was still behind.

Often, managers in corporations with extensive catalogues of generic training fail to thoroughly analyze the many components of a problem. In these environments, participants sometimes attend training on the chicken soup theory of education: "Well, it couldn't hurt." Such training seldom works and is not systemically linked to strategy or results, and is therefore the first thing to be cut when times get tough.

It follows that the least likely training to be cut is that for which the need is abundantly clear. For example, in the early 1990s, Heinz USA completed basic skills and technical training of its existing workforce for its new Pittsburgh plant. To achieve a strategic advantage, the new plant was automated and computer-controlled. This created a clear need for computer skills and the basic math skills to back them up. It would be difficult to imagine Heinz canceling this training because of a recession. Similarly, it would be unlikely for workers who needed these skills for their new jobs to be too busy for training.

Why training is not integrated into the organization

No one is taking the system-wide view.

When I first began learning about management, I discovered that managers were responsible for accountability and development, for making sure that their people achieved results and grew into more challenging jobs that came from business growth. Now, business growth is still elusive, accountability originates in computerized cost reports, and development is the responsibility of those with PhDs in industrial psychology or instructional design. Training has become the purview of staff specialists and outside consultants. Other specialists look at organization development, compensation and the reward system, and strategic planning etc. Sometimes, no one looks at the organization system as a whole.

It is therefore possible to have sales training preaching the value of team selling while accounting moves salespeople to individual commissions based on order volume. Likewise, supervisors can return from training and be asked, "Where'd you learn that? We don't do it that way around here!"

For training to work, it must fit into the language and context of the organization. Ideally, training needs should be tied to desired strategic results. As important, however, is that newly learned skills must be supported by congruent organization structures, reward systems, and managers who speak the same language and help their people fine-tune these new skills.

Integrated training is viewed as too expensive or too difficult to execute.

I once participated in a four-year project to train 400 managers and senior sales people in the individual behaviors needed for working in teams. The program was taught cross-functionally because it would be expensive and logistically difficult to have entire work groups close down for four days. The program was extraordinarily well received. Generally, interdepartmental teamwork improved and some individuals reported "transformational experiences." However, functional teamwork, the key unit for company results, remained unchanged.

The company later held two-day action learning offsite meetings for intact work units where teamwork skills were taught in the context of solving real work problems. These sessions were sometimes stormy, but the results were astounding. Not only did teamwork improve, but all teams reported measurable performance increases, some as much as 50 percent. One could ask, of course, whether the second training would have been as effective without the common language created by the first, but it was clear that expense and logistical difficulty were less appropriate design criteria than organizational integration.

How to make training work in your organization Put training into perspective.

Training is neither panacea nor placebo. Insist on proper analysis of all components of a problem whose solution *might* include new knowledge or skills.

Make the need to learn abundantly clear.

This may require many individual and organizational actions, including but not limited to:

- Linking training needs to strategic objectives
- Linking training needs to new job specifications
- Encouraging an attitude of lifelong learning
- Coaching, counseling, or otherwise providing feedback to individuals to help them *choose* to learn

Take the system-wide view.

Consider training in the context of all the systems, structures, and management behaviors necessary to support it. When reviewing training costs, compare total costs, including rework if the training is inadequately designed or unsupported. Also,

- If you are a manager, learn training technology.
- If you are a trainer, learn the business.
- If you are a CEO or senior executive, advocate regular rotation of managers through training jobs and place trainers in line jobs.

In his 1991 book *The Work of Nations: Preparing Ourselves for 21st Century Capitalism*, former Secretary of Labor Robert B. Reich describes our world as "changing from high volume production to high value-added service" and this new environment as one where a "nation's assets are... its people's skills and insights."

It is imperative that business invests in training that works. We can't afford to push stacks of hundreds into the shredder.

CHAPTER 39.

VISIBLE LEADERSHIP

A pologies to those who say I talk about the transformational privatization of British Airways way too much. They're right. I do talk about BA too often. But that's because the BA change effort was a huge success.

There are many reasons for BA's success:

- Margaret Thatcher _was_ the burning platform: "I can sell you off in little pieces. . . or we can sell your stock to the public. It's your choice. . ."
- With its deep pockets, the British government was willing to spend whatever it took.
- It was driven by the pride of the people working for the "Fly the Flag" and "World's Favourite Airline."

The transformation strategy was described as the three-legged stool:

- The basis for executive compensation changed from activity (number of flights and load factors) to results (customer service and profits).
- Performance appraisals changed to include customer service and staff emotional support, measured by a 360-degree feedback system normalized for rater bias.

- There was also a substantial amount of training to communicate the change and build values, knowledge, and skills to support it.

As a young project manager, I helped design and deliver the Passenger Group Programme, which taught customer service. I helped design Managing People First, which taught the top 10 percent of the airline how to lead the change; these leaders then ran the change projects that drove the transformation. As preparation, I attended Putting People First, the opening program, three times, which everyone at the airline went through to learn the connection between managing the emotional needs of employees and customer service excellence.

There was a lot of training. To me, the most interesting thing about it was that Chief Executive Colin Marshall was there. Colin (later Sir Colin, and then Lord Marshall) attended every single session of Managing People First. He was at all three sessions of Putting People First that I attended. (He made about half of them himself, and executive team members made the rest.)

"Visible Leadership" was one of Colin Marshall's watchwords (along with "Visionary Leadership" and "Caring Leadership"), and he certainly lived it. He didn't come naturally to this persona. I remember his somewhat awkward first session, arriving in his pricey suit and tie, haughtily asking his Training Director, "Get us a cup of tea, won't you, Paddy?" Over three years, he became collegial. He arrived for the change project presentations, took off his jacket and tie, and rolled up his sleeves ("Alright, ladies and gentlemen, let's hear what you have").

As previously discussed, training is overused and misused in many organizations, which dooms it to failure. Colin Marshall saw training as central to BA's transformation, and his visible presence at that training was critical to the success of the change.

With other clients, I was often asked to develop and deliver training that was allegedly "a central part of our transformational change," only to discover those words were hollow. No senior leader ever showed up at the training; they couldn't tell you the content even if they were involved in approving it. Such training often excited individual participants, but it made no transformational change in the company.

In the late 1990s, General Motors fell in love with BA's Managing People First. They hired us, copied much of the material, and called it Leadership Now. The program drew rave reviews from participants. Roger Smith, then CEO, never showed up at Leadership Now, nor did any member of his executive team. Thirty years later, GM's bankruptcy caused it to transform.

During the same period, I was also at Short Brothers, the aircraft manufacturer in Belfast, which Mrs. Thatcher was privatizing. Shorts liked the name Leadership Now and used the GM moniker for its training. The firm had much more success, was ultimately acquired by Bombardier, and still builds fuselages for Canadair regional jets today. CEO Roy McNulty showed up at every program. He embodied the change, and his people loved him for it.

In my last years of consulting, I was engaged in two large transformational training programs, one at an oil company trying to reduce risk and one at a financial services firm interested in becoming process focused. Both clients invested a great deal of money in these training programs. Getting senior managers to come to address the class was in both cases difficult. No CEO nor any member of the executive committee ever showed up at either training program. Both programs were highly rated by participants, but failed to produce lasting organizational change.

I recognize that a lack of Visible Leadership may not be a causal factor in that failure. Leadership may not have been committed to the change or may have harbored the belief that the training was "for them," an expression of disrespect for their employees. Still, correlated factors bear investigation because they often reflect a root cause. It is unlikely, for example, that Jack Welch's constant presence at the Crotonville Leadership Development Center explains the greatness of GE in that period, but his involvement did communicate what he thought was important. It also role-modeled that importance for other leaders. To this day, General

Electric believes that teaching is a core leadership competency. I know a chemical plant manager who personally leads quarterly leadership training and who has built pride in his organization by sending people from his plant to other plants all over the world to share what they have learned.

I also know that executive time is expensive and that attendance at already pricey training sessions makes it even more costly. The training costs at British Airways were substantial, but Colin Marshall saw them as critical to the change and showed up at every leadership workshop and everyone saw how much he changed in the process. At one point the unions challenged the expense, and a hard-bitten shop steward who had been included on the change team said,

"Pricey? Yeah, mate, but we were re-educating our Chief Executive and you know how expensive that can be."

People laughed and the objection dissolved, because the point was made.

You can't delegate change leadership. If learning is a part of your company's transformation, be a role model, be visible, **and show up**. Connect with the people who will embody the change. Talk with them about the importance of what they are learning. Share your own struggles with the change. But mostly **listen to them** and answer their questions. I guarantee it will be well worth your time.

SERVING CUSTOMERS

I n business, customers make everything happen. And so I have an almost religious view that serving customers is what business is about. Yeah, yeah, we are there to make money and we must treat our people well, but our purpose is to deliver value to customers as <u>they</u> define it, and deliver that value in a way that confirms that we understand them. Usually, that means a business leader asked them what they needed and listened. So I consider customer focus a prerequisite for a leader.

Some people always thought of me as a salesman. Despite mild intro-version, I'm able to talk with people from all walks of life. I'm genuinely interested in what they have to say. I sold enough in my life to know that I was better in a long-term relationship sale rather than a "one-call-and-close-sale." It took me a while to warm up, I guess.

Sales and customer service are often viewed as different. Salespeople acquire the customer, and customer service representatives (CSRs) keep them happy after the sale. I see both positions as serving the customer and creating/maintaining a relationship. I consulted to a lot of businesses that named their salespeople "relationship managers" and charged them with deploying a team of specialists to serve all the customer's needs. But a business leader is salesperson and CSR in chief.

So why my focus on customer service? As a young man I often worked for tips. In my early teens I caddied at a YMCA caddy camp serving the Oyster Harbors Golf Club on Cape Cod. At fifteen I worked the counter at Howard Johnson's. At twenty-one, I did what a lot of aspiring actors do - waited tables, tended bar, and drove a cab. I learned that listening to customers and responding was rewarding, i.e., people gave you money.

I found myself in a variety of selling environments. In high school, I worked at a gift shop as a stock boy, but graduated quickly to sales clerk because I knew the stock and liked talking with customers. When I became a booking agent, I sold on the phone, serving both the "client" speakers and the "customers," college lecture chairmen. After business school, I sold training to training managers and sales managers. As an independent consultant, I sold consulting projects for myself and colleagues.

However, even as an independent consultant, I would walk away from a consulting sale that I believed wouldn't solve the customer's problem. If I could not be genuinely helpful, or if I couldn't help the client build internal capability to execute sustainable change, I'd just pass on the work and tighten my belt a little. That was a source of frustration for colleagues who worked with me, but serving customers was a big part of how I defined myself. And should be a big part of how a leader defines himself or herself.

CHAPTER 40

THE POWER OF LEADER-CUSTOMER INTERVIEWS

his is the Information Age, the era of bar codes, databases, People Meters, perceptual mapping, and a host of big data quantitative market research techniques that can deliver more data about who buys products and why than at any other time in recorded history. I was therefore unprepared for the power of a rather simple customer focus technique: I just asked leaders to talk to customers and tell their colleagues what they learned.

What astounds me is that this simple exercise created in-depth discussion of:

- Strategy, especially profound strategic change
- Quality
- Service
- Market segmentation and niche marketing
- Competition
- Internal and/or marketplace issues

In 1984, while working on the BA transformation, I interviewed customers in the ticket queues at Heathrow Airport about service. As you might imagine, interviewing people who are waiting in a queue can produce some hostile reactions. In leadership meetings my efforts to relate the depth of that anger was met with disbelief. This airline had customer service reports detailing that satisfaction with queue length was a substandard 4.3 on a 5.0 service problem survey scale, so these data were not news, but the data just didn't appear that bad. Somehow, I enticed a few executives to accompany me on queue interviews. Their perspective changed dramatically and action quickly followed.

Some years later, I facilitated a meeting for a rep firm that sold advertising time on radio stations to media buyers at national advertising agencies. The firm was changing strategy and moving toward calling on higher-level senior agency personnel to ask for a different kind of service. Existing customers (agency media buyers) resisted the reps calling above their heads, and so the rep firm's salespeople resisted as well. They wanted the strategy rescinded. I said to the account executives, "Just go talk to one media planner and one media executive; get to understand their needs. Take notes or record the meeting. Then we'll talk about it."

Everyone came back understanding that these higher-level customers understood little about the radio medium and yet decided on media long before the plan ever reached the traditional customer, the media buyer. As a result, the meeting was spent strategizing on how to resolve different customer expectations (not lobbying to abandon the controversial strategy).

Another time I facilitated a one-week leadership development session for a domestic automaker. As a group we had jawboned about perceived quality and dealer relations and had just endured a mind-numbing presentation of domestic auto market segmentation, complete with darkened room and colorful slides of a thirty-six-customer-segment matrix.

The lights came up and Pete, the cigar-chewing national sales manager for the luxury marque, spoke up in New Jersey brogue: "That was really pretty. It's just when I meet a person in the showroom, I have a hard time figuring out which one of those pretty colored boxes he's supposed to be in."

My colleague and I said, "OK, go out on the street here in Detroit and talk to some customers. You have two hours. Come back and tell us what you've learned." What came back were reports of many aspects of the customer experience: one executive brought a dealer who ranted about how it feels to try to tell Detroit anything; another told how a man eloquently described quality as the care of his wife and child; and others recounted a panoply of real customer needs that placed customers with others of similar needs (in segments that could be represented graphically as little colored boxes).

This is not a technique meant to replace statistically valid quantitative market research. It produces qualitative, anecdotal data that personalizes the information of a quantitative study. It brings executives face-to-face with customers to gather real data and then report to their colleagues. This first-hand experience inspires action in a way that reading results from the linear regression in the quantitative data often fails to do.

In all these examples three elements are present:

1. Executives were engaged in a group meeting where the objective was to solve problems associated with implementing strategy.
2. The executives gathered the data themselves. In some instances I helped them by suggesting some questions, but they conducted the interviews.
3. They collected (through note taking or recording), analyzed, synthesized and then formally presented the data to their colleagues.

This exercise can also help to build customer relationships. My experience was that customers usually are flattered to be asked their opinions. Further, they will expect action on the issues they raise: don't ask passengers how they feel about standing in line if you're not prepared to get another ticket window open, even if you must man it yourself.

I've experimented with several structures for bringing customers and executives together:

- **The customer site visit** - Select executives visit a customer site to determine how their product is being used.
- **The invited customer tour** - Select customers are given a tour of the executives' site, and asked about service and quality strategies. This is not a sales pitch and will backfire if you corner customers and bombard them with product bells and whistles.
- **The informal chat** - Select customers are invited to discuss their needs as a focus group. An executive is present even if there is a professional facilitator. It is also beneficial if the setting is informal; this means armchairs and no one-way mirrors.
- **The scripted interview** – Select executives agree in advance on the type of information needed and questions to be asked of customers. This can eliminate spontaneity but will standardize the data for comparison purposes. If a large qualitative study were to emerge, then sample selection and content analysis of data would become issues. (It is possible to get carried away with what is a simple exercise.)
- **The recorded interview** – This is like the interview described above, except the executive asks the customer for permission to record and then asks a few softball questions to put the customer at ease. In one instance, a customer's soliloquy about the effect of quality on his family produced an emotional connection I don't believe any executive presentation could have matched.

Video also can be an effective tool. I saw video used to demonstrate what a small businessman wanted from a commercial bank lending officer.

I also saw a California retail bank manager load all his people in a bus on a Saturday and drive around interviewing customers and residents in his resort community, taping the entire event.

Video brings special challenges. Sometimes people ramble, so editing may be required.

Also, you really want the customer to forget about the tape, so a stationary tripod is best for interviews. If someone is acting as your cameraman ensure that he or she doesn't get carried away with unnecessary zooms and pans. Further, while a little home video is refreshing, more than fifteen minutes will pale compared to Disney and you will lose your audience.

These days with smart phones we all carry audio and video recording devices in our pockets. However we should always practice before using them for interviewing and to ask permission from the person being interviewed. As effective as audio and video can be, I believe that for the purposes of this rather simple exercise notetaking is sufficient. I most often leave this decision to the executives.

In my view, the content and structure of the data gathering are less important than the presence of all three of the previously described elements. There must be a *forum to use the data,* the **executives must gather it themselves,** and, finally, the **executives must present the data and its implications to their colleagues.**

In so doing, executives
- Take responsibility for the data.
- They humanize the concept of being "close to the customer."
- They personally engage customers, and as a result of that interaction,
- They can choose to use their leadership to improve the customer relationship.

Flying into the old Hong Kong Kai Tak airport -CNN photo

CHAPTER 41

CREATING A DELIGHTFUL CUSTOMER EXPERIENCE

I n the late 1990s, I visited Hong Kong for the first time. I was consulting on Continuous Improvement for a global financial services firm and had just come from spending two weeks in suburban Tokyo with its new acquisition, an efficient property and casualty company that kept all its records on 3x5 index cards. My corporate client team had been horrified by this practice and spent the entire time I was there disparaging their "backward" Japanese colleagues. The Japanese firm had superb processes and an admirable customer service ethic, which had created a large and growing share of their home market. On the flight into Hong Kong I was anxious, concerned the client would destroy sterling customer relationships in their blind drive to automate for efficiency.

As we approached Hong Kong, I was immediately distracted from my worry. This was before Gordon Wu had built the gleaming new Hong Kong International Airport on Cho Lap Kok Island. As I flew into the old Kai Tak airport, I looked out from my window seat and observed office workers in high-rise office buildings seemingly six feet from the tip of the plane's wing. My eyes grew wide with anticipation of a unique experience.

I had read a lot about Hong Kong, from James Clavell's novels *Tai-Pan* and *Noble House,* to Frank Welsh's history *A Borrowed Place,* to travel guides like Lonely Planet's *Pocket Hong Kong.* It was the latter that recommended the immersive and inexpensive experience of the Chinese bus, which, traveling for business, I had absolutely no intention of taking. Then I came outside into the ninety-degree heat to find a taxi line that stretched around the width of the terminal. I was not enthusiastic about the sixty-minute wait; I changed my mind about the Chinese bus.

I got on the bus along with Chinese grandmothers and multiple generations of children. It was clear that I was the only non-Asian, the only person in a suit and the only person who had luggage not appended with many plastic and paper bags. I told the driver I was staying in the Central District at the Mandarin Oriental Hotel. He nodded and smiled at me in a way that said, "I have no idea what you just said," and directed me with elaborate pantomime to put my luggage in the rack at the front and sit down. He spoke in Chinese to everyone else and I began to think that this was a colossal mistake.

An ancient Chinese woman sat next to me and offered to share her street food. I politely declined, shaking my head and thanking her in mime, recalling previous times I'd strayed from tourist areas to the real local environment where no one speaks English. My discomfort escalated when I realized that the stop announcements were recorded and in two different Chinese dialects, presumably Mandarin and Cantonese, neither of which I understood.

Just as my anxiety was peaking, I thought I heard English. Yes, it really was English. But what was it saying? "Centra. .strict. . ndarin. . .rienta. . otelle." While I was completely befuddled, trying to decipher this cryptic message, my seatmate poked me in the ribs and pointed to the driver, who was gesturing for me to get my luggage and get off the bus. *Ah, it was my stop.*

I'm no stranger to the bustle of cities, but Hong Kong had infinitely more of it. I stood on the pavement in the Central District, no doubt looking very confused. The bus driver honked his horn and pointed in the direction he was going, smiled again, and drove off. I took this to mean that if I walked in that direction, I might come upon my hotel, and sure enough, after walking about two blocks, I could see the marquee for the Mandarin Oriental Hotel. But just as I was starting to feel comfortable, a man in a maroon uniform took my computer bag from my shoulder and my Rollaboard suitcase from my hand. I tried to say "No," but he just shepherded me toward the door and disappeared with my luggage. I was swivel-heading around looking for him when a tall woman with straight black hair in a blue blazer took my hand, smiled, and said, "Welcome to the Mandarin Oriental Hotel, Mr. Culler. I'm Ming, please follow me."

"But my bags. . ." I stammered.

"Don't worry. They know the way."

I followed her to the dark wood-paneled elevator, redder than mahogany, very rich looking.

"But don't we need to check in. . . ?"

"We'll take care of that."

We got off at the fifth floor and stopped briefly to admire an antique Chinese porcelain vase, Ming pointing out some fine points. Then she took me to my room and opened the door made of the same red wood. My luggage was in the room on a luggage rack by the bed.

"But how . . . ?"

"It's magic," Ming smiled. She took my passport and wrote down information quickly.

"What time would you like your wake-up call in the morning? She asked. I calculated my morning schedule and replied, "7:00."

I remember wondering if she had my credit card but perhaps I had given it when I reserved the room. Ming handed back my passport and started to leave, turning at the door.

"Would you like some tea, Mr. Culler? Yes? Chinese or Jasmine? Jasmine then. Thank you and I hope you enjoy your stay. If you need anything, my name is Ming."

After she left I turned to unpack and there was a knock on the door. *Oh, she's forgotten something* I thought, but when I opened the door it was the Jasmine tea.

I was impressed, but a hotel room, however luxurious, is still a hotel room and there was unpacking to do. I busied myself and got ready to go to a client meeting, which turned into a dinner. I arrived back at the hotel after 9:00 p.m. and was a little surprised that the doorman wished me a good evening by name. "Have a good evening, Mr. Culler." But it was late, and I went to bed; I was flying out in the morning.

My wake-up call came precisely at 7:00 a.m. "Good morning, Mr. Culler. And Happy Birthday!" I was shocked. How did they know? Then I remembered that Ming had taken information from my passport.

I went for breakfast in the coffee shop. The hostess took my room number and wished me a Happy Birthday.

My meal was a bit late and I was rushing for a plane. When I asked for the bill, the waiter said, "There is no charge, Mr. Culler."

"No, really, it doesn't matter that it was late, I ate it all. . . ."

"Well, we <u>were</u> late. Think of it as a birthday present. Have a very Happy Birthday, Mr. Culler!"

So how does such a delightful experience happen? It happens by a carefully planned process and disciplined execution.

The bus driver signaled to the bellman that a guest was arriving.

The bellman read my luggage tag and phoned Ming, who greeted me in the lobby by name. She paused to admire the vase so that the luggage could arrive in the room. The tea is made on each floor and she simply told the tea servers, "Jasmine for Mr. Culler."

The process was impeccable, and the execution inspired. Ming observed that the next day was my birthday and communicated that to everyone at the hotel. How does a company create such great service? They hire the right people and they train them.

Some will say, Oh, this is Hong Kong before the transition to Chinese rule (1999). Others will say this is only an Asian tradition. But my experiences in other Hong Kong hotels before and after transition were quite different from the Mandarin Oriental, and my stays in other Mandarin Oriental hotels outside of Asia since were similar to that of my stay in Hong Kong. My conclusion? Service is in the corporate culture.

There are many companies that pride themselves on exceptional service - American Express, Southwest Airlines, USAA, Nordstrom. Most have strict criteria for hiring that include a positive attitude, empathy, genuine friendliness and care for others. It isn't impossible to train these personality traits as skills, but it is simpler to select for them.

Most companies known for customer service are values-based. They have a clear idea of why they are providing service. They know what the right thing is, so when they train their people to always do the right thing, it is a clear instruction.

Jan Carlzon, the former CEO of Scandinavian Airline System, SAS, wrote about "moments of truth" with the customer. These are opportunities to excel – a birthday greeting, a late meal comped when a customer is in a rush, a waived fee, a gift to a valued long-term customer. Each gesture surprises the customer and creates a lasting positive memory.

Not everyone gets this. Consider my experience the next night at a large chain hotel in New York City. My plane was late, and I got to the front desk at 3:00 a.m. Upon hearing my name, the desk clerk smirked, "Oh, do you have a color TV at home?" (Culler-color, get it?) I wasn't amused, but my displeasure grew when he informed me that they had given my guaranteed room away.

"Late arrival is only good till midnight. But don't worry, we got some rooms." He then proceeded to give me a key for a room that had another couple in it. They were not amused.

The desk clerk told me that "the girl on days didn't enter it into the computer." He found me another room, this time smaller and situated right next to the service elevator used for trash removal starting at 6:00 a.m. As I said, some companies and people just don't get it.

As a society we are moving toward a seamless electronic sales and service process, which takes the costly human being out of the transaction. Some companies hide call center phone numbers and direct people online to chatbots. Some companies measure call center representatives on metrics like average handle time or success cross-selling customers to new products during service calls, and <u>not</u> on service, customer satisfaction or call resolution.

In the future, will we still have processes and people who create a surprising and delightful experiences for our customers? I hope so. I like to feel that my business is valued. I like surprises. Even now, I am thrilled to be wished a "Happy Birthday" by complete strangers. It's like cake and ice cream, but without the calories.

WORKING WITH CONSULTANTS

There will be some who say that including working with consultants in a book for new change leaders is self-serving. Maybe they are right. But first, I am retired and second, there are scenarios in which I would recommend *not* hiring a consultant. For example, if you know how to do the work and/or have the time to learn, **don't hire a consultant.** Also, if you are abdicating a difficult change task and are trying to ensure that you have someone to blame, **don't hire a consultant.** However, from my experience and the experience of colleagues, I know that consultants can add value to companies.

Leaders may seek a consultant who is familiar with a particular issue the company is facing.

Or a leader might just want experienced heads and hands to help his company through a rough period of change. Or he or she might believe that the organization could use someone to teach them how to master skills that they haven't needed in the past but need now.

These are all valid reasons to hire a consultant. If you hire the right consultant for the right reason and manage the relationship well, you will doubtless get value.

But as Hamlet said, "Aye, there's the rub."

Some leaders hire consultants over and over again to do the same thing - a new strategy or a new organization every two years or so. I believe if you are doing that you should bring those skills inhouse. Likewise, some companies try multiple continuous improvement or innovation initiatives, using a new methodology each time; I believe companies should pick **one** methodology and stick with it.

There are leaders who hire a consultant and delegate the entire relationship to a junior person, never seeing the consultant again until the report is presented. In my view, this is not delegation but rather abdication, and it is unlikely to produce lasting results.

If you are thinking of hiring a consulting firm, the first question is – Why?

There are basically two types of consultants: content and process. Typically, content consultants provide information and answers, and process consultants help you build capability often by the Socratic method – by asking questions. I have a bias for process consulting, but sometimes what you want is an answer or a different perspective.

Simply put, if you are looking for information, hire a content firm; if you want to build capability, hire a process firm. Be suspicious of firms that tell you they are both; from my experience, combining those two approaches is beyond rare.

What follows are two chapters that address working with consultants:

- How to get the most value from working with a consultant
- How to form and build an internal consulting firm in order to bring consulting skills inhouse

These two chapters won't tell you everything about working with consultants, but they are a good start.

CHAPTER 42

HOW TO GET THE MOST VALUE FROM A CONSULTANT

Over my long career, I was employed by five different firms and also worked for myself in a variety of different structures. I didn't see every possible variation on the consultant/client relationship, but I saw a lot. I started out as a content consultant - providing information and giving answers. I ended up as a process consultant, asking questions and helping build capability. I didn't know it then, but in my first year of consulting I saw both ends of the spectrum in terms of clients getting value from consultants - or not.

My first consulting project was while I was getting my MBA at the London Business School. I worked for a consultant at the London office of a Boston-based firm doing a product-and-market evaluation for a commercial vehicle assembler located in the north of England near the Scottish border. It was, I suppose, sold as a consulting project on the cheap, five mid-term business school students, one partner (Dick), and one part-time principal (Basil).

Dick chose me as Data Secretary of the LBS team. I really don't know why; what he said was, "Harrumph, whenever you bring five people together, one emerges as a natural leader." I was a few years older than my classmates; I talk a lot; and Dick and I were both Americans. Nevertheless, I accepted his explanation and, in fact, ate it up big time. I got to manage the schedule and make sure we hit deliverables while Dick was in Provence for four weeks. And after a few "don't 'manage' me, Alan" moments I learned to be helpful with teammates, the team got the work done and we all had a lot of fun in the bargain.

The greatest advantage of the Data Secretary role was that I sat in on client meetings and worked closely with a client team that included the heads of marketing and manufacturing. The CEO and I scheduled bi-weekly updates, which I led, but the entire joint team attended. And I coordinated the report and attended the final presentation. The LBS team did have weekly access to Basil, but mostly we were on our own.

The client company made tractor-trailer trucks, forty-four-ton "articulated lorries" in British English. Their market positioning was "heavy-duty": thick steel, big Gardiner engines, the kind of truck that would stand up to heavy use. They wanted to expand to building thirty-two-ton, eight-wheel vehicles like highway construction dump trucks and big city garbage collectors, and possibly build sixteen-ton distribution vehicles, the kind of box van that distributes groceries, toys and, well, everything really. (They are what U-Haul rents the most and are the high-volume vehicle in the market.) We found that the market would accept heavy-duty eight-wheelers, but not heavy-duty sixteen-ton trucks because extra weight adds fuel cost and reduces payloads, and distribution is a thin-margin business.

We interviewed dealers, truck fleet owners, competitors, and trade association people; we pored over sales and pricing data with our client team members. Every other week we met with the CEO and members of his team. By the time we produced our report and presentation, the client understood much of what we had to say. Dick came back from

Provence and demonstrated why he was a partner by adding many insights we hadn't considered or discussed with the client. The client was pleased.

My second consulting project was another LBS student cheapie working for Dick – a desk-study of the market for automatic transmissions in buses in the developing world. I was again Data Secretary, and the LBS student team numbered eight. Basil was more hands-on, and Dick didn't go on holiday. Everything I'd thought I'd learned about how consulting projects worked was different.

The CEO, with whom the project had been arranged, delegated it to a junior marketing manager. After the initial meeting with Dick, the CEO wasn't visible until the final presentation. There was no client team, no bi-weekly updates, no interaction between the client and consultants, not even with Dick or Basil, from the kick-off meeting to the final presentation. We reviewed twenty-six bus markets across the world and identified eight that were ripe for automatic transmission sales. We produced a one-hundred-page report according to detailed specifications from the client, including a separately packaged three-page executive summary, fifteen copies, all professionally printed and bound with a particular Pantone color cover and delivered one week before Dick's presentation. I remember Dick being unhappy after the presentation. "We'd scheduled two hours and he cut me off after forty minutes," he grumbled.

These two projects were conducted four months apart. About a year later I had the opportunity to go back to the first client as part of another project. They had started building and selling the eight-wheeled vehicle and were assembling a sixteen-ton distribution vehicle for a Japanese manufacturer.

I was quite excited and called Dick. Serendipitously, he told me he had just visited our second client's CEO. "You remember the ninth market that we argued about?" he asked. At the time I felt strongly that we should include in our recommendations a market where all the elements of a national bus system were present (city, county, and intra-city) but were owned by different entrepreneurs. "One consolidating acquisition would put it in play," I had said. Dick had argued against inclusion because the market didn't currently meet the clients' strict specifications. In the end, he agreed to a footnote in the report.

"Well," Dick said, "I told a bus operations firm in Cincinnati about that and they bought out the three entrepreneurs. I went to tell the CEO that the ninth market was now an option."

"What happened?" I was getting excited.

"It took me three months to get an appointment and when I did he gave me fifteen minutes and smiled in my face and pointed to the maroon binder on his bookshelf. I think it was dusty. They <u>haven't</u> <u>done</u> <u>anything</u>."

Now forty-something years later, I still think about the stark difference between these two clients. Frankly, that comparison caused me to go back to school and study leadership and change.

The difference? Leadership engagement

In the previous examples, the first CEO had weekly meeting with a group of grad students. He assigned a senior manager to work with us, not the marketing manager who had opinions of his own on this subject.

The second CEO gave us the impression that he couldn't be bothered. He delegated to a junior marketing person who adopted the CEO's aloof attitude and was rarely available. The second CEO cut the presentation short and hadn't read the report. Most especially, he <u>took</u> <u>no</u> <u>action.</u> According to Dick, there were no follow-on automatic transmission sales to existing or new buses in our eight recommended markets. It was not clear why.

Occasionally consultants are hired to promote or discredit someone's pet idea or to get a board member off the CEO's back. And maybe something like that was underlying the second client's lack of interest and action. Maybe the disengagement was not the cause of the inaction, but a symptom of what was a foregone conclusion from the beginning.

After many years as a consultant, I learned that clients most often hire consultants for three primary reasons:

- For a particular expertise – a skill perhaps that they don't use enough to hire inhouse
- As fill-in resources because staff resources are too busy
- As a partner to make something important happen

Of course, as a strategic process consultant I always wanted to be in the last category, but I worked on projects in all three. I think of consulting as a helping profession. So in the spirit of being helpful, if you hire a consultant here are some ideas to think about:

- Be clear about why you are hiring the consultant:
    - What are your expected outcomes? What action will you take based upon these outcomes? (And maybe who might take it and when?)
    - What role do you expect from the consultant: expert, extra resource, or partner?
- Be open with your consultant about the answers to these questions.
- Have a plan to bring the consultant's process inhouse:
    - What can you learn?
    - Who should learn it?
    - What will they do with this new knowledge?
- Roll up your sleeves and engage with the consultant yourself. If you don't have the time to do this, delegate to someone who can devote the time, but make sure this person engages and arranges for you to interact (and not just at the final presentation).
- Resist the pitch for additional work that comes at the end of most every consultant project presentation until you have implemented what you have planned.

Approach hiring even a temporary consulting resource as the opportunity to increase your organization's capability; plan for it, and act on the plan. Ask the consultants you hire to help you grow your capability. Many consultants - not all - will partner with you in this way, but their answer to this request may guide your choice of whom to hire.

CHAPTER 43

FORMING AN INTERNAL CONSULTING FIRM

"Why on earth would you help a client take the work inside?" The year was 2006, and I had just received my first consulting engagement helping a client form an internal consulting firm. A former colleague, a partner in another small consulting firm, was incredulous that I would agree to such an assignment. Like a lot of expert consultants he wanted to protect the dollar value of his expertise.

When this consultant and I worked together previously, our firm had lost business when a service offering commoditized, i.e., clients either hired our people directly or took our presentation materials and trained their staff to replace us. Our answer was to rewrite our consulting contract to specify that the client could not hire our people or use our materials internally during the project and for two years after it ended. This never worked. Now I was abetting a trend to eliminate consultants.

"You're poisoning the well!" he said, perhaps a bit louder than necessary.

Now all these years later, I still believe an internal consulting firm is the right answer for many leaders. The clients that I helped form internal firms used fewer consultants overall, but they also didn't use consultants over and over for exactly the same type of work. They developed internal capability as they improved performance. Consultants help with things the client hasn't yet learned to do themselves.

Why develop an internal consulting firm?

Despite my colleague's fears, I never encountered a client who said that they brought expertise inside to reduce consulting spend. Most of these clients were medium-sized firms and larger, over $200 million in annual sales and one thousand people or more. But I have seen smaller firms hire a single consulting manager who screened and managed independent consultants as if they were building an internal department. What united all these models is that the firm wanted to grow a critical competency that they foresaw needing, such as Reengineering, Continuous Improvement, or Innovation. Serial acquirers often hire strategy consultants to run their strategy department and develop due diligence and integration management capability. Some holding companies or private equity groups set up internal operational assistance staff.

Often these groups are run by experts with a specialized skill; others are staffed with extra junior "pairs of hands." Still others staff a combination of permanent hires and contractors much like a big body-shop temp agency. But many of these units are set up like consulting firms, with client development models, content and consulting skills training, and the infrastructure to develop and build firm capability while achieving results for clients. These internal consulting firms appear successful and worthy of a closer look.

What kind of consulting firm?

External consulting firms come in many shapes and sizes; some are generalist and some are specialist. Some differentiate themselves by a particular service offering, e.g., Economic Value Added, or Balanced Scorecard. Some have products like off-the-shelf training programs or software. But the most interesting and relevant difference between types of firms is that of Content vs. Process.

Content consulting starts with a mindset of *solving a problem for the client*. Consultants do analysis, draw conclusions and make recommendations. Acting on those recommendations is the responsibility of the client. In content firms, there is a focus on knowing – smart people reign. Analytical frameworks help the client understand what you are telling him. Client team members' roles are usually administrative (scheduling meetings, processing invoices) and data collection, and only consulting leaders attend final presentations. Sometimes a content consultant will do an early demonstration of how to implement recommendations, but generally they want to move on to the next engagement sooner rather than later. Change management in a content firm is often user training at the end of a project.

The mindset of process consulting is to *teach the client how to solve the problem*. As a result, client teams tend to be larger and the work tends to be shared. There is a focus on listening and helping. Often a process consultant is a "coach." Process consultants talk about inputs and outputs as well as process steps. Change management starts early, and the consultants usually work with the client longer.

When forming an internal consulting firm, ask yourself: should it be a content firm or a process firm? The kind of firm you have in mind will dictate whom you hire and the infrastructure you set up. I favor setting up an internal process consulting firm because I saw more clients implement and achieve results with this model. But either model works, though some disciplines lend themselves more to one model than the other. For example, Strategy and Analytics are often content-structured departments; they do the work for you. Organization development and process improvement are often process-structured departments.

Can you be both content and process?
I worked for three firms that sought to combine content and process

consulting: strategy development with strategy implementation, or the analytical with the behavioral. In one I was considered the strategy content guy in the organization discipline because I could talk content or process. In another, a partner described me as "the best facilitator I've ever seen, but doesn't have an analytic bone in his body." It always sounded like such a great idea to combine these two streams of consulting, but in my experience it never worked. Content people have answers and process people have questions and the only thing they have in common is little use for each other. So from the point of view of an internal firm, I'd suggest choosing either content or process and not combining approaches.

Purpose: doing vs. teaching

If you are stuck on this decision, ask yourself, "Why do you want to form an internal firm?" If the answer is that you want staff specialists to <u>do</u> technical work for the line, then you are most likely building a content-oriented firm. If the answer is to <u>teach</u> or to <u>build capability</u>, then a process-oriented firm is a better fit.

Service offering

The large generalist consulting firms pride themselves on being able to solve every problem, using every known methodology or framework. However, most successful internal firms start with a single service offering and often a single methodology or framework. For example, if members of a company group are forming a strategic assistance firm, not only do they avoid operational improvement work, but they work with a single strategic methodology such as Michael Porter's industry and competitive analysis (5 Forces), or Chan Kim's Blue Ocean Strategy (Innovation focused), or Michael Treacy and Fred Wiersema's Value Disciplines (Customer Intimacy, Product Innovation, Operational Excellence).

Similarly, continuous improvement groups pick Lean or Six Sigma while innovation groups select Human Centered Design, Agile, or TRIZ, etc. Flexibility as to service offering and methodology is an advanced concept, kind of like spin in tennis. ("First, learn to get the ball over the net, then you can try to slice.")

External firms grow by adding new methodologies (different ways to solve the same problem) or service offerings (different problems to solve). They tend to grow this way AFTER they build an identity for solving a particular kind of problem in a particular way. Internal firms should start simply, one methodology or service offering at a time.

The Consulting Pyramid*

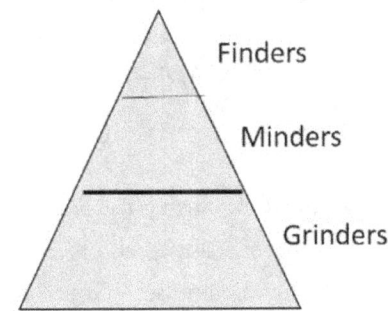

*Source: Balancing the Professional Services Firm
David Maister

Structure

In *Managing the Professional Services Firm*, David Maister describes the structure of consulting firms as a pyramid, divided between those who sell the work (Finders), those who manage projects and the daily interface with clients (Minders), and the often junior consultants who do the work (Grinders). Maister notes that the shape of the pyramid is determined by how mature the service offering is; established methodologies can be taught more easily to juniors and so pyramids are broader at the base. In the internal firms that I saw, the methodology was often established and the base was very broad.

Compounding a base-heavy structure is the fact that in the least successful internal firms, Minders and Finders are in short supply. For example, some Six Sigma implementations have only Black Belts, whereas successful Six Sigma structures have:

- Yellow Belts (often in the business) who work on large projects
- Green Belts who work on small projects and coach Yellow Belts
- Black Belts who work on more complex projects and coach Green Belts and Yellow Belts, and
- Master Black Belts, who find the work and structure improvement efforts with the business leaders according to strategic need

There is often a Six Sigma Program Manager who reports directly to a C-Suite executive (Chief Executive Officer or CEO, Chief Operating Officer or COO, Chief Financial Officer or CFO and so on) and who ensures that improvements focus on the C-suite's strategic priorities.

Client development

A pitfall for an internal consulting firm is the Field of Dreams assumption: "If you build it they will come." People who form an internal consulting firm assume that the internal businesses will just see their expertise and automatically use them. Nothing could be further from the truth.

A business leader must recognize the need for help and that the internal consulting firm can provide it. As a founder of the Human Potential movement, Carl Rogers once said, "Help that isn't asked for is seldom perceived as help. It is looked at as interference at best."

Also, the "because Papa said so" model – a single CEO directive in the form of an email announcement - doesn't work either.

The most successful firms have people who meet with potential internal clients and frame needs in a statement of work with clear objectives, expected outcomes, measures, and a timeline. This is equivalent to the partner role in an external firm.

Hiring and training

Who is hired to work on projects depends on the service offering and structure. Some successful internal firms have hired consultants from external firms; some have hired and trained internal people. Others have a combination of internal and external people who work on a full-time, part-time and/or contractor basis. Clearly whom you hire dictates training needs.

Everyone must understand not only the service offering, but also the consulting model with its requisite consulting skills, staff and client management. And classroom training by itself does not a consulting firm make. Planning the learning infrastructure, as well as creating the toolkit, project history, and databases with search capability, all make learning easier.

The best internal consulting firms rotate line people in and out of the firm to distribute expertise throughout the business. General Electric CEO Jack Welch demanded that all his leaders above a certain level become a Six Sigma Black Belt. Many went on to become Master Black Belts who trained as well as coached. This made for an integrated approach.

Owning results and funding the firm

Perhaps the trickiest issues around internal consulting firms are who owns the outcomes and who pays for the work. This also depends on whether the firm's approach is content or process consulting.

If a client buys a recommendation but fails to implement, he or she may blame the consultant. When a Black Belt turns the improvement over to the process owner and the process owner doesn't maintain the control plan, who is responsible?

These issues must be discussed and worked out prior to starting the firm and reinforced in the client contracting process.

Who pays and how? Over the years, I saw multiple payment schemes. Some companies hold the consulting firm costs centrally below the contribution line for which the businesses are held accountable. Some allocate costs to everyone whether they use the services of the internal consulting department or not. Some have service level agreements between the firm and the client with cross-charges based upon either time used or the results delivered. I also saw benefit- or gain-sharing agreements, i.e., "I saved you $x, $.3x accrues to my budget, $.7x accrues to yours."

These are all brown dollar funding arrangements (internal allocations vs. real money exchanges) but they still can have a huge impact on the bottom line for which businesses are held accountable. It is imperative that the implications of funding decisions be discussed with customer business leaders. The American colonial war cry is a good guideline: **"No taxation without representation!"**

My message to firms thinking about starting an internal consulting firm is not unlike my message to firms contemplating outsourcing: think about the infrastructure and expertise needed to <u>manage</u> the operation. There can be huge benefits, but they don't drop automatically to the bottom line. Someone must ensure that the business uses your service and that the customer is satisfied. If the consulting business were easy, everyone would do it.

Consultants are sometimes described as arrogant. In my experience, arrogant people are often deeply insecure. They work hard to sound knowledgeable because deep down they are afraid they know nothing. I learned over the years to quickly get up to speed in an industry so that I could have an intelligent conversation with people in that industry. But I didn't delude myself into thinking that I could do their jobs better than they could. In fact, I often said:

> I've worked as a consultant for a long time. I've listened to you and many others like you across many industries. As a result I've become quite good at <u>talking</u> about work. I've also developed a real respect for those who actually <u>do</u> <u>real</u> <u>work</u>, and I never assume that I have your knowledge or skill. So if what I say helps you to improve, great. If not, let's find another way, and then I will pass on your words to others.

Underlying this statement are, once again, the two core values of consulting:

- Be Helpful
- Focus on Results

I found that these fundamental attitudes and values make for a great consultant and the absence of them creates most of the negative stereotypes of the profession.

SNOOZE FACTOR ANALYSIS

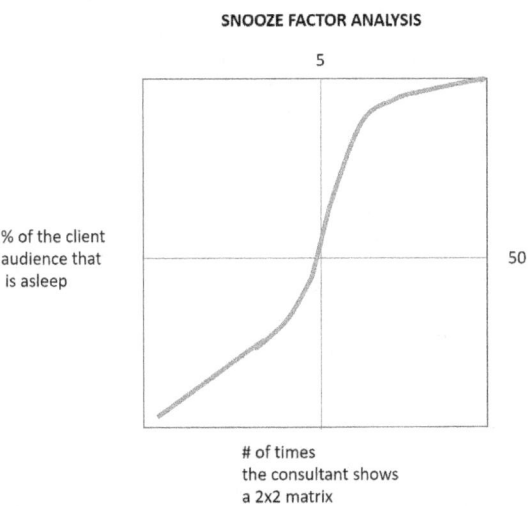

Frameworks, processes, and other tools

Consultants love frameworks. A framework is a tool that structures analysis and simplifies the communication of results. The classic 2x2 matrix, for example, has been used by consultants so often that it evokes consultant jokes like the snooze factor analysis at right.

If you are among those who <u>love</u> frameworks, remember that the vast majority of people don't think this way. Alfred Korzybski, the early twentieth-century philosopher, described the human difficulty understanding two dimensional representations of reality: "The map is not the territory."

Similarly, remember that the Excel model is not the business, and the analytical framework is not the solution. People need to be brought along with your way of representing the problem and/or solution so that they fully engage, discuss and decide.

GETTING READY
TO LEAD CHANGE

L eaders need to be good at envisioning, to see and explain the compelling case for change and what the changed organization will look like for each and all.

They need to attract followers with their vision and values as described in the previous chapters. They need to communicate, **to listen first** and then speak in a compelling way.

They also need to work on themselves.

Someone once told me, "Wherever you go you take yourself."

The person proceeded to give me advice about self-knowledge as a foundation for being a change consultant. Much of that advice is valuable for those leading change from within an organization:

- Be aware of how you think and how you frame issues.
- Understand your way of taking in information and making decisions, but do not assume that others think and make decisions in the same way.
- You must be prepared to change yourself if you want to help others choose to change.
- Always think about whose help you need and how to encourage them to collaborate.

But first leaders need to think. The next chapter "Thinking about Thinking" outlines some of what that means.

Then they need to unify. Times of change can be quite fragmenting.

Much of my work as a change consultant was called leadership alignment. At least that is what we consultants called it. Clients called it things like "getting everyone on the same page," or "singing off the same hymn sheet," or 'breaking down silos" (inward-looking functional departments or divisions).

In the chapter "Silo-Busting" I shared how I brought people together. Alignment and integration are key leadership skills. However this is tricky because too much alignment produces group think and limits innovation.

CHAPTER 44.

DON'T BE THAT GUY: AVOIDING LEADERSHIP DYSFUNCTION

An idea I've beaten to death in this book is that managers and leaders differ:

- Managers work in a steady state environment and are accountable for getting the work done and for developing their people and improving their skills.
- Leaders work in an abnormal environment - change, emergencies - and are accountable for direction and for getting people to follow, "Hey guys, this way, follow me!"

There's a reason why the military always talks about leadership; they are preparing their workers for war, the ultimate abnormal environment.

In business, management skills and leadership skills are often expected from the same person, and that person is usually a boss. Over my career the business press has progressed from talking about management skills as leadership skills. I think this is for three reasons:

- Nobody wants to be the boss or be bossed. Managers and supervisors are looked down upon; everybody wants to be a leader.
- We live in an increasingly abnormal business environment of constant change: new technology that transforms industries overnight; mergers and acquisitions and other structural changes; and shifts in societal norms, customer and worker attitudes and expectations. As someone once said to me, "There is no steady state!"
- In this environment, peer leadership has increased in importance, and direct lines of authority have had to respond accordingly. As someone else once said to me, "You can't tell anyone what to do anymore!"

So, everyone is a leader, and everyone has an opinion on leadership. But not everyone is cut out to be a leader, and there are some bad leaders out there. Here are a few of the dysfunctions of leadership:

- **Unclear, poor, and/or wrong direction**: People will forgive a leader who is wrong if he or she admits it or is transparent about what is a guess. Lack of clarity and its resulting confusion is less forgivable, especially if followers pay for the consequences. Symptoms include:
    - **A vision that keeps changing.** Evolution is to be expected in uncertain times, but wild swings in the way a leader talks about the change implies the leader doesn't understand the vision, and hasn't admitted that.
    - **KPI of the week.** Most organizations have too many key performance indicators. The change should have two to four KPIs at most on which the leader focuses. At British Airways it was customer service (as rated by JD Power) and profit.
    - **Tunnel-vision and trivia.** This is evidenced by a leader who, for instance, picks apart cost minutia in an innovation that will lead to doubling market share and profit.

- **"He doesn't want to lead you; he just wants you to follow him."** This was a quote about the villain Grindelwald from the movie *The Secrets of Dumbledore*. It describes a narcissist who craves the adulation of followers, but gives nothing back. He sees no value in others, but feels entitled to their worship. It is all about the leader when it should be all about the direction, the vision, the mission and the followers.

Symptoms of this leadership style include:
  - **A leader who values flattery and loyalty over truth-telling**. If the suck-ups always get the best roles, the most time with the leader, the biggest budgets, and most praise, then there is no one who will say to the leader, "This isn't working."
  - **A leader that explodes at bad news.** This person blames and denigrates the messenger. If you hear, "You tell him" or "Uhn-uhn, not me, you tell him," then the leader gets only honey-glazed info-crap. In this situation no news is not good news.
  - **Pseudo-empathy.** Some leaders have learned how to fake a genuine interest in followers. They say things like, "That must have been tough for you, but. . ." "I hear you, but. . ." Ignore anything said before the "but," no matter how sensitive it sounds.
  - **True anti-social behavior.** I'm enough of an optimist to believe that while some people call their bosses psychopaths or sociopaths, these are clinically rare in the workplace. There are some people who have the gift of sensitivity but misuse that gift to feign emotions; if combined with verbal acuity they can be quite manipulative.

If you work for someone that can elate you one day and then pinpoint your weaknesses and/or verbally eviscerate you to the point of tears the next, forget that it is an exciting place to work. Run away, far and fast.

But what should you do if you are the leader, if it is your job to make some part of the change happen? Here are a few ideas:

- **Don't be that person.** If you see yourself displaying any of the dysfunctions above, stop and get help. Help could be a friend, a coach, training – whatever it takes.

- **Focus on the direction, vision, and mission of the change**. People will pay attention to what you systematically pay attention to, measure, and control on a regular basis. Make sure it's the right thing.

- **Be clear about what you role model.** What's most important? Getting it right the first time or try-it-fix-it-try-it-again? Big Picture or sweat the small stuff? If you're running innovation and/or improvement initiatives, learn the methodology and do a project yourself. What you do people will emulate.

- **Control how you react to bad news, set-backs, incidents, and crises**. Don't shoot the messenger. Thank the people who bring bad news and tell the truth.

- **Give time and resources, rewards and status to people who tell the truth.** I once saw a leader make a joke out of SUWI (suck-up with integrity) vs. SUWOI (suck-up without integrity). The leadership team had felt required to flatter the previous leader regardless of truth or the good of the organization (SUWOI) and this leader was asking for just the opposite - truth and the good of the organization. The SUWI/SUWOI joke turned that around in two meetings.

- **Recruit, select, develop, and promote people who do the right things and do things right.** The people who make the change happen, get results (do the right things) and build good processes (do things right) should end up running the changed organization.

Remember, as Dr Edgar Schein pointed out, leaders shape culture by establishing what is important: "Culture is the long shadow of leadership behavior." Make sure your shadow is one that serves your people and the change you intend them to make.

CHAPTER 45.

THINKING ABOUT THINKING

I travelled for a lot of years. Still to this day, I get in the car, and my wife says, "Where are you going?"

"Oh,. . . I'm driving to the airport."

I turn the car around, as she whistles the theme song of Ray Bolger, the Scarecrow in the Wizard of Oz, "If I only had a brain."

This is the kind of mistake that comes from being on autopilot. It happens to us all, like when we walk into a room and suddenly can't remember why we wanted to go in there.

In his book *Thinking Fast and Thinking Slow*, Daniel Kahneman describes two thinking processes: System 1 (automatic processing) and System 2 (focused conscious thought). System 1, automatic processing, accounts for 90 percent of our brain activity, and System 2 does the other 10 percent. It is a good thing that this is true. Imagine having to drive to work with the same brain activity that you had when you first learned to drive a car: *OK, now ease off on the clutch, give it a little gas, not too much, watch out for that car on your left, give the bicycle a little more room, you're coming up to a stop sign so start slowing down.*

Our conscious brains are very powerful. When we focus we can calculate, evaluate, solve problems, plan, and execute plans. But our conscious brains can **only do one thing at a time.** So we switch out of System 2 into System 1 as quickly as we can; our brain goes on autopilot.

Our autopilot brain still makes decisions and directs our actions, but it does so based upon the frequency with which it has made a particular decision in the past.

It is also susceptible to suggestion. What our unconscious brains see is often what we expect to see. "That light was <u>green</u>, officer." This selective perception can cause us to see things that aren't there or to not see things that are there based upon our expectations.

In my work with leaders in the chemical, and oil and gas industries, I spent a lot of time thinking about "brain failures." It turned out that a substantial percentage of Process Safety Incidents resulted from brains on autopilot or expectation-based inspection.

So, I believe leaders need to get control of their thinking. They must use their conscious brains to focus on what's important and to run periodic checks on their automatic processing brains.

This is a critical requirement in light of the overwhelming amount of information available to us. Some of this is driven by ubiquitous technology and some is driven by the lionizing of multitasking. I often saw "ability to multitask" as a specific requirement on entry-level management job descriptions. That said to me "we know we're giving you too much to do; we just expect you can do a bunch of things at the same time."

Let me be clear. **Multitasking is a myth.** What we are doing is switch-tasking, rapidly switching between our conscious brain and our automatic processing brain. Switch-tasking has been shown to degrade overall productivity, decrease working memory, and compromise the ability to focus.

So as a leader, your first act is to get control of your thought processes. Create space where you can use your working memory effectively. Review emails at regular times, say, 10:00 a.m. and 2:00 p.m. Quit saying, "My door is always open." Maintain your accessibility to your people, but occasionally close your door, and find time to think about how you think.

Self-awareness is the foundation of leadership. How could we expect someone to follow unless we understand how we ourselves think, behave, and come across to others? It all starts with thinking.

Remember Jung's two primary brain functions? The first is perceiving - the way we take in information; the second is deciding - the way we draw conclusions from that information and prescribe action. He further broke each of these functions into preferences, two ways most people *prefer* to take in information, or decide and act.

Do you prefer to take in information in an ordered, organized, step-by-step way or are you more comfortable skipping around and reading between the lines? There is no right or wrong way here, just differences between people.

Do you prefer to decide things by weighing pros and cons, or making spreadsheets or balance sheets? Or do you most often decide things by comparing expected outcomes to deeply held values, often about people? Again, there is no right or wrong and these are *preferences,* not absolute irrevocable personality traits. It's like left-handedness. Some of us have stronger preferences for our handedness than others, but left-handed people often become more ambidextrous because they live in a right-handed world.

By now you may be thinking, *Oh, he's going to push the Myers-Briggs Type Indicator.* The MBTI is an instrument that measures Jungian brain function preferences together with an understanding of external orientation (gravitate toward people and things) or internal orientation (toward concepts and ideas). I do like the MBTI as a way to understand differences among people, but I think it is misused to select people for jobs or compose teams. It is much better used to understand one's self or as the basis of discussion between people trying to understand each other.

There are many models for the way people think that I like as well - David Kolb's Learning Style Inventory, Ned Hermann's Whole Brain Model, Stuart Atkins' LIFO, The Gallup Strengths Finder, to name a few. I am agnostic as to the analytical model leaders use to think about their own thinking. However, I do recommend that a leader try to understand how he or she naturally thinks and to become more mentally ambidextrous. For example, to push the limits of how you think about strategy, use the Michael Porter Five Forces of Industry Structure model <u>and</u> the value engineering approach of Chan Kim and Renée Mauborgne's Blue Ocean Strategy.

A client once said to me, "I like having you around because you think of things that would never occur to me. You see the impact of my decisions or actions long before they happen." This is one of the nicest compliments I ever received. I think Fred valued my intuition and perhaps my "emotional intelligence" (to quote Daniel Goleman). But the subtext of what he said was: "You think weird!"

It's extremely useful for a leader to be surrounded by others who think weird. Recognize your own thinking patterns and the limits of your cognitive flexibility and hire people who fill out your flat sides. The drive for diversity in organizations is not just to create a fairer workplace. It is also to create a more complete thinking style, a collection of people who can think about an issue from many different perspectives in order to produce better decisions and more sustainable results.

There is one place where thinking flexibility doesn't work: in problem solving. Problem solving requires two different kinds of thinking:

- Divergent thinking, where
    - The objective is the quantity of ideas
    - You suspend all judgment
    - You use tools like brainstorming and lateral thinking
- Convergent thinking, where
    - The objective is the best idea
    - You group and combine ideas, evaluate ideas, and plan execution of ideas
    - You use tools like affinity diagrams, prioritization criteria matrix, and critical path method

Leaders must insist that these two types of thinking be kept separate in solving problems, generating innovation, and improving processes. Just as "that's a dumb idea" poisons idea generation, "here's another thought" derails idea selection and planning.

Thinking about our own thinking involves introspection and strives for flexibility, either within ourselves or within our team. It also requires the discipline to focus on the right type of thinking at the right time.

It isn't intended to turn us into the smartest guys in the room (that's what the guys at Enron used to say, and that didn't work out too well), but rather to recognize that none of us is as smart as all of us. And to give us the kind of confidence the scarecrow felt when the Wizard of Oz gave him a diploma:

> The square root of the hypotenuse of an isosceles right triangle is equal to the sum of the square roots of the other two sides. Oh Joy! Oh Rapture! I've got a brain.

Yes, I do. And it is mine to expand and to use.

CHAPTER 46

PEOPLE ARE DIFFERENT? REALLY?

"That's why Baskin Robbins has thirty-one flavors of ice cream." That was how my friend Brad explained that people are different to his six-year-old daughter. Brad's daughter has now graduated from university, but I used his Baskin Robbins analogy a lot over the years.

We've always known people are different and we humans have been trying to analyze and categorize those differences for a long time.

History of categories of people differences

In 500 B.C.E. Alcmaeon of Croton theorized that differences in people were due to humors, bodily fluids: blood, water, choler / bile, or phlegm. About the same time Hippocrates - the father of medicine – calculated ratios of humors, wrote them down and popularized the theory.

This paradigm held power until the nineteenth century and we still have these words in the English language: sanguine (too much blood, overly warm and optimistic), melancholy (too much water, tears and sadness), choleric / bilious (too much choler or bile - bad tempered, nasty), and phlegmatic (too much phlegm, stuffy, stolid, unemotional).

Wilhelm Wundt and William James pretty much invented psychology in the late nineteenth century, both saying that differences in the human mind explained differences in people. Wundt, a structuralist, said differences in the brain and body were best studied through an inside-to-outside scientific approach . James, a functionalist, believed studying behavioral function from an outside to inside analysis would yield better results. Both structuralists and functionalists were concerned with the conscious mind.

Sigmund Freud dwelled upon the unconscious, basic drives affecting behavior like sex and the fear of death, which were common to all people. He theorized that differences were caused by these drives and the degree to which socialization (super ego) constrained them.

Carl Jung hypothesized a collective unconscious containing archetypes that guided all people. He also identified two mental functions, taking in information and making decisions, and posited that differences in these functions might be inherited.

BF Skinner ushered in Behaviorism, which says all behavior is determined by experience. Most of Skinner's experimentation was conducted with rats in mazes - probably the best analogy for contemporary organization life.

Despite rich experimentation in psychology, early management theory assumed people were the same and that motivation was delivered by a method used with mules, a carrot dangled in front of the nose and a stick applied to the rear end.

We came a long way in management theory in the late twentieth century, although too many are stuck in the muleskinner mindset of performance management. Carrot and stick still rules.

Psychometrics used by companies
Some companies use the Intelligence Quotient (IQ) test to select and sort workers despite the fact that it is culturally biased and measures language, deductive analysis and spatial problem solving rather than general intelligence.

Other companies use personality tests such as Caliper, 16pf, California Personality Assessment, etc. These tests typically measure extroversion, emotional stability, agreeableness, conscientiousness and openness to new experience.

It is often the case that companies use IQ tests and personality tests without the input or interpretation of psychologists trained to administer them.

Tests that show differences among people are a cottage industry. I'm going to highlight four that I think have value: Meyers Briggs Type Inventory (MBTI), Life Orientations (LIFO), DISC assessment personality profile, and Gallup's CliftonStrengths.

Myers-Briggs Type Indicator (MBTI)

As noted, Carl Jung theorized two conscious brain functions: perceiving, or taking in information; and judging, making decisions on that information. Katherine Briggs studied with Jung. She later expanded the Jungian concept of cognitive function and added research on internal or external focus and lifestyle (do you prefer taking in information or deciding and acting?)

In 1954 her daughter Isabel Briggs-Myers codified this work into the Myers-Briggs Type Indicator. Each function or orientation is a continuum between two different preferences.

The word preference is key. It is like right or left handedness. Some people have such a strong hand preference that their non-dominant hand is quite limited. Some people are ambidextrous.

The resulting four continua are each defined by two poles representing extreme answers to questions:

Where do you get energized?	
I – internally - world of concepts and ideas Introvert-----------------------	E – externally - world of people and places ---------------------------Extrovert
How do you prefer to take in information?	
S- facts confirmed by senses step by step Sensing -----------------------	N – connections, associations - skip around ---------------------------- Intuiting
How do you make decisions?	
T – logical ordered process, +/- charts Thinking ----------------------	F – comparing impact on people and values ---------------------------- Feeling
How do you prefer to live your life?	
J- deciding and acting in a planned way Judging-----------------------	P – learning and experiencing as it comes ------------------------------Perceiving

This taxonomy produces sixteen personality types, each with strength of preference. For example, I am an ENTP, but I am only marginally an E and P, and at the top of the scale on N and considerably above the mid-point on T.

I used the MBTI more than any psychometric assessment in my consulting with leadership teams. It is well researched and documented as to statistical validity and the reliability of individual questions. Critics say the theory was created from thin air. Perhaps, but it rings true.

What I like about MBTI is that absorbing information and making decisions are critical to business, and being aware of differences avoids misunderstanding and unproductive conflict.

I also like that the instrument doesn't portray introverts as shy, broken people. Introverts relate and converse just like extraverts, but are simply more energized by thinking and reflecting.

Life Orientation (LIFO)

The LIFO assessment was created in 1967 by Drs. Stuart Atkins and Allan Katcher and is based upon the psychological research of Erich

Fromm, Carl Rogers and Abraham Maslow. I was introduced to LIFO at Gemini Consulting induction training and we used it with client teams.

The LIFO instrument places your life orientation among four categories:

- Supporting - Giving - people who strive to include others, be helpful, and fair
- Controlling -Taking – people who strive for competence, results, direct action
- Adapting - Dealing – people who strive for harmony, know people, are flexible
- Conserving - Holding - people who strive for the right answer, are analytical, slow but sure

The report shows a person's primary mode and a secondary fall back if under stress. For example, my profile is supporting-giving primary and adapting-dealing secondary. Apparently I'm prepared to be helpful at most times, but turn into a conflict negotiator under stress.

"Tell me what you want. Let's see if we can find a win/win."

However, my controlling/ taking score is also high, so under time pressure, I sometimes just take charge to get things done. This either shows that I'm tough to be around, or reveals the limits of self-report personality instruments.

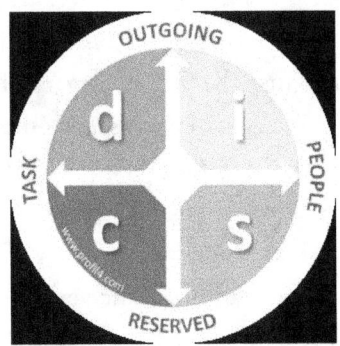

DISC Assessment Personality Profile

The DISC assessment was created in 1956 by industrial psychologist Walter Clarke, and is based upon the 1928 research and theory of William Moulton Marston.

The report places a person in four categories with a percentage score:

- Dominance – Directing: people who use force to overcome resistance
- Inducement – Influencing: people who use charm to overcome resistance
- Submission –Steady: people who accept and accommodate resistance
- Compliance – Cautious: people who carefully follow directions to overcome resistance

DISC theory concerns managing an environment and so is context dependent. There are only four categories. My DISC scores are within one percentage point of each other, clouding interpretation and making strengths and weaknesses difficult to determine.

CliftonStrengths by Gallup

CliftonStrengths was created in 2001 after much research by Donald O. Clifton at the University of Nebraska. Clifton's intention was to study the personality traits of the "best of the best" so companies could hire according to those strengths. The Gallup Organization, known as a pollster but having deep survey data expertise, acquired Clifton's company Selection Research Inc. and together they created the Clifton Strengths-Finder, now known as CliftonStrengths.

CliftonStrengths has been widely adopted by the coaching industry. Building upon your strengths to overcome your weaknesses is a positive approach. The current version has 177 paired comparison questions over 34 strength domains.

The report urges the respondent to pay most attention to the top five identified strengths. My top five strengths (Learner, Empathy, Achiever,

Strategic, and Communication) aligned with my perception. So either I know myself or my self-delusion took over as I answered the questionnaire.

Issues with psychometric personality assessment

Theory base, reliability and validity. Critics of these and other psychometric personality assessment often focus on the origins of theory or the statistical reliability and validity studies of the instrument. It is true that many of the theory origins are subjective and some instruments test better for reliability and validity than others, but there are other issues.

Subjectivity. All are self-report questionnaire data, i.e., my perception of myself. Therefore the answers are inherently subjective and prone to cognitive biases such confirmation bias, i.e,, finding what you expect. If you want to find out how well you know yourself (free of confirmation bias) ask for feedback about your strengths from others who know you. Also do you have rater bias? Some start in the middle of the questionnaire scale and never move more than one point; some use the entire scale, but are skewed to one side or the other, which makes comparing relative strengths problematic.

Non-predictive results. Some companies use these instruments to hire, staff teams, promote and sometimes fire people who "don't fit." The results of these tests by themselves do not produce the objective predictive data to justify those decisions beyond a reasonable doubt.

Best uses for personality assessment

Personal development. A good use of these instruments is to learn about yourself. Will you only learn what you already know? Maybe, but treat results as a starting point. For another view, talk with others about them – a significant other, friend, teammate, coach, or your boss.

For example, I score myself particularly low on LIFO Conserving - Holding and DISC Compliance – Caution, which might imply I am a spendthrift. My wife says that doesn't ring true, especially on my cheap days.

Team formation. I wouldn't use these instruments to select members for a team; that should be based on capabilities and connections. However, comparing and discussing results can help a team form a working approach that respects differences and capitalizes on strengths.

What about career planning?

Could knowledge of one's strengths cause us to apply for a particular job? Yes. Could an MBTI type or a DISC or LIFO profile guide you in what jobs to seek? Yes, but interest, skill base, and opportunity might be more important.

What to do about differences among people

In ancient Greece the Oracle at Delphi was a kind of psychometric testing and leadership coaching center. To help the leaders who came from far and wide to ask her advice the Oracle had a measurement system (animal entrails divination) and a theory base (147 maxims of the Oracle). She also had a contractual disclaimer in three maxims enshrined on the entrance, which are not bad advice for those evaluating themselves and the differences among people:

- **Know thyself** - get the opinions of others in addition to self-report.
- **Nothing in excess** - don't overuse assessments that pigeonhole people.
- **Surety brings ruin** - allow for change of circumstance, personal growth, and adaptation. People will always surprise you.

People are different. They will always surprise you if you ask their point of view, or background. I used Brad's "That's why Baskin Robbins has 31 flavors" with my six-year-old granddaughter. She said, "I know, and it would be a very boring world if we were all the same."

Yes, it would.

CHAPTER 47.

HELPING PEOPLE THROUGH CHANGE

This picture comes from an article I wrote for *Transformation Magazine*, a publication of Gemini Consulting. At the time, I thought the article was my definitive statement on "everything you needed to know about change."

When I think back on that article, it was about large-scale change that happened all at one time; it had a distinct "here's how you <u>make</u> change happen" top-down orientation. Some of my later work in innovation and improvement was more organic and added more bottom-up work with change teams and internal consulting groups.

This drawing originally came from that top-down orientation. I started with Gemini's Emotional Cycle of Change, the 'U' shaped curve:

- Uninformed Optimism
- Informed Pessimism
- Informed Openness
- Informed Optimism

Gemini used this change emotion curve to educate its consultants and client teams about what to expect. It is roughly based upon Elizabeth Kubler Ross's stages of grief, and it fits with what some people go through in change.

HELPING PEOPLE GO THROUGH CHANGE

Company

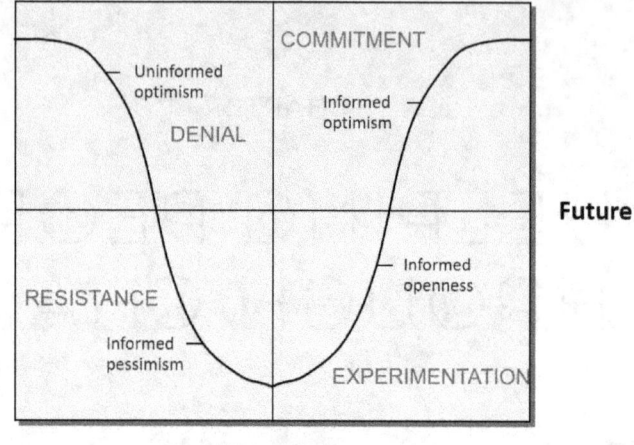

Personal

Source: *A Change Process*, Alan Cay Culler 1997,
Adapted from Gemini Consulting and
Managing Organizational Change, Cynthia Scott, Dennis Jaffe, 1989

Source: "In Praise of Followers" by Dr. Richard Kelley, *Harvard Business*

I combined this with the Scott and Jaffe quadrant model that explained what happened at various stages in a change process:

- If you were in denial, you might be looking backwards and at the way the company used to be. This aligns with Uninformed Optimism.
- If you were resisting, you were looking back at your personal situation, what you had lost. This aligns with Informed Pessimism.
- In order to move on, you'd need to experiment with different personal roles with a future focus. This aligns with Informed Openness.
- Finally committing or recommitting to the company with a future focus aligns with Informed Optimism.

My thought in combining these two models was that leaders could help someone focus on the future and the company, and then move the change along. What I wrote communicated that I wanted people to get through all this messy emotional stuff and change the company. Yikes.

How I look at this drawing today: people's reactions to change
I recognize now how naïve that was. Saying to someone struggling with change, "Hey, you just need to focus on the future and the company instead of the past and yourself" isn't likely to be successful.

Some people actually do grieve the loss of their identity that was wrapped up in the old company preacquisition, or their old way of doing things pre-change.

Elizabeth Kübler Ross's Five Stages of Grief are:
- **Shock**, including disbelief and denial
- **Anger**, directed at the deceased, self, or lashed out at anyone
- **Bargaining,** with God, the medical community, family, "If I do this will you save him (me)?"
- **Depression,** "Nothing will ever be the same again, I can't go on"
- **Acceptance,** "It's over; life goes on."

Since I created my diagram, I have lost both parents, one sister, one nephew, and a close friend and business partner. I have grieved and been around many others who are grieving.

I have worked with people in companies going through acquisitions, including hostile takeovers. I have coached business owners whose business failed. I have reorganized companies, seeing people who've been transferred after devoting their lives to one business unit or function, a move that radically altered their business identity. I observed many people go through the "Emotional Cycle of Change."

It doesn't matter which curve you are on; whether you are grieving loss of a loved one or emotionally processing change, these things are true:
- **It is an individual journey**. You are processing your emotion, something only you can do.

CHANGE LEADER? WHO ME?

- **It isn't a straight line or a one-way journey.** You bounce back and forth between phases.
- **You can get stuck in one phase.** "De Nile [denial] is not just a river in Egypt," is funny for a reason. And perhaps you know someone stuck in anger - Louis Black's comedy and his role in *Inside Out* are parodies of that.
- **You can't just skip to the end**. Some individuals might spend less time in one phase or another, but the emotional journey is the same.

There was a time when I made fun of organizational development consultants who conducted funerals for the old ways, carrying certain values forward into the new. I still think it's a little woo-woo, but I understand the usefulness.

In truth, I saw the remnants of denial in employees who did not say goodbye to the old. British European Airways (BEA) and British Overseas Airways Corporation (BOAC) still each had different British Airways logos eight years after they became BA. At BP everyone asked where you came from - Amoco, Arco, etc. Some workers wore overalls with their old logo, years after the acquisitions.

How I look at this drawing today: paths of discovery
While not a roadmap for leaders to direct people, this drawing could be useful to individuals facing a change.

- I could write down my individual reactions and place them in the appropriate quadrants
- I could view the past to future as a personal path and a company path
  - What am I leaving behind? What is the company leaving behind?
  - What am I carrying forward? What is the company carrying forward?

- What new is created for me/us in the future?
- What are my choices, options, degrees of freedom?

A team might use the drawing in the same way if they choose to do so.

If asked, a leader, a coach, or a consultant might use this as a process with an individual or a team.

To be helpful to those grieving or having difficulty with change, a leader might:

1. Wait to be asked.
2. Start by just listening.
3. Summarize what you have heard.
4. Assess where someone is on Elizabeth Kübler Ross's Five Stages of Grief.
   - Someone in Shock or denial mostly needs someone to listen.
   - Someone in Anger may need to vent, but counseled not to be threatening to self or others.
   - Someone in Bargaining may be feeling survivor's guilt or taking too much responsibility for the negative effects of the change. They might be asked what that sounds like, and if they really think it will help.
   - Someone in Depression might be directed to professional help.
   - Someone moving toward Acceptance might be encouraged to experiment or to act on things they are committed to in the new order.
   - Prepare for, and try not to judge, backsliding and revisiting.
5. Prepare for, and try not to judge, backsliding and revisiting.
6. Avoid saying things like "Get over it," "Move on," "Let's look at the bright side. At least you have _____" or "Relax and enjoy it.

Remember:

Expect people to be different. Some reactions to change might be predictable, but not all.

Change must be a choice. A person needs to see the compelling case for change for himself or herself as well as for the company.

Help must be asked for. Some people will work their way through change on their own. Some may talk with their friends. If they turn to you for help, as their leader it is a time to listen. Then ask questions and perhaps – perhaps – offer answers.

CHAPTER 48.

LEARN TO FOLLOW

Lately, I've been reviewing my life. I suppose that might be expected for someone my age. After all, looking back is easier than looking forward, reflecting is easier than planning to change and at seventy-five-plus, there's a lot to review.

The presenting cause for all this navel-gazing is my new "career" as a writer. I'm midway through writing three books: *Traveling the Consulting Road; Change Leader? Who Me?;* and *Wisdom from Unusual Places.*

In actuality, the first book could have been called *My Mistakes as a Consultant.* This book, my second, could be titled *My Mistakes Leading Change,* and the upcoming third book *My Mistakes in Life, plus some interesting people who tried to set me straight.* Are you sensing a theme?

Perhaps my biggest mistake leading change is that I denied that I was leading anything. As a result I gave too little thought to why anyone would follow me.

Truth be told, for much of my life, I was a terrible follower. I battled anyone who had the slightest bit of power over me. I used to joke as an independent consultant that I work for myself because I discovered I'm a lot nicer to clients than I am to bosses.

And I taught leadership

I designed and ran workshops about leading change for corporate managers. I emphasized attracting followers by joking "Are you a leader? Or just delusional? Look over your shoulder. Is there anyone there? Well then . . ." I don't think I spent enough time on followership.

Following can be an act of leadership

I wasn't always a poor follower. Several times in my life, I was committed to an idea, a leader's vision, the purpose of an organization. I worked hard to get stuff done, not just stuff I was assigned to do, but stuff that aligned with the vision. I built my own competency and asked for help when I needed it. I encouraged peers to have the same spirit and confronted anyone who veered away from the vision.

I experienced good followership in many contexts, Boy Scouts, the theatre, Habitat for Humanity house building, and in every job I had, from factory worker, waiter, and booking agent to trainer and consultant.

Recently, I read a *Psychology Today* blog post by Dr. Ronald Riggio, professor in Leadership and Organizational Psychology at Claremont McKenna College, entitled "In Praise of Followership." Dr Riggio referenced a *Harvard Business Review* article "In Praise of Followers," written by Dr. Robert Kelley of Carnegie Mellon University, which I had read when I lived in Pittsburgh in the late '80s. I reread that article.

Here are some points from each:
Dr. Riggio:
- Research on leadership has paid little attention to the critical role of followers.
- Leaders and followers co-create leadership in a specific context. There is no leadership without followers.
- It is imperative that followers support the leader when the mission is a good one or stand up to the leader when the path and goals are wrong.

Dr. Kelley:

- A good follower has active behavior and independent critical thinking.
- Good followers self-manage well.
- Good followers commit to the vision, the organization, the purpose or the mission.
- Good followers build the competencies they need to deliver.
- Good followers are courageous, honest, and credible.

Nowhere does either professor recommend sucking up to a leader, blind loyalty, only delivering news the leader wants to hear, or putting up with a toxic environment.

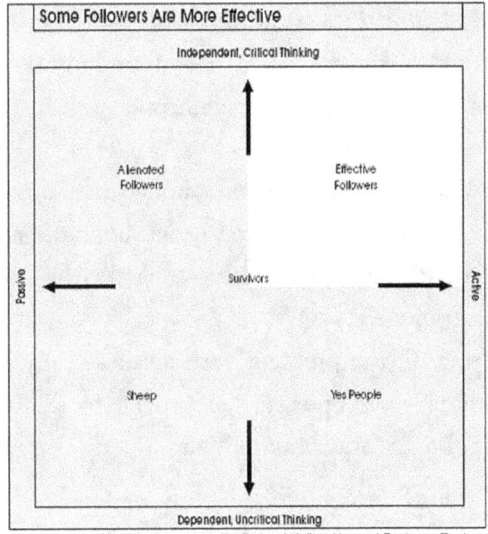

Source: "In Praise of Followers" by Dr. Richard Kelley, Harvard Business Review, November 1988

Learning to become an effective follower

Dr. Kelley uses a matrix to evaluate follower behavior.

Effective Followers (upper right quadrant) show independent, critical thinking with active behavior patterns.

Followers Kelley calls Sheep (lower left quadrant) are too willing to accept whatever the Leader thinks or says.

Those he calls Yes People (lower right quadrant) operate from fear or seek approval, betraying the requirement for courage and honesty, and losing all credibility as a result.

Alienated Followers (upper left quadrant) display passive-aggressive behavior. When I failed as an effective follower, my particular failure mode too often fell into this quadrant with passive-aggressive behavior I might have described as righteous indignation. Over time I learned how to disagree agreeably, as Kelley recommends, but it took me far too long.

According to Kelley, effective followers confront leaders constructively. I have done more than my share of confronting, sometimes more constructively than other times. Perhaps my best follower behavior, though, was in getting stuff done. I learned early to deliver on what I was assigned and to look for things that needed to be done and just doing them. That trait increased my workload, but it bought me some forgiveness for my disagreeable disagreement.

Some of my best follower behavior I honed in leaderless groups, or teams where the leadership role rotated according to the skills and knowledge needed. I also learned a great deal from facilitating groups and keeping my opinions to myself.

I'm still working on the problem with authority, my counter-dependent behavior thing. I'm helped in that struggle by the fact that as a retiree I have fewer bosses, and as an old man others just shake their heads and smile when I get obstreperous.

I've also learned that "do as I say not as I do" doesn't work with children and grandchildren, so they're lousy followers too, but . . .

. . . maybe some of you, dear readers, can learn from my mistakes. **Learn to follow.**

CHAPTER 49

SOME FINAL THOUGHTS

"Who wants to be a leader, anyway?"

The truculent twenty-something manager in my change leadership workshop went on to complain, "I can't do anything to make my people happy and I can't do anything to make my boss happy."

As it turned out, the next slide on deck was the Machiavelli quote mentioned earlier about how change has no constituency:

There is nothing more difficult to take in hand, more
perilous to conduct, or more uncertain in its success,
than to take the lead in the introduction of a new
order of things, because the innovator has for enemies
all those who
have prospered under the old order, and lukewarm
defenders
in those who might do well under the new.

"It's more than that," he said. "I'm sure there is a plan for this change, but somehow it's up to us to just <u>figure</u> <u>it</u> <u>out</u>!"

Others jumped in and I let the group complain for a bit. Change is tough. Once I facilitated a leadership group one level below the C-suite at one of the world's largest corporations. Their combined annual budget was bigger than many countries and yet they complained bitterly about "those guys up there." It was one of the few times I can remember losing my temper.

"Guys! You do realize that for a hundred thousand people in this company, YOU are _those guys up there_!" They stopped whining.

Ultimately both the executive group and the millennials came around to taking action on what they could, and asking for information where they needed it. Sometimes leaders just need to hear the message of the quote attributed to Thomas Paine, the Revolutionary War period pamphleteer. "Lead, follow, or get out of the way." Or, more recently, as Bob Dylan sang, "Don't stand in the doorway, don't block up the hall... For the times, they are a-changin'."

Sometimes a leader will be required to lead changes – being clear about direction and bringing followers along. And he or she will have to just figure out what hasn't been thought of or thought through. A leader will also be required to follow sometimes; following enthusiastically is a kind of leadership too.

I have seen huge corporations change successfully. I have seen leaders emerge from the ranks and do amazing things. I have also seen people who should be leaders obstruct or otherwise block change. Leadership is a choice for those who lead change and for those who choose to follow. I hope that these stories of leaders help others choose that adventure.

ADDITIONAL RESOURCES:

This book represents my point of view on change leadership evolved over thirty-seven years as a change consultant and a work life of forty-five years. Change leaders must be prepared to change themselves, to expand their knowledge and skill, to improve themselves, and to help their organizations improve and innovate. They must absorb a great deal of information and help their organizations integrate new information.

Here are some resources that influenced me:

Leadership

Bennis, Warren. *On Becoming a Leader.* Fourth Edition. New York, NY: Basic Books, 2009. The first of the late Dr. Bennis's books on leadership, originally written in 1989, contains wonderful advice and case examples.

Covey, Stephen R. *The Seven Habits of Highly Effective People.* New York, NY: Simon & Schuster, 1989. This book has sold millions of copies and has spawned an entire industry of leadership self-development. It is definitely worth a read.

De Pree, Max. *Leadership is an Art.* New York, NY: Crown Currency, 2011. De Pree was the chairman of office furniture company Hermann Miller and wrote several books about servant leadership. This is the best and a classic.

Frisch, Bob. *Who's in the Room? How Great Leaders Structure and Manage the Teams Around Them.* San Francisco, CA: Jossey-Bass, 2021. Leadership decisions about change and about hiring consultants. Frisch makes the point that these decisions are often made by an executive and a few close advisors, "the team with no name," and improving process and structure will lead to better decisions.

Gerstner, Louis V. *Who Says Elephants Can't Dance? Leading a Great Enterprise Through Dramatic Change.* New York, NY: Harper Business, 2002. This is an excellent description of the turnaround of IBM that Gerstner led. It's more than a little egocentric and ignores the role of the expanding economy of the dot-com era, the massive workforce reductions at the time, and the substantial financial gain Gerstner received during his tenure, but it lays out the process of saving a company.

Kleiner, Art, *Who Really Matters: The Core Group Theory of Power, Privilege, and Success.* New York, NY: Currency/Doubleday, 2003. Written in the immediate post-Enron collapse era, Kleiner demonstrates that there is a core group of individuals in every organization who really run things. Senior leaders are in the group, some board members, maybe a key investor, customer, union leader or supplier, but these people direct the corporation to serve their interests, sometimes positively sometimes not. Change requires this group.

Sinek, Simon. *Start with Why: How Great Leaders Inspire Everyone to Take Action.* New York, NY: Portfolio/Penguin, 2009. There is a series of Sinek's books that are excellent, but this one is the first and the best at helping leaders make change.

Springsteen, Bruce. *Born to Run.* New York, NY: Simon & Schuster, 2016.

Zaleznik, Abraham. *The Managerial Mystique: Restoring Leadership in Business.* New York, NY: Harper Collins Publishers, 1989.

Zaleznik, Abraham. "Managers and Leaders: Are They Different?" Boston, MA: *Harvard Business Review,* 1977.

Followership

Kelly, Robert. "In Praise of Followers." Boston, MA: *Harvard Business Review,* November 1988

Riggio, Ronald E. "In Praise of Followership." *Psychology Today,* March 2023

Change

Burke, W. Warner. *Organization Change: Theory and Practice Sixth Edition*. Thousand Oaks, CA: Sage Publications Inc., 2023. Perhaps the best textbook on change in organizations by one of the leading lights of organizational development.

Gladwell, Malcolm. *The Tipping Point.* New York, NY: Little, Brown and Company, 2006. Gladwell explains how change happens when a critical mass of opinion leaders adopt an idea. Gladwell's book *Outliers,* published in 2008, explains the importance of timing and practice.

Heath, Chip, and Dan Heath. *Switch: How to Change Things When Change is Hard.* New York, NY: Crown, 2010. A good explanation of how to manage the emotional limiters to change.

Johnson, Spencer and Kenneth Blanchard. *Who Moved My Cheese? An A-Mazing Way to Deal with Change in Your Work and Your Life.* New York, NY: G.P Putnam and Sons, 1998.

Kotter, John P. *Leading Change.* Boston, MA: Harvard Business Review Press, 2012. Also, *The Heart of Change was* written with Dan S. Cohen (same publisher and year). There are a lot of books about change models that talk in terms of steps or phases. Kotter describes the requirements for successful change.

Lippitt, Mary. *Leadersheep: Saving the Herd, A Fable about Successfully Executing Change.* Charleston, SC: Palmetto Publishing, 2024. A fun fable about a sheep dog saving a herd of sheep from starvation lays out her five-component framework for getting everyone on board and successfully making change happen. Dr. Lippitt has written many other books on leadership and change. This is the simplest, but her common sense rings true.

Litwin, George H., John Bray, and Kathleen Lusk-Brooke. *Mobilizing the Organization: Bringing Strategy to Life.* London: Prentice Hall / Simon & Schuster, 1995. A book, to which I contributed, tells the stories of some of the most important change projects of my early career.

Phelan, Karen G. *Who Moved My Holy Hand Grenade: Everything I*

needed to know in business I learned from Monty Python and the Holy Grail.
Mahwah, NJ: Lineson Publishing, 2013. A humorous sendup of change
management theory that contains very helpful advice in spite of itself.

Sax, David. *The Revenge of Analog: Real Things and Why They Matter.*
New York, NY: Public Affairs/ Perseus/Hachette, 2016. Sax reports on,
and forecasts a reaction to, the digital revolution in which people return
to analog forms such as vinyl records, crafts, and small retail shops. He
expands on this in his 2022 manifesto *The Future is Analog* wherein he
argues for more human-scale business and society.

Change consulting

Culler, Alan Cay. *Traveling the Consulting Road: Career Wisdom for New
Consultants, Candidates, and Their Mentors.* West Orange, NJ: Unusual
Wisdom Press, 2023. This book is tailored to consultants, but has more
depth on change methodologies and tools.

Maister, David H. *Managing the Professional Services Firm.* New York,
NY: Free Press, 2007. I first encountered the concepts in this book as a
series of monographs written by Maister in the 1970s. I referenced them
in the chapter on internal consulting firms.

Maister, David H., Charles H. Green, David L. Galford. *The Trusted
Advisor.* New York, NY: Free Press, 1981. This work contains their version of the Trust formula.

Strategy

Ansoff, H. Igor. *Corporate Strategy.* New York, NY: McGraw-Hill, 1965.
There are many excellent books by Ansoff on strategic management, but
this is the one that started it all.

Frisch, Bob, Logan Chandler. "Off-sites that Work." *Harvard Business
Review*, June 1, 2006. A perfect roadmap for preparing for and facilitating a strategy off-site.

Jemison, David B., and Phillippe Haspeslagh. *Managing Acquisitions:
Creating Value through Corporate Renewal.* New York, NY: Free Press,

1991. A detailed plan for integration.

Kim, W. Chan, and Renée Mauborgne. *Blue Ocean Strategy.* Boston, MA: Harvard Business School Publishing, 2004. INSEAD professors demonstrate how to differentiate your business so you have no competition.

Porter, Michael. *Competitive Strategy.* New York, NY: The Free Press, 1980. Porter details the industry analysis that should help businesses decide whether or not to enter an industry and how to differentiate their business.

Quantitative continuous improvement

Deming, W. Edwards. *Out of the Crisis.* Cambridge, MA: MIT Press, 1982. Dr. Deming, the guru of the quality movement, has the best prescription for managing continuous improvement.

Gawande, Atul. *The Checklist Manifesto.* New York, NY: Picador/Macmillan, 2010. Using medical examples, Gawande describes how to ensure outcomes by making sure that all important activities are completed on time.

Gonick, Larry, and Woollcott Smith. *The Cartoon Guide to Statistics.* New York, NY: HarperCollins Publishers, 1993. A fun way to learn statistics? That sounds like an oxymoron. It isn't.

Lynch, Richard L., and Kelvin F. Cross. *Measure Up: Yardsticks for Continuous Improvement.* Malden, MA: Blackwell Publishers, 1991. A good description of how to choose the best metrics.

Spear, Steven J. *The High Velocity Edge: How Market Leaders Leverage Operational Excellence to Beat the Competition.* New York, NY: McGraw Hill, 2010. Spears earned his PhD writing about the Toyota Production System. Building upon this example he describes how to accelerate change.

Innovation

Drucker, Peter F. *Innovation and Entrepreneurship.* New York, NY: Routlege/HarperCollins Publishers, 1985. One of the most read of Drucker's books provides no-nonsense how-tos for running an innovative business.

Hamel, Gary. *Leading the Revolution: How to Thrive in Turbulent Times by Making Innovation a Way of Life.* Boston, MA: Harvard Business School Press, 2000. Hamel has written many excellent books. This one is memorable for the detailed blueprint for the Royal Shell internal venture capital system used to fund innovation.

Kelley, Thomas, and Jonathan Littman. *The Art of Innovation: Lessons in Creativity from IDEO, America's Leading Design Firm.* New York, NY: Doubleday, 2001. Stanford University's Human Centered Design model described in detail.

Michaelides, Dimis. *The Art of Innovation: Integrating Creativity in Organizations.* Cyprus: Performa Productions, 2007. Michaelides offers an artistic presentation that drives innovative thought through image and symbol.

Organizations, teams, climate and culture

Burke, W. Warner, and George H. Litwin. "A Causal Model of Organizational Performance and Change." *Journal of Management* 1992; 18. Thousand Oaks, CA: Sage Publications Inc, 1992. This is the first publication of the Burke-Litwin Model, a collaboration of my mentor George Litwin and Warner Burke during the British Airways transformation 1984-87. This open systems model drove a great deal of my work in change and is continually cited at the best description of organizations transactional and transformational elements.

Butler, Ava S. *Mission Critical Meetings.* Tucson, AZ: Wheatmark, 2014. Tips for meetings.

Collins, Jim. *The Good to Great* series (*Good to Great, Built to Last, How the Mighty Fall, Great By Choice, Turning the Flywheel*). New York, NY: Harper Business 2001-2020. Peter Drucker advised Collins not to form a consulting firm because then he would have to "feed the beast," i.e., continually look for clients. Collins' research has arguably made a more significant contribution than if he had been on a client acquisition flywheel.

Heskett, James L. *Managing in the Service Economy.* Boston, MA: Harvard Business School Press, 1986. The first of several books by Heskett explaining service businesses.

Katzenbach, Jon R., and Douglas K. Smith. *The Wisdom of Teams.* Boston, MA: Harvard Business Review Press, 1993. This is the definitive book on teams. Katzenbach has many excellent books on a variety of leadership and organizational topics. The follow-on book *The Discipline of Teams* by Katzenbach and Smith includes an excellent chapter on their research into virtual teams.

Kleiner, Art, *The Age of Heretics: A History of the Radical Thinkers Who Reinvented Corporate Management.* San Francisco, CA: Jossey-Bass, 2008. This book describes the historical research and practice of what we now think of as contemporary management theory. I read an earlier edition of this book and was so impressed that I summarized it for training new consultants. This edition bears a forward by Dr. Warren Bennis.

Lencioni, Patrick M. *The Five Dysfunctions of a Team: A Leadership Fable.* San Francisco, CA: Jossey-Bass, 2011. A good description of team dysfunction and what to do about it written in story format.

Litwin, George H., and Robert A. Stringer, Jr. *Motivation and Organization Climate.* Boston, MA: Harvard Business School Press, 1968. Organizational culture has become both a ubiquitous buzzword and an excuse for an inability to change. Litwin and Stringer demonstrate how relatively easy it is for managers to create a high-performance climate.

Peters Jr. Thomas, and Robert H. Waterman. *In Search of Excellence: Lessons from America's Best Run Companies.* New York, NY: Harper Row, 1980. This book sold one million copies in its first year, unheard of for business books at the time. *In Search of Excellence* started a trend of looking at current success and generalizing. While some of the original companies have fallen on hard times, many of the principles in *Excellence* are still relevant, i.e., "bias for action, close to the customer, simultaneous loose-tight properties."

Pugh, Derek S., and David J. Hickson. *Writers on Organizations.* London: Sage Publications, 2007. This book has short summaries of organizational and management theory. I used these summaries in an earlier version of this book to educate new MBAs on organizational and process consulting.

Schein, Edgar H., with Benjamin Schneider, Richard O. Mason, Ian Mitroff. *Organization Culture and Leadership.* San Francisco, CA; Jossey Bass, 1985. This classic has been revised many times, most recently (5th Edition 2016) with Peter Schein, published by Wiley in New York. In this book Schein lays out his research, models and leadership behaviors that shape culture.

Senge, Peter. *The Fifth Discipline.* New York, NY: Currency, 1990. Senge explores the integration of systems thinking and participative management.

NEWSLETTERS/WEBSITES
AND BLOGS

Wisdom from Unusual Places https://widomfromunusualplaces.com/blog/ is my blog with my latest thoughts on change consulting, leadership, and stories about working, living and loving.

BizCatalyst 360°, https://www.bizcatalyst360.com/ BizCat is the creation of Dennis Pitocco. It is a publisher of hundreds of writers, and a media company, and a community of people who want to change the world. I am grateful to be a featured contributor and member.

On Human Enterprise, http://www.onhumanenterprise.com/ is the blog of Niko Canner and Incandescent Consulting.

Visual Capitalist, https://www.visualcapitalist.com/ is a subscription website with some of the best graphics for information I've seen.

Ken Blanchard's blog, Leaderchat, https://resources.kenblanchard.com/blanchard-leaderchat, is an extensive blog by the author of the *One-Minute Manager.*

ACKNOWLEDGEMENTS

In my life, I have had lots of help. I am not an easy person to help so let me express my gratitude to all who have supported me or tried to support me even if I appeared less than grateful at the time.

The following people have been instrumental in bringing this book to fruition:

I am grateful to Charlotte Wittenkamp for early review and feedback and for much advice on self-publishing. I am grateful to Bob Musial for his review and structural feedback of a later version.

Thanks to Dr. Mary Lippitt for review, encouraging feedback, and support, and to Dennis Pitocco, Founder and Chief Imagineer of BizCatalyst 360° for publishing my writing, and for his praise. I am grateful for Dr. W. Warner Burke for his review and for teaching me about Organization Development (OD) at Teacher's College, Columbia University and through his writing. Thanks to my client Bob Yardis who engaged me at two different companies and wrote advance praise for this book.

Thanks to Dr. George H. Litwin, friend and mentor who first gave me opportunities to learn about change and leadership, and wrote advance praise for this book.

Thanks to my friend and colleague the late Dr. Richard W. Taylor who taught me more about continuous improvement than anyone.

I am grateful to Lisa Monias of South River Design team for the cover and interior design and to my son, Zac Culler for his logo for my blog and the publisher imprint.

Most of all thank you to my wife, Billie Smith Culler. Billie earned her living as a business writer and editor for more than twenty years. I am extremely fortunate that she has been my first reader, my first and second to nth editor. She has shown amazing patience when I whined, resisted, and ignored her editorial advice only to accept it from someone else later. She has encouraged me, pulled me out of discouragement periodically, and supported my writing, even when it took time away from our time together. Thank you, Billie! This book wouldn't have happened without you.

Even though I had a great deal of assistance with this book, any errors are my own and probably due to my obstinate rejection of offered advice.

Thank you also to all those clients and consulting colleagues who taught me about change and leadership over my many years in change consulting.

ABOUT THE AUTHOR

I am the son of old technology and new, a printer dad and computer programmer mom. I was a lower-middle-class kid in an upper-middle-class Boston suburb, saved from perpetual punkdom by an interest in theatre. I went to college in Kentucky, married young, became an actor, turned booking agent, bought two houses, all before thirty. I then sold my second house, two cars, and everything else we owned, and moved my wife and two young children to London to get an MBA. We had a third child there. I interned at a consulting firm and got a job at a training firm, moved to Pittsburgh, got fired, rehired in Boston, and then got involved in the British Airways turnaround and privatization. I started working for myself as an independent consultant in Pittsburgh, first to try to save my marriage, then to be close to my children after my divorce.

Only then did I begin to think about change. It's funny that when you start to think about something you see examples everywhere and understand your life experiences in a new way.

When I began thinking about work I was in a play. In high school I was in two musicals and thought *Hey, maybe I don't have to grow up. I could become an actor for a living.* I studied theatre as an undergraduate at Centre College. There I learned to observe people in order to portray them. That skill turned out to be quite useful later as I became an organizational change consultant. What I didn't learn was how to get work as an actor.

So I went to work as a booking agent for celebrity speakers. I learned to sell, which fed me as a consultant. I also learned that the famous and powerful are just people, who want you to listen and help if you can. This turned out to be useful later when talking to CEOs.

With absolutely no roadmap, I decided to become a consultant and went to the London Business School. Later I studied Organization Development with Dr. Warner Burke at Teachers College, Columbia University.

I worked for five firms: Harbridge House (acquired by Coopers & Lybrand, now part of PwC); The Forum Corporation (now Achieve Forum, part of Korn Ferry); HRI (Dr. George Litwin's firm, which had the British Airways contract, was acquired by Forum to form Strategic Action Services); Gemini Consulting (now Capgemini Group); and Katzenbach Partners (McKinsey spin-off, start up, ultimately acquired by Booz & Company, Strategy &, now a part of PwC).

I first became an independent consultant in 1987 and ultimately spent twenty-three years of my thirty-seven-year consulting career working for myself in a variety of structures: as sole proprietor; in partnership as Morton Culler & Company; and founder of a confederated network of independent consultants, Results-Alliance LLC.

In 2018 I retired to write stories and songs. My other books are *Traveling The Consulting Road* (2023) and *Wisdom from Unusual Places* (coming soon).

I now live in New Jersey with my wife Billie and our dog Pip. We take as much opportunity as we can to see our five children and five grandchildren.

You can read more about me at https://www.alanculler.com and read more of my writing at https://wisdomfromunusualplaces.com.

INDEX

www.ingramcontent.com/pod-product-compliance
Lightning Source LLC
Chambersburg PA
CBHW070546130626
46556CB00001B/29